Blood Trails II

THE TRUTH ABOUT BOWHUNTING

UPDATED AND REVISED

Blood Trails II

THE TRUTH ABOUT BOWHUNTING

UPDATED AND REVISED

Ted Nugent

This labor of love book is dedicated to my incredible family. My dad, Warren H. Nugent, for introducing me to Fred Bear, my first bow and arrow, and fathering in me the fundamentals, not so much of bowhunting, but more importantly about the mandatory need in life to be accountable. My saint of a mother, God rest her soul, Marion D. Nugent, for more than could ever be written in a mere lifetime. Love, patience, understanding, support, thru thick and thin, and an undying sense of joy in the face of anything and everything. To my brothers, Jeff and John, and sister Kathy for rounding out that family spirit that has represented strength and a bonding of life and togetherness that so many people are denied in this short-lived scheme of things called life. My beloved Starr, Sasha, Toby, and Rocco, who have always been my drive and meaning in everything I do. My loving wife, Shemane, who has supported and helped in the most demanding of times, beyond the call of duty. I am so lucky to have the strength of family in everything I do. I love you all with all the God-given power I have within me, now and forever. Thanx for letting me go hunting all the time.

I ALSO DEDICATE THIS BOOK TO FRED BEAR

"There I was, back in the wild again. I felt right at home, where I belong. I had that feeling coming over me again, just like it happened so many times before. The spirit of the woods is like an old good friend. It makes me feel warm and good inside. I know his name and it's good to see him again, because in the wind he's still alive!

Oh Fred Bear, walk with me down these trails again. Take me back, back where I belong. Fred Bear, I'm glad to have you at my side my friend, and I'll join you, in the big hunt before too long, before too long.

It was kind of dark, another misty dusk. It came from a tangle down below. I tried to remember everything he taught me so well. I had to decide which way to go. Was I alone, or in a hunter's dream? The moment of truth is here and now. I felt his touch, I felt his guiding hand. The buck was mine, forever more!

Oh Fred Bear, walk with me down the trails again. Take me back, back where I belong. Fred Bear, I'm glad to have you at my side my friend. And I'll join you in the big hunt before too long, before too long.

We're not alone, when we're in the great outdoors. We got his spirit, we got his soul. He will guide our steps, guide our arrows home. The restless spirit forever roams.

Because of Fred Bear, we'll walk down those trails again. He takes us back, back where we belong. Fred Bear, we're glad to have you at our side my friend, and we'll join you in the big hunt before too long. Because in the wind, he's still alive.

Hey Fred, let's go huntin'. Talk to me Fred. I hear ya. Fred, you go up that ridge, and I'll go down in the swamp. We'll get that buck!" [1]

"If today's teenage thrill seekers really want to get a thrill, let them go up into the Northwest, and tangle with a grizzly bear, a polar bear, or a brown bear. They will get their thrill that will cleanse their soul." (Fred Bear, 1964)

[1] *From the song "Fred Bear" by Ted Nugent, copyright 1989, Broadhead Music ASCAP.*

Front cover image: Ted Nugent   Back cover images: Ted Nugent

Published by: Woods N' Water, Inc.
Peter and Kate Fiduccia
P.O. Box 550
Florida, NY 10921

Printed in the United States of America
10 9 8 7 6 5 4 3 2 1
ISBN: 0-9722804-7-2

CONTENTS

Dedication iv

Preface/Introduction by Ted Nugent: Over 40 Years of Bowhunting vi

Introduction by Bob Munger: Lifelong Hunting Companion
and Friend of Fred Bear ix

Introduction by Inspector Frank Mitchell: Inspector for the
Detroit Police Department and Avid Bowhunter xi

Ted Nugent's World Bowhunters By-Laws xii

Prelude xiii

Equipment xiv

The Hunting vs. Anti-Hunting Game 1

Mother Nature Is a Bitch, But I Still Love Her 11

Ask Uncle Ted How to Maximize Your Spirit of the Wild 19

Nuge's Favorite HuntStories 35

Highlight Hunts

■ A Miracle Triple on Barbary Sheep of Texas 133

■ A Trophy for Rocco 136

■ Annual Baptizmal Deer Hunt 139

■ Bowhunting Boy Scouts 142

■ Buckos Encontado 143

■ Family Hunt Celebration 148

■ Frozen Pork of the Virgin Tundra 151

■ Naked Soul 153

■ Nyala–The Most Beautiful Antelope in the World 157

■ Rock 'n' Roll Wild Boar Hunting–Hogmando 161

■ Snowhogs 165

■ The Beast from Nowhere 171

Why I Hunt 175

Hunting Techniques 183

Recipes 191

Teditorials 199

Afterthoughts 233

About Ted 237

It could have been whiskey, it could have been drugs. But NO!! I was a teenage hunting addict. There, I've said it. It's not a pretty picture (to some). But like I've always said, if Elvis would have been a bowhunter, he would be alive today. If all this hunting is the worst thing I ever do (and it is), I'll go straight to heaven. In Genesis 9:3. God said to Noah, "All moving things that liveth shall be meat for you." Genesis 27:3. "Now therefore take, I pray thee, thy weapons, THY QUIVER AND THY BOW, and go out to the field, and take me some venison." Then He goes on about some great recipes He likes for "savory meat" and stuff. Pretty damn clear to me folks. Sounds like a little venison whackin'. There is not a man, woman, or a child alive who has not caused a blood trail. Think about it. All life lives and prospers off the death of other life. If you don't get it, put this book down and continue wandering aimlessly in your bullshit little fantasy world. You're a fool. However, if you embrace the more meaningful pursuits of this wonderful life, like I do, join me in a review of one hundred memorable bowkills of big game around the world. Every one of my thousands of hunts, kill or no kill, represents an unforgettable, lasting impression of the relationship man and beast share on this planet.

Though these stories deal with the kills, they in fact represent a small fraction of my hunting adventures. As it turns out, my most memorable and enjoyable hunts, for many different reasons, were excursions where no kill was made. Rather, a lasting relationship was formed, an inner peace was realized, or just an imprinting, unforgettable sunset was experienced. The bonds I have made with myself, family, friends, and the Lord are the real trophies of hunting. Always have been, always will be. It's the spirit of the wild! And I got it.

We have a responsibility to use our intelligence in our God-given role as caretakers and stewards of the animals. Being at the top of the food chain puts us in direct control, when everything is right, of this most intricate of life's equations. With compassion and forethought, we can continue to progress with our enviable success at managing game populations in the face of overwhelming odds, like the wanton destruction of wild ground (habitat). Hunting is conservation. Here, in 2004, the entire world is in awe of the incredible stability and even growth of America's game animals. Historic game ground, like Africa, has a hit-and-miss pattern. Countries like South Africa, Zimbabwe, Tanzania, and Botswana have great success also, because they encourage animal value, through sporthunting operations. Kenya is ashamed of itself, as it should be, for in 1970 when hunting was a big part of the economy, it boasted the wonderment of over 150,000 African elephants. Then they banned hunting in defiance of professional hunters', scientists' and biologists' historical data. Today that number has been reduced by ninety percent. Thanks a lot. This has happened over and over again around the world. The truth being rammed down our throats is that those who would ban hunting do so not because they love or want to save any animals, but because they, at any cost, want to protect their comfortable ignorance. The simplest, most unthinking way is to just hate hunters. Time has proven that it is the hunter who is the steward of animals; we are conservationists, willing to get in there and get the job done. We do what is right and good for the big picture of wildlife. Animals cannot be cuddled one at a time, but rather, managed within the confines of reduced planetary habitat based on the carrying capacity therein. I am a hunter. This is how God designed me and the world I live in. I will continue to live this life and fight for what is right.

OVER FORTY YEARS OF BOWHUNTING

I started twanging the one-string 'bout the same time as the six-string. There was some sort of bow and arrow in my hands as young as six or seven I'm sure. I was cocked, locked and ready to rock, doc! Got my first guitar around the same time, and both have remained my favorite weapons to date. I can kill my dinner with either at any time I please!

When the other kids were playing army, tag, hide and seek, cowboys and Indians, and all those other games, I was down at the Rouge River exploring Skunk Hollow with my wrist-rocket or bow and arrow, whackin' river rats and other big game. My longbow was about twenty-five pounds, and the cedar arrows were bought for ten cents apiece by the handful. I would collect pop bottles along the road 'til I had enough cash, head into Redford, run up Grand River Avenue into Miller's Feed store, and buy my favorite thing in life: Nice, new, feather-fletched cedar arrows. As I broke them, I'd simply resharpen them with my pocketknife. And boy, could I shoot! Something about the untainted mind of youth. For when I snapped that arrow back to the corner of my mouth, Zippo! I could hit anything I looked at. Purely instinctive.

My cousin, Mark Schmitt, witnessed a whole bunch of outrageous shots. Running squirrels on telephone wires, flying birds, starlings, pigeons, rabbits. Talk about whackin' and stackin'! I was dangerous. Rats, coons, possum, skunks, pheasant, quail, even sparrows helped sharpen my eye as a kid starting out. Remember, John James Audubon learned all about birds and animals first hand the same way. He would kill them to study them. Me too. I learned real early all about wildlife, hands on. By the time I was ten, I knew every songbird by sound and flight characteristics. It was, and still is, fascinating.

It was the time of rebirth of hunting with the bow and arrow. My father, Warren, gets full credit for introducing me to archery. Like many archers of the period in the '50s, he was a casual, recreational bowhunter, inspired by the master pioneers, such as Saxon Pope, Art Young, Howard Hill, Ben Pearson, and the all-time great, father of modern-day bowhunting, the one and only Fred Bear. Fred was (still is) my hero. Back then, when our family would make our annual trek north to the big woods near Gladwin, Michigan, along the Tittabawasee River, for our fall camping and bowhunting adventure, I was filled with visions of Fred Bear stalking giant grizzly bears. In those days of bowhunting infancy, we didn't know much about technique or approach. Never killed a deer, that's for sure. But we would see them, and I was clear in my vision, a vision that will stay with me the rest of my life. We would shoot the first aluminum arrows to come on the market. We would learn to sharpen the famous Bear Razorhead, Bodkin, MA3, Zwickey, Howard Hill, Hilbre, and the few others that were in this new market. These were the pioneering, "point-man" days of Rock 'n' Roll and bowhunting, and I was seeking the eye of each storm.

Forty years later, the fundamentals have not changed. Woodsmanship, and persistent stealth will get you your buck, nothing else. The Chinese had string-release aids in 400 AD. A form of recurve bow as well. If you've got a bow in one hand and an arrow in the other, obey the laws and rules of fair-chase, then I'm with you. We are all bowhunters. And we have our work cut out for us in this day and age. Stick together and spread the truth of our love and respect for the critters we coexist with, and we will safeguard our heritage for our children and our children's children.

Bowhunting is the future of outdoor shooting sports; and the future of bowhunting is in the hands of today's young people. Share the spirit of the hunt with them. Get these people the hell out of the city, away from the malls, the street corners of drugs and drinking and death. Cleanse their souls in the wonderment of the great outdoors. Establish some accountability. In a decayed, service-oriented society, this last vestige of hands-on culpability may be our only hope to teach us we can't keep pissin' in our own soup.

Those of us who are smart enough to walk the pre-dawn forest, touch the ways of the wild, kill our own food, cut our own fuel, grow our own fruits and vegetables, change our own oil, raise our own kids, and think our own thoughts will be the salvation of the globe. Pretty potent stuff for a smelly old bowhunter, huh? When meat is only procured in a cellophane package, heat is increased by turning a dial, and automobiles are serviced by signing a check, one inevitably loses complete touch with what has actually taken place. Not me. Not bowhunters. I've encountered a major load of my fellow human beings over the years, and the top one thousand are all bowhunters. Peaceful, intelligent, responsible and caring individuals who wouldn't interfere or complicate another's life for nothing. That is because our peaceful, senses-articulating sport keeps us tuned into the world around us, and shows how we fit in.

This book isn't going to be a comprehensive life history of Ted Nugent the bowhunter, but rather a rundown, a review if you will, of detailed data surrounding 120 arrow hits on big game. Let me just state for the record just who I think I am. I am just another smelly bowhunter. Not great, but deadly. I am by no stretch of the imagination a trophy hunter. My homes are filled with dead critters, all magnificent and bursting with graphic memories, some even record-book status, but that was just good fortune. You see, my idea of a trophy bowkill is one that walks by in range. On a few occasions, the big ones strolled on in, and I whacked 'em. I sure ain't no Fred Bear or the like. Guys I know like Bob Fratzke, Doug Walker, Bryan Schupbach, Claude Pollington, Bruce Cull, Myles Keller, Dick Mauch and many others are much better bowhunters than I will ever be. Either that, or they are lucky as hell!! I know I am sometimes. But I hunt real hard, real often, and always get an absolute chill thrill each time I'm out there. And more importantly, I'm learning all the time. Stealth and awareness of your surroundings will determine the extent of your bowhunting experience, and your success in kills.

Think, listen, smell, touch. Aspire to become one with the primeval dirt. Relinquish the modern burden of damaged senses. The concrete jungle, electronic war-zone of 2004 modern living must be escaped and compensated for. What works best for me is to stop, shut up, and take a long pause as I enter the hunt zone. Even if it's within spittin' distance of a city or neighborhood, abandon those city feelings. Pretend your life depends on the kill. "I do not hunt to kill, but rather kill to have hunted" (as quoted from the Spanish philosopher Ortega y Gasset). The predator within, when allowed to surface, will make you a better person.

Cover ground with your eyes, not your feet. Don't step on anything you can step over. Do not try to stalk thru a clearing, but rather skirt the edges, or just hustle thru and get it over with. Avoid silhouetting yourself. Keep in the shadows. Spend as much time as possible in the wild, as wild as you can get. Learn the ways of the wind. It will be your number-one friend or foe. Breathe deeply and slowly. It's a long way back to your predatory instinct. The bow and arrow can be mastered to the point of near-perfect accuracy. If we apply ourselves, we can become expert hunters, attaining the ultimate goal of swift, clean, humane kills. To kill is not necessary to have hunted, but to aspire to kill cleanly is the only killing goal. We've got what it takes if we use what God gave us. We are a specialized predator, capable of effective, intelligent, and uniquely compassionate killing. Keep those broadheads razor-sharp, keep those senses razor-sharp, and put forth the effort to do it right.

Ted Nugent

INTRODUCTION

LIFELONG HUNTING COMPANION
AND FRIEND OF FRED BEAR

Fred Bear and I found out that Rock 'n' Roll stars come in several colors—this one came in "camouflage." At first it was hard to believe. How come we two old coots are running with the racy young "Dude?" It was hard to adjust to a long-haired wild Indian in deer camp. Fred was afraid he might spook all of our deer. When he arrived, he had three bird dogs and six speakers in his Bronco. He also had the wrong brand of bow for our "Bear Camp." Fred said he figured the dogs would range out for about a mile and, with the stereo speakers at full volume, would be heard at the South gate, which was two mile away.

This was many years ago, shortly after Ted walked into Fred's office at Bear Archery in Gainesville, and announced who he was and the reasons for his visit. Fred related to me that Ted told him he had made a special trip to Florida because Fred has been his lifelong idol. Fred said he thought the least he could do was to invite him to our deer camp. Fred sort of apologized to me, like he'd done something wrong. We were both apprehensive, almost really hoped he'd turn Fred down—but he didn't! The day before the season, Ted came sweeping in like the Siberian Express. We saw the cloud of dust coming down the runway. It looked like a DC3 had landed. (Ted had arrived.)

You won't believe this! Ted announced that he didn't come to hunt! "I came up to hear the yarns that you guys spin about your hunting experiences in the 'good old days'."

You won't believe this either! We never left camp opening day of the season (except to train Ted's dogs).

Fred had to be one of the world's best storytellers. All of them had his special non-heroic, modest humor. Fred should have been a stand-up comic. We laughed 'til we almost cried.

Fred was the farthest from the "boastful bowhunter" that I've ever met. Ben East once told me, "Fred's the toughest guy to get a good story out of." When I asked him to tell about his exciting bear hunt, Fred would say, "Well Ben, there's really not much to tell. The bear came along and I shot him and he fell down!" Now how the hell do you make that sound exciting?

Ted is a wild man in the Rock 'n' Roll world, but he's ALMOST normal when he's in a hunting camp, and don't ever try to out-do him in the woods because he's a tiger and a real pro—you'd probably wind up in second. He said, "You know, I can't decide which I like most, bowhunting or Rock 'n' Roll."

As a gesture of appreciation for his first invitation to Grousehaven, Ted came up with a real production. He announced that on Saturday night he was making an Oscar Award presentation to Fred. Ted and I feel very lucky to have had the opportunity to spend many years with Fred.

We were all very impressed with the effort that Ted made with his project. As they say, if you want to get the job done—ask a busy guy. Fred told me later that he thought that Ted was quite a guy. "I like him for what he is," he said, "and I think he'll do a lot of good things for the future of bowhunting." I could not have put it better. It makes me tired just to hear about Ted's treks, back and forth from Hollywood to Michigan, squeezing in trips to Africa, working his hundreds of concerts and personal appearances, his work on drug-fighting campaigns, sport shows, opening an archery business, publishing a magazine, writing a book, (all while he's building a new house), plus the local hunting trips, writing for newspapers, and . . . etc., etc., etc.

As a bow-hunter for some fifty years, I would like to lend my thoughts on what I think is going to happen in 1990s to the bow-hunters. I think most bow-hunters have a down feeling from what happened to the California bear season (which neither Ted nor his video had anything to do with). The least that may be gained by this action is to teach us that a good representative from the bowhunting world must maintain a friendly position with the conservation department, the legislators, and the lobbyists, and have current information about prospective changes of the game laws. The most important thing that the bow-hunters must do is to maintain a group of top-quality people to represent them.

As I have previously stated, if you want to get a job done, ask a busy man. Ted Nugent, in my opinion, is this type of guy. He also has the rare virtue of being able to speak his mind, and these expressions are sometimes the first to be heard.

—Bob Munger

American bison, 1996

INSPECTOR FOR THE DETROIT POLICE DEPARTMENT AND AVID BOWHUNTER

Ted Nugent, Rock 'n' Roller, is a dedicated professional musician and a great sportsman, but to me, Ted means a hell of a lot more. Ted is a person who loves and represents the outdoors. He has spent most of his life studying nature and has dedicated himself to knowing just what Mother Nature has to offer him and his fellow human beings. Together, we can live and exist in harmony if we, as a people, would get out from behind the desk, off the couch and into the woods, and get to know the real meaning of the balance of nature.

At the same time, Ted has never compromised his time and love for his family as is illustrated so well in his very popular quote, "I take my kids huntin', so I don't have to hunt for my kids." This simple quote has a very profound meaning in today's corrupt, drug-infested society.

Ted knows the meaning and significance of teaching our young people the importance of fairness, whether it relates to our everyday living or to maintaining the balance of nature—to go out and hunt, but take only what you need, leaving the remaining balance for sportspersons of tomorrow. This is typified so well in Ted's statement, "When you cut your own wood, the fire is much warmer, but you don't cut down all your trees."

I have had the privilege of listening and watching Ted speak to large audiences and have also talked one-on-one with him at his home, as well as in a dimly lit hunting cabin in Michigan's Upper Peninsula, regarding hunting and a drug-free environment. It is obvious that what he has to say comes from the heart. When he speaks out against drugs, he has a sincere desire to promote a positive "clean-living" lifestyle, and to show today's youth, and the old as well, that there are alternative highs with which our great nation is blessed. Ted demonstrates this desire in the promotion of his Bowhunters Against Drugs. He further shows his devotion to our youth by working to establish a camp for kids in Northern Michigan. He strongly believes that every kid needs to be taught archery, canoeing, fishing and the love of the outdoors, as these can be positive alternatives to help him, or her, combat and change the menaces that threaten them in society.

Ted takes a lot of heat from the anti-hunting, ridiculous, out-of-touch-with-their-environment people who can't see or understand the real world beyond their country clubs, the Hollywood theater, or Disneyland. The half-witted, hypocritical, activists protest against wearing furs, but at the same time are sporting their expensive leather shoes. Ted never wavers, he stands up, speaks out loud and defends our God-given right to intelligently manage our natural resources.

To sum up what Ted Nugent stands for, it is simply **FUN!**—good, clean fun. Go out into the woods, hunt, stalk, shoot straight and take your time. Have fun, kill or no kill. But most of all, do your homework, learn to be safety conscious, know the laws, rules and regulations, and **do not** infringe on other's rights. Never take anything for granted. Be prepared when the moment of truth comes, which can only be achieved by practice, practice, practice. NEVER drink or touch drugs EVER, and keep your senses finely tuned at all times.

Ted's advice is to go slow, stop, look and listen, see the flowers, birds and squirrels, and you will see it is pretty nice to find that there is so much, much more in the woods to supply you with a thrill than just the rush back to camp to tell others about your kill. Learn to take it easy, enjoy the outdoors, and you will hunt a whole lot longer and have a lot more **FUN!**

—*Inspector Frank Mitchell*

A SPORTSMAN'S CREED

All members agree to:

1. Enjoy yourself, live it up, have fun!
2. Abide by all laws and regulations governing the states and provinces of our designated hunting area, living a code of ethics honorable to our sport.
3. Insist on and practice utmost safety rules.
4. Abide by the rules of fair chase, always giving the game the benefit of the doubt, never pursuing while restricted by topography, water, deep snow, or constricted by limited fence.
5. Conduct ourselves with manners and consideration for all others, refusing to tolerate drugs and the misuse of alcohol both in the field and out.
6. Strive diligently at our sport, with the legal equipment of our choice, to maintain a proficiency and accuracy to optimize quick, humane kills.
7. Follow up on all shots, persevering to eliminate the loss of any animal.
8. Responsibly utilize the products of the game we harvest, appreciating the God-given flesh, hides, bone, horn, and antlers with respect and dignity.
9. Share the wonderment of the outdoors and conservation with others, especially the young, in word and action, signing up new members at every opportunity.
10. Go beyond the call of duty in policing the ranks of outdoorsmen and women, never accepting or allowing abhorrent, illegal, or detrimental behavior from others.
11. Put more into the wild than we take out, assisting in habitat conservation and helping at every opportunity.
12. Pick up after inconsiderate people and keep the wild litter free.
13. Be ultimately conscientious of the wildlife and restrict our bag even more than the law demands when the animals need the help.
14. Stand strong and proud, with action, letters, and phone calls in defiance of ignorant people who wish to force their mistakes on society and wildlife, in detriment to all.

Respect, value, and safeguard the great outdoors.

Good huntin'.
Bowhuntin' forever!

ENTER THE KILL ZONE

Only recovered kills will be dealt with herein. If you hunt, you have a deep responsibility in your natural role as a reasoning predator to kill with regard and respect for your quarry. I know my life would be less if it were not for the whitetail deer and all other game I have encountered. In this book, there will be, I'm sure, many references to whackin', gut piles and other sundry slang that reflects a suspicious attitude on my part. Let me explain (even though the vast majority of you know that I'm just havin' fun). Bottom line is, I am just havin' fun. I hunt to feel the thrills involved that I've often mentioned, certainly for the premium meat I get, but most importantly because I really enjoy myself throughout the many maneuvers involved. I mean no disrespect to the sport, to its participants, or the critters. The baseball fans don't REALLY want to kill the umpire. The football fans don't REALLY want anybody's head ripped off. I'm sure. They are just getting into it and HAVING FUN! Get it? I do. (I'm not really a gut-pile addict, I don't think!!)

A hunter must aspire to attain and maintain a proficiency, in hopes of never wounding an animal. At the same time, we must psychologically be prepared for the agony of lost game. If you hunt, it can and most likely will happen. I have painfully lost animals. The difference between a lung/liver shot and a gut shot can be an inch. Under field conditions, few of us can expect consistent accuracy to these exacting tolerances. I hunt a lot and am improving all the time. I try hard to. On a recent twenty-day African bowhunt, I killed twenty-three head of big game. I failed to recover four hit animals. I saw two of them days later and am confident they fully recovered; the others I'm certain perished (and made their way back to the earth, via predators and scavengers). I certainly cannot take full responsibility for such a fine record because I had a phenomenal native South African tracker, Elliot Nzaine, assist on a few BloodTrails I would never had effectuated. If only all of us could have available such a talented helper (unfortunately, he got whacked himself by a jealous neighbor), I'm sure lost game could be reduced by 90%. I'm confident that hunters lose less game than domestic production procedures account for.

The kills contained in this book all have one thing in common. Each game animal has a vital organ or prime blood vessel sliced by a sharp broadhead. Conversely, every animal I'm aware of that has ever been lost, did not. Some high-chest hit animals can bleed one hundred percent internally even though double-lunged, and make for a no-Blood Trail situation. I hate this. For shots within twenty-five yards, I recommend using a string-tracking device. Practice is necessary to determine at what range your arrow flight will be affected. When utilized properly, these string trackers can make the difference between recovered and lost game. (Persevere, By-Law number seven.)

Study, in detail, the anatomy of your intended target, and shoot to drain the critter of life expeditiously. There is nothing more wonderful in this world than a Blood Trail you can follow without stooping over! The only certain way to accomplish this is with RAZOR SHARP BROAD-HEADS. I take great pride in my sharpening method, and/or choice in quality arrowheads. Just for the record, I will repeat the obvious. Once you shoot a hunting broadhead, you cannot expect it to be sharp enough to hunt with until you resharpen it perfectly, or replace the blades. On Bear, Zwickey, Satellite Titans, Whackmasters and other leading knife-edge heads that are resharpenable, there is a specific way to maximize a deadly edge. I take a six-, eight-, or ten-inch fine mill bastard file, and stroke the edges with a forward motion on alternating sides, flipping it over and over. With decreasing pressure, I finally, barely remove the slight burr. For the finishing touch, I take my angled stone block, like the Tru Angle or Grayling, oil it up good, and push it forward for a few more light strokes. This is, in my opinion, the deadliest of penetrating edges. I do not use the insert for a four-blade, but prefer a two-blade to squirrel right on through.

Good luck, shoot straight. Whatever you do, do it right and have fun.

EQUIPMENT

Whatever works for you. It has to feel right, and fit you as an individual. There is so much diverse gear out there, it could drive a newcomer nuts. Pick up Fred Bear's *Archers Bible and Field Notes,* Larry Wise's technical books on bow and arrowhead tuning and Dave Holt's *Balanced Bowhunting.* Read them all. But most importantly, dig. Hands on. Go to your friendly local archery pro shop and try all the equipment you can get your hands on. It is such a subjective decision, only trial and error will determine the best tools for you. Watch out for the gomers out there though. You will be able to quickly tell you are in their presence. The minute they claim only one bow or one head is the only one to use, get out of there. Look for helpful, courteous assistance in choosing your gear. I have shot, I'll bet, every bow on the market. There is some real quality stuff out there. There is also many tons of debris that has little value to the serious bowman. Be careful. Let effectiveness, not colorful advertising, be your guide. I have drawn a few simple conclusions as to what I naturally grab when I head out to bowhunt. The name of the game is to kill outright. To do this you need stealth, accuracy and deadly force. Stealth comes with attentive time in the wild, feeling your way back to your predatorship. Accuracy only comes with accumulated practice time, shooting under varied circumstances. And most importantly, deadly force means a strong, razor-sharp broadhead clean thru the vital organs of your quarry. In one side and out the other. Killing clean and fast is the name of the game. Maybe the big (and small) predators can play around with their half-dead victims, but man has the responsibility and intelligence to whack 'em good. Face up to accountability. The rest of society pays for their mass killings. The kill isn't everything, but a clean kill is my favorite part! Here is what I have come to use as of hunting season 2004:

- Renegade Nuge Bow 53#
- Easton aluminum arrows of varying sizes 2016, 2115, 2213, 2315
- Gold Tip 5575 & 7595
- Game Tracker Carbon Xpress
- Vapor
- Beaman Hunters
- Arrow Dynamics
- Magnus Broadheads Nugent Blade & Stinger 100's
- Scott Release, Tru Fire
- Bodoodle, Golden Key Futura & NAP rests
- Martin Super Quiver
- Sims Vibration Labs Accessories
- North Starr Tree Stands
- Invisiblind Groundblind
- Honda
- Outdoor Edge Knives
- Inhibitor Rust Proof
- Black Mountain Socks

- Snake Skin Illusions
- Mossy Oak Camo
- Scent Lok
- Glenns Deer Handle
- Innotek Training Devices
- Primos Calls
- Buck Grub
- Temptation Lures
- Purina Deer Feed & Blocks
- Buck Stop Lures
- Georgia Boots
- Field Line Packs
- Xtreme Scents
- Natures Essence
- Black Death Scents
- Hard Hunter Minerals
- Bio-logic
- Jurrasic Seeds
- Wildlife Innovations
- Overdose of Attitude!!

Equipment is such a personal thing. I AM NOT TRYING TO SELL YOU ANYTHING. The only reason you should buy any bowhunting tackle is because you, as an individual, so choose to, based on hands-on, utilitarian effectiveness. Period. My stuff has my signature on it for one simple reason. I like it, and feel it is the best for me. Everyone should do the same. One thing I do guarantee, my stuff is all primo equipment. I believe it is the best out there. And I promise you, it works.

Study all the laws carefully. Go slow. Think deeply of the consequences of your actions, before, during, and after the hunt. Go proudly into the wild, for you are the blessed of the earth, the caretakers, the guardians. You are at the top of the food chain. We've got the complex brain. Use it to the limit. Now get out there and whack something for ol' Ted. It will make me, and you, oh so happy! I AM THE WHACKMASTER. TO THE HUNT. Live it up.

Black ram, Young Ranch, Texas, 2000

THE
Hunting vs. Anti-Hunting Game

We had pheasant for dinner last night. Venison steaks the night before. Wild game every day of the week. For Thanksgiving at the Nugent ranch, we sat down and gave thanks for our family and friends, our health, home, and the wildlife we live amongst. Then we shared a meal of turkey. We are hard-working, tax-paying Americans. (Oh, those taxes!) We ate turkey just like everybody else, at least 99% of everybody else. Only our turkey was a wild bird I shot with my bow and arrow. Not a Butterball, but a natural wild, free-ranging creature. After many hunts, I finally put all the elements together to release my arrow and harvest our Thanksgiving dinner. I feel like an idiot when I even bother asking "What did we do wrong?" Of course, the answer is a resounding NOTHING! Nothing wrong at all. In fact, in all honesty, our bird was a better bird, procured in a better way. Certainly more delicious and healthier for us. Pure. Perfect.

The harsh reality of the animal-rights freaks is that they are not just after hunting and hunters. People for the Ethical Treatment of Animals (PETA) and other brain-dead animal-rights goofballs do not want to just ban fur coats. They are not out to save wildlife or any animals. What they demand is clear. PETA, Fund for Animals, and most of the others, have admitted their goals are the elimination of ALL animal use. Chicken dinners, burgers, leather shoes and all leather and wool clothing, zoos, pets, dairy products, medical research, milk and cookies, everything! I watched a professional biologist on the National Geographic TV special on the African elephant the other day make the wildest, most offensive statement I have ever heard. In the face of overwhelming evidence that Zimbabwe and other southern African countries were having great success at managing their INCREASING elephant herds via controlled hunting and cull operations, PLUS feeding and clothing thousands of hungry people, she nonetheless stated, and I quote, "I would rather see the elimination of ALL elephants, than ever allow any killing." There you have it in a nutshell. Or should I say nutcase!? These imbeciles really do not give a damn. They admittedly would allow the elimination of a species, just to mindlessly cling to their self-serving, ignorant bliss. They would deny their child a polio vaccine shot because the needle hurts! To allow wildlife management policy, or any policy for that matter, to be implemented based on this irrational, irresponsible stupidity is the ultimate mind crime. All thinking members of our society should let their voices and their beliefs be heard, and insist on conscientious, sound reasoning to guide decisions on such far-reaching issues. Fools like Paul McCartney, k.d. lang, and the Go-Gos should stick to their drugged-out shallowness and leave important decisions to people willing to seek out and act upon the truth. It is criminally inclined, left-winged hippies like them at *Rolling Stone* magazine that preach insults such as "ban fur, legalize dope" that expose them as the assholes they truly are. They must be ignored and left to blabber their insults into the night. Like Hare-Krishnas, confined in their little cages at the airport, we can tolerate their expression of opinions, but never let obvious wrong get its foot in the door.

10-point whitetail, Michigan, 2000

I could not attempt to write anything in this day and age about bowhunting without including this raging cultural conflict, or should I say war? Hopefully, I expect common sense to prevail in the actions as well as the minds of my fellow man.

Even though I have not given up all hope yet, I am always astounded at the lunatic fringe and their dangerous screams in defiance of what is right. When so-called leaders of our society recommend a dress code in response to inner city children murdering each other over jackets and new tennis shoes, I get scared. Somewhere in my mind, I would like to think that maybe, just maybe, we could enforce law against murder and eliminate these heinous criminals from our streets. Dress code indeed! A 1989 bear-hunting ban in California was one such idiotic success for this small, but loud and obnoxious, anti-hunting group. A grand bear-hunting tradition flourished in California, with a stable, and in many areas, growing bear population. But again, showing their total lack of concern for the wildlife, they ignored the facts. These zealots just plain don't like hunters, to hell with the critters. Even when shown the irreversible damage their mistaken actions have caused in the past, they continue to force their uneducated fantasy on the wildlife, and those of us who truly love the wild.

Look at the embarrassing track record of the extremists when it comes to the hunting issue. Here in the U.S., the Great Swamp Wildlife Refuge in New Jersey is the last piece of wild ground remaining in that portion of the state. Wildlife flourished and everyone took pleasure in the beauty of the wild area. Deer hunting was the tool by which the game department maintained the size of the herd to conform within the carrying capacity of its limited habitat. And limited it is. Like ALL habitat in the world, there is just so much left.

The Great Swamp deer and other animals could not go further east, because there was a landfill. They could not go south, because there was a toxic dump. They could not go north, because Manhattan was across the river. To the west were endless housing developments, malls, neighborhoods, highways, and nowhere to go.

Each year, the regulated hunter bagged hundreds of healthy, beautiful animals; partook in a safe, wholesome sport, harvested valuable, quality venison, and had a rare opportunity to accomplish something good for the big picture and everybody in general, especially the deer. And never forget that when the deer herd is kept in check properly (an easy thing to do), the entire ecosystem will always benefit. Plants, songbirds, small game, the air, water, soil, natural filtering and purification procedures, and overall beauty are safeguarded and assisted. But the left-wing morons would have none of this. Around 1970, they took their ridiculous posters and banners, and paraded at the refuge entrance, protesting the assumption of cruelty to the deer. What simple-minded jerks. Their signs read things like, "Hunters, show your manliness at home in bed, not in the woods with a gun!!!" Can someone please tell me what the hell that means? Of course good old Bambi was well represented. My prime goal is to get a one hundred percent natural video of Bambi getting half-whacked by a coyote, and slowly eaten alive coming out of his mother's ass, killing ma and junior in all its blood and gore reality. And then

"The youth of America must be educated to the wholesome and valued world of hunting and conservation," Ted Nugent, Kamp for Kids, August 1998.

11-point whitetail, Texas, 2002

having the coyote smile into the camera. A little reality is just what these gomers could use, close up and natural like. Animal-rights idiots should have the truth forced up their arses and down their throats.

Meanwhile, the protestors actually succeeded in getting a judge (why wasn't I surprised) to halt the hunt after a couple of years of protesting. The sportsmen's clubs of that state went on the offensive, because they cared. Led by Lou Martinez and the United Bowhunters of New Jersey, they prepared to expose the truth. With the direction of the Wildlife Legislative Fund of American (WLFA), they countered the protestors face-to-face, and accomplished positive impact. They knew the realities of the situation because, like the vast majority of hunters, they are in touch with the overall scheme of things out there. For every action, (or lack thereof), there is a reaction. And in a finite, microscopic setting like this, the violent reality was swift in coming.

Within only a short few years, hunters were able to document on video the disastrous effects of the hunting ban. Deer were shown dying of malnutrition, with huge tumors and deformities. Vegetation was stripped away, and took with it the smaller animals and birds that relied on it for food and shelter. Surrounding homes experienced intolerable incidents of yard and ornamental landscaping destruction, and highway fatalities skyrocketed. Overall, they were left with a mess on their hands.

Eventually, with the facts shoved in their faces, the courts again opened the refuge to regulated hunting. Thank God the truth prevailed. But here is the clincher. Immediately, the scum were back, demanding no hunting!! It was so obvious that they just plain didn't give a damn about the animals or what was right. The courts continue to support the hunt, yet every year, in decreasing numbers, the protestors show up with their stupid signs babbling on and on, giving everyone a good laugh, and keeping us on our toes to the fact that fools will show their ugly ignorance no matter what.

The list of horror stories goes on and on. Again in the late 1970s, Cleveland Armory and his dope-smoking hippie nerds came stumbling down to Florida. Terrible rainstorms had flooded an entire area of the Okeechobee Everglades. Wildlife was stranded on isolated patches of high ground, and it was clear a massive die-off was right around the corner. The state game people were swift in assessing the situation, and wisely chose to issue special hunt permits to reduce the overwhelming pressure on the constrained remaining land. It was obvious as hell what had to be done. Failure to reduce the animal numbers would have guaranteed the unnecessary starvation of large numbers of critters. A disaster waiting to happen.

The decision to cull was made by caring professionals. People and equipment were ready to go. WHAMO! Along came the shitheads. A restraining order from the court threw a wrench in the whole works. Time was running out. In fact, some animals were already perishing. Swift action was of the essence. Because of the admirable track record of the Florida Fish and Game boys, a compromise was struck. The gomers could attempt to live-capture the deer and other animals by hand (good luck) and the hunters could select-shoot some deer, based on careful scrutiny and direction of the sportsmen's clubs and game department officials.

The line was drawn. On one side, the animal protectionists would try to "save" individual deer. And on the other side, the sportsmen would cull a certain portion to balance the land/herd condition. The results were exactly as we predicted. The hunters harvested (killed) about one hundred deer, about the same amount as

12-point whitetail, Michigan, 2001

10-point whitetail, Michigan, 1998

usual for the hunting season in that zone. Later, when the waters receded to normal levels, the herd condition was very healthy and stable. On the other hand, the ensuing fiasco at the hands of the anti-hunters was disastrous. Of the hundreds of deer they attempted to rescue, eleven were handled, six of which died in transport to higher ground, and the other five were traumatized, incurred broken limbs and eventually escaped. Good job, clowns. Talk about worthless, dangerous buffoons. If there was any common sense justice out there, these idiots would step forward with their recommendations, and they would get slapped silly and be sent packing. Did I mention how much I dislike these people? You can rest assured that they will ignore the truth and experiences of the past, and continue to attempt this crap over and over again. They just plain do not care. We should never let our guard down, for if these maniacs progress in their dastardly plots, everyone will lose, especially the animals.

Let's try to keep it simple. I need food. Good, healthy, delicious and nutritious food, for my family and myself. I know how to get it, legally, effectively, enjoyably and the way God told me to do it. I merely grab by bow and arrows, and hunt. Ninety-nine percent of society understands and supports this practice. Because there are so damn many of us crammed onto this planet, man has worked up a system to raise and provide this type of demanded food for those who choose, for whatever reason, to take advantage of this service. It is called farming. A good, clean life-style for sure, but somewhat compromised by the sheer numbers involved.

Basically, my fellow Americans place their orders in loud, clear voices: WE WANT CHICKEN, FISH, BEEF, LAMB, TURKEY, DUCK, GOOSE. WE WANT IT D-E-A-D. WE WANT IT RAISED IN PENS AND CAGES. IT'S OK IF THEY HAVE TO LIVE IN AND EVEN EAT THEIR OWN SHIT. INJECT THEM WITH ANY CHEMICALS YOU PLEASE TO GROW 'EM FAST AND PRETTY, KILL 'EM ALL, ONE HUNDRED PERCENT. WE WANT BLOOD, FLOWING LIKE A RIVER, SPLASHIN' ON WHITE APRONS COAST TO COAST, KILL, KILL,

KILL, BLOOD, BLOOD, BLOOD, GET THE JOB DONE, AND HAVE ALL WE NEED BY TUESDAY! THANK YOU VERY MUCH! That, ladies and gentlemen, is the real meaning of slaughter. Mass efficient slaughter. And it is necessary to supply the demand. Kill, and we will pay. The hard-working farmers of this country have a damn good system worked out in response to the people's demands. You want it, you got it.

OR! Like those of us who prefer, they could shut up, relax, stop, look, listen, smell, touch, and feel the original pulse of the primeval wild that is there for the living. Take hold of the senses God gave us and that we have nearly ruined. Save 'em. Use 'em. Hone 'em back to life. Utilize, with intelligence and common sense, those resources that were put here for us. CONSERVATION IS "WISE USE."

Hunting is a sacred function. A special responsibility for special people who can shoulder it, in a very special role from a higher source. Take a look around us. There are more deer, elk, bear, caribou, buffalo, antelope, turkey and geese than there have been in one hundred years. Modern regulated hunting IS WORKING! Even in the face of ever-decreasing habitat, our trained, hunter-paid-for, qualified game biologists have safeguarded and managed the balance of wildlife and the needed wild ground to support it. Sometimes, they've done too good of a job. But like all government agencies, multi-level and questionably motivated pressure sources have oftentimes hamstrung their efforts.

In Michigan and states like Pennsylvania, New York, Wisconsin and others, in excess of 60,000 deer carcasses are recovered each year from the highways. And that is with increased, record-breaking harvests (hunter kills) for many years in a row. I believe,

9-point whitetail, Texas, 2002

7

Red hartebeest, South Africa

from personal experience and discussions with wildlife and law enforcement officers, that Michigan's real road kill number is beyond one hundred thousand per year. Most deer/highway deaths result in the animal running out of sight before it dies. Include in these statistics the five or more human fatalities, just in Michigan, each year, and you realize very quickly how serious the population dynamics of some species must be considered. The National Highway Safety Council reports more than four hundred thousand deer are killed by vehicles a year, resulting in more than two hundred human fatalities. Small game by the billions!

And you want to know why this many deaths occur? Many years, nationwide, too many big game animals starve to death as well. It's simple. A few heartless big mouths, pissin' and moanin' from their apartments somewhere, claim Bambi can live forever if the big bad hunter would just not kill his mommy. Misguided, bureaucratic controlled fish and game personnel make bad decisions in fear of reprisal and/or heat. Damn shame. I say, either the non-hunting public gets off its complacent ass and figure out the truth, or just stay out of it. Lack of information steering a decision could, and in fact has caused great harm to the wild that I love. And I've had just about enough of it.

It would be simple management procedure to establish hunting seasons and bag limits based on habitat and individual species population dynamics. Unnecessary gross losses due to starvation, road kills, dog and predator kills, and various other causes could be better controlled by giving out more kill permits for hunter utilization. There is no reason to subject animals to what is basically a forced, prolonged, agonizing death due to habitat restrictions. I know from hands-on experience how deer, for example, can be specifically managed and maintained in exacting proportion to their land support capability. There are many hunting clubs in this country and abroad that have succeeded in developing near-perfect, balanced game herds by using proven methods. The health and superior quality of their animals attest to the techniques available that could in fact be applied by our game departments, if the anti-hunter assholes would just leave us alone. But alas, there does not appear to be much relief on the horizon.

In the meantime, I implore my fellow sportsmen and women, or anybody who truly cares about the wildlife, to take the battle to heart. Put this book down right now for a little while and write a letter to the newspaper, the game department, TV, magazines, everybody, and get the demand in their faces that we want what's best for the critters. Help focus attention on habitat destruction, attempted hunting closures where it isn't necessary, gun confiscation or limitation, or any issue you are fed up with. The day of complacency and apathy should come to an end right now. Let your voice be heard. Each individual CAN AND MUST make a difference. If just the Nugent Rock 'n' Roll bowhunters took pen in hand and attacked, we would blow some minds! DO IT NOW! For ol' Ted, and bowhuntin', for yourselves, and ultimately for the critters. We have made a big enough mess of things already. It's not too late if we get going. It will take a pen in hand, with a clear vision of what we want, to get the job done. And it will take a special breed of people to take the initiative. That special breed is us. Let's ROCK 'EM.

Mother Nature
Is a Bitch,
But I Still Love Her

For the umpteenth time I was perched twenty feet up in my favorite oak tree with a hawk's eye view of the rolling farm country in southern Michigan. The crops were harvested, as they always are, and the surrounding countryside was beginning to take on the depleted look of winter. The eleven whitetail deer had spent the last fifty minutes melting out of the woodlot's shadows into the remnant cornstalks on the swamp's edge. A feeding ritual seeking out scattered grain in America's cropland represents survival sustenance to these animals. Farming technology has all but eliminated spillage and makes for slim pickings in these fields. The deer meandered up and down the cornrows obviously finding little to eat. One of the yearlings was munching steadily on a small pile of grain apparently spilled where the combine left the field. The remaining deer joined him.

As I've seen so many times before, the oldest and largest doe of the group rose up on her hind feet and came down swiftly with a flailing front hoof onto a younger deer's back. WHACK! One by one, she eliminated the competition and became queen of the hill. Wildlife writer and photographer friends of mine have documented numerous occasions where death to offspring has resulted in dominance over scarce and preferred food during the hard months of winter in typical whitetail habitat.

I don't need some concrete-jailed animal protectionist to tell me about "animal families" and the wonderful world of Bambi. There is no such thing. I've spent over forty years in the real world of wildlife and I've witnessed Mother Nature's scheme first hand. Boar bear will eat their offspring at nearly every opportunity. Male lions will do the same. In the wild, there is no life without death and, nearly always, that death is violent and unforgiving.

My family and I do not consume commercial or domestic meat. We only eat what I kill myself with bow and arrow or firearm. There are more elk, wild turkey, whitetail deer and pronghorn antelope in America today than there were ninety years ago. It's all a matter of habitat and its carrying capacity through the winter months. In my home state of Michigan, there are over 65,000 deer carcasses removed annually from the state's highways. The number is over 75,000 in Pennsylvania. Of course, these numbers only represent those that are killed outright, and most wildlife and law enforcement officers agree the number could be double that if wounded animals that die out of sight are included. That means that we have paved over, and overwhelmingly compromised, historical wildlife range.

Each year, in nearly every state of the nation except California, where they have an out-of-control mountain lion problem, the deer-hunting harvest figures continue to grow. Because of habitat reclamation, improved forest management and timber-cutting operations, combined with agricultural land set-aside policies, many wildlife populations are at all-time highs.

The ignorant anti-hunters and so-called preservationists continually harm and threaten wildlife by their insensitive knee-jerk, make-believe claims. Even in the

Toby Nugent, Black Bear, Canada, 1999

face of undeniable documented proof by trained scientists and biologists, these dastardly factions are still trying to stop concerned sportsmen's Great Swamp annual hunt in New Jersey to maintain a healthy deer herd within the confines of the remaining finite habitat.

It's easy to be swayed by a photograph of a cute raccoon with its foot in a trap in your favorite magazine. In an irrational attempt to save the little animal, otherwise well-meaning people are funding the perpetrators of these horrible lies. Does anyone truly believe that the minks for fur coats, deer for venison burgers or pheasants for my dinner died any deader than Holly Farms drumsticks, Big Macs, or your favorite leather

Double bag, Pollington's Buck Pole Ranch, Michigan, 1999

jacket? So many times I have been subjected to pathetic tirades by so-called do-gooders, veggies and their ilk, condemning me for putting an arrow through my dinner, with their feet in dead stuff. A portion of the cost for their shoes went directly to the killer.

Unless a person lives on another planet, they directly contribute to death every day of their lives. The protestors of the Great Swamp hunt eliminated, through displacement and ultimately death, untold numbers of living things in the grand scope of human encroachment as they populated their paved, sewered, toxic-dumped, manicured-lawn, fertilizer-poisoned, permanently altered little neighborhood. All the hunters and trappers in the world will never catch up to the wildlife body count victims of just golf courses in this country. Hunters, fishermen and trappers pay for wildlife management, for all to appreciate via their license fees and self-imposed taxes.

Everyone wants to save lives. In the big picture of planet Earth, saving a species is far more important than the close-minded, short-sighted saving of a few lives. The

9-point whitetail, Claude Pollington's Buck Pole Deer Camp, Marion, Michigan, 2003

African country of Kenya, against sound historical management pleas, stopped sport hunting in 1972. At that time, there were 150,000 magnificent elephants found throughout the country. There were thousands upon thousands of rhinoceros. Then the hunting stopped. Along with the hunting stopped the flow of funds to manage these and all wildlife in Kenya. Today, there are but small remnant groups of animals found only in the sightseeing tourist areas. Without funds generated by the sportsman's licenses and related expenditures to pay for an ample number of game wardens, the illegal poaching business has run rampant. Only now, in a

Double sika stags, YO Ranch, Texas, 1999

"No Hunting" zone, is the African rhino on the verge of extinction. Yet in the country of South Africa, where sport hunting is still a way of life, the black rhinoceros and white rhinoceros both maintain a viable breeding population.

These classic confrontations are often repeated around the globe. The modern-day sports hunter has not been responsible for anything close to the extinction of any animal. Even the American bison, whose numbers approached one hundred million in the 1700s, would be no more numerous than they are today, if for no other reason than the wave of human encroachment. The cattle and sheep industry would have seen to that. Not to mention the alteration of their sustaining habitat throughout the continent. Never forget, that it was hunters like Theodore Roosevelt and his hunting buddies who created the concept of wildlife refuges in this country and in the world. Kruger, the famous African leader and hunter, established that great park. Even so, after meeting with the manager of Kruger National Park in the Republic of South Africa, I learned that over one thousand cape buffalo and

Ted, Shemane, and Rocco

one hundred elephants are killed within the park some years to balance the carrying capacity with the mouths to feed.

I used to say that it's not a very pretty picture, just a necessary one. But now, considering what lessons have been learned over such a long period of time, it really is a pretty picture. We must stop equating death and blood in the wild as something undesirable. Anything that benefits God's creation is truly desirable.

The predator sometimes chooses its meal as its meal is being born, taking the mother down as well. This is not wrong. This is not painful. This is not ugly. This is, in fact, the beauty of life. The predator gets his meal; the prey species is made stronger through the cull. An entire chain of biological events takes place when addressing the big picture and improving life.

The devil is out there preying upon you, in the name of God, so he can afford private planes, multiple homes and a wardrobe that only a big-time pimp can appreciate. There are other devious bastards who will try to sell a bill of goods in the name of saving cute little animals' lives so he, too, can make a lot of money.

I do not believe that these so-called friends of animals give a damn about the animals whatsoever, but are taking advantage of our human instincts to help the critters. If you really want to help wildlife, buy a hunting license, buy a fishing

5x5 bull elk, Young Ranch, Texas 1999

8-point whitetail, Michigan, 2000

license, send a check to the National Wildlife Federation, send a check to the Wildlife Legislation Fund of America (WLFA), Ducks Unlimited or your state wildlife agency.

Don't go down to the pits at the Indianapolis 500 and tell anybody how to adjust their fuel injectors unless you've spent some time, a lot of time, with fuel injectors. Any life you lead can be enhanced, and much more appreciated, if you spend more time in the out of doors. If you truly want to help, first you have to know how. Take a drive out in the country. Get out of your car and put

16

some earth under your feet. Meet a farmer and learn the ways of the land. Contact your local trappers association or hunting club. Touch that part of life that all our lives come from and will determine where our lives will go. The old miners used to keep a small bird in a cage deep down in their mineshafts to monitor the oxygen quality in their work place. The condition of wildlife in our fragile environment today will foretell the potential quality of our lives in the years to come.

Healthy wildlife is intelligently managed wildlife. Within the altered structure of modern land use, it is now in the hands of man. Mother Nature used to have a buffer zone when she had the whole world to play with. Now, a judgment mistake on her part could have a devastating effect on what may be a pocket population of wildlife. Leave it to her, and the bitch could really mess things up! Modern wildlife-management techniques, based on population dynamics and winter range carrying capacity, must be adhered to intelligently to ensure the wonderful beauty of wildness for generations to come. I don't know about you, but I'm going hunting.

Fallow buck, Texas, 2003

Ask Uncle Ted
HOW TO MAXIMIZE YOUR SPIRIT OF THE WILD

Q1 Dear Blood Brother Ted, I've read your books and watch your various TV appearances and have noticed that you have a very unique and wonderful way with words. I was wondering if you could give your definitions of some catchphrases you use quite often: True North and Spirit of the Wild? Thanks a lot, *Ed Weber*

A Thanx for you support, Ed. TruNorth refers to our spiritual compass setting guiding us to always do the right thing, whether anyone is watching or not. Spirit of the Wild identifies the ever mystical wonderment and dynamic of God's creation that is all around us, most emphatically beyond the pavement where nature thrives and our intellect guides us to function as reasoning predators in His Tooth, Fang & Claw world. Pursue 'em both the very best ya can!! Good luck, Blood Brothers, Ted

Q2 I'm new to hunting and I'm planning to go on my first hunt in September. I'm looking to buy your Nugent Blade broadheads, but I'm unsure of which grain to choose. Which is better for the average hunter, the 100- or 125-grain? I know that the 100-grain will be light and can give more speed, but there can be disadvantages as well. What is your preference also? Thanx, *Heath*

A Welcome, my friend, to the Spirit of the Wild Blood Brother campfire. Know that you are embarking on a wonderful journey to a higher level of awareness as a reasoning predator that will upgrade your overall quality of life. I assure you! Archery and bowhunting can be an exacting discipline, and the tuning of our personal choice in equipment is critical. I highly recommend that you ignore considerations of speed in choosing your gear, and focus on grace, feel and effectiveness in accuracy and stealth. A silent, accurate arrow is what brings home the sacred spirit backstraps, believe me. My 53-pound Renegade bow delivers a 500-grain arrow at a plodding 200 fps, but I kill consistently. It is much more about predator radar than it will ever be about speed. Test your combination of arrow and broadhead to be sure they fly true. That's all that matters. Though you will be told otherwise, large, hi-profile, hard helical feathers will best stabilize and steer your hunting arrows. The weight, stiffness and length of your arrows will be determined by your bow design, draw length and bow weight. Test extensively to discover THE killer setup for your own style of shooting. The mystical flight of the arrow will come in due time as you put your heart and soul into being the archer/hunter you can be. Give it your best and let me know how ya do. Good luck!

Q3 First thing I would like to say is a BIG thank you for all that you do for the hunting world. I appreciate all the things that you invest your time and name into to help protect our rights and to further our sport. Second, I would like to say what a HUGE fan I am of your music, your videos and your Spirit of the Wild shows. I have watched every video you have produced and I never miss your show. If I could partake of your wisdom for a few moments,

9-point whitetail, Michigan, 2003

I had a few questions. A little background on the bow I shoot: I shoot eighty pounds, I prefer medium weight arrows, I shoot Muzzy three-blade fixed blade broadheads, use a whisker biscuit rest, use twenty-eight-inch arrows, use all the Sims products available, use a release, and I enjoy shooting long distance when I practice. I am currently switching to carbon arrows (due to arrow longevity) and I was wondering what type of fletching I should use with them. I have never used carbon before and don't really know much about them. I was wondering if I should use four-inch or five-inch vanes, three or four fletch, and right helical, left helical or straight fletch? I currently use 2317 Easton XX78 aluminum arrows and 125-grain broadheads, and was wondering, with the slimmer and lighter Easton evolution arrows I am planning on making the switch to, will the 125-grain broadheads effect my long range flight, and if that would effect the flight of the arrow, would I be better off switching to 100- or 75-grain broadheads (which I really would prefer to stay at 125 grains to keep my arrow weight up a little bit if possible). One last thing is I was wondering what you think of the new single cam bows. My own personal thoughts on them is that they pull uncomfortably for me, torque unbalanced when shot. Could you suggest any bows that are available with twin cams, and available up to eighty pound draw? (I shoot eighty pounds because it is the only weight I have ever felt comfortable pulling back, and I have no problems pulling it straight back repeatedly.) Hopefully one day I will get to meet you and shake your hand to thank you for all you do for hunters everywhere. Keep up the good work. Thanx, *Joe*

A Thanx back at ya Joe for your kind words. In this cultural war against hunting and gun rights, I pray every hunter and gun owner will stand up and fight for our God-given rights together. Let's pray that day comes soon. If you're not a member of the NRA, you're no friend of mine. I can summarize your concerns by highly recommending to you to always shoot the equipment that FEELS best for you. All bows made in America today are ultra quality. You sound like you know what you like, so stick with it. As long as you shoot eighty pounds comfortably, your long-range practice fun will be fine no matter what bow, arrow or broadhead combo you choose. I do suggest you use five-inch hi-profile feathers on carbon or aluminum when hunting for maximum arrow stabilization. Hard helical, R or L, is best. Trial and error will guide your decision.

Q4 Uncle Ted, I am sixteen years old and live in mid-Michigan. My buddy Tim and I are die-hard bowhunters. Every year we have trouble locating bucks the first couple weeks of the season, before the rut starts warming up. We hunt between feeding grounds and bedding areas of the beast during these hard times to no avail. We see a lot of does and occasionally a spike but no shooters. I was wondering how you set up for the early season. *Ryan*

A I luv teenage bowhunters!! Salute to you guys!

12-point whitetail, Sunrize Acres, Michigan, 1996

Michigan whitetails, especially bucks older than a year and a half, are the smartest animals in the world. Finding a mature buck before rut time is tuff for all of us. It takes an amazing amount of smart scouting and thinking outside the box. The most traveled trails in your area are NOT the trails to hunt. Go deeper. Look for the nastiest puckerbrush hellzone you can find, use the wind, be silent and do not crowd the area. Go early, stay late, stay back, climb high into a crows nest tree and use your binos to figure em out. Do not underestimate the midday hours, as that is when the smart old boys make their moves as they pattern us. Spend more time afield and get ready for the moment of truth! And get all your young friends to join ya in the great outdoors so they can discover the joys of our Spirit of the Wild!! Good luck!

Q5 Ted, I have a poor retrieval rate on bow-shot hogs. I shoot a 72-pound Golden Eagle, and have complete pass thru more times than not. The last pig I shot was eight paces from me, I put it right behind his shoulder, angling forward. He dropped in his tracks squealing like a proverbial stuck

pig, and got up and ran like hell. My pard' and I tracked blood for about four hundred yards until the blood ran out. I use a Muzzy 100-grain three blade and have had great luck with it on these South Texas whitetails. Of the last ten pigs I've shot, I've lost three. South Texas is infested with wild hogs. I know that stuff happens and it's a part of

Jurassic Pork: Free-range wild boar, Texas, 1995

the game. I was just wondering what you do, that I may not be doing, to help on recovering wounded game. Keep the wind in you face, *BK*

A Losing game is every hunter's worst nightmare, but let me remind you, that God's deadliest predators, lions, eagles, hawks and owls lose more critters than they bring home! Do not despair!! Now, here's the simple system I use to bring 'em home. It's all about shot placement. Period. Of course, you must be in full shot preparation before the game gives it to ya, so be sure you are ready to rock. I say my little three-step pre-shot prayer where I, One-Pick a spot; Two-Breathe to relax my form and anchor; and Three-Release with my back muscles for a killer shot. Hit one-third up from the foreleg armpit, broadside or quartering away, you got pork on the ground my friend. Make that xtra effort to perfect your shot sequence and your recovery rate will soar!! Good luck!

Q6 **Sir, I am a right-handed person with a cross-dominant eye. (My left eye is dominant.) Over the past several years I have been having problems adjusting the sight pins on my right-handed bow for accuracy. So far I have been able to hit the target effectively but with a lot of compensation for sight picture. Do you think I need to change to a left-handed bow or what can I do to fix the cross-dominant problem involving sight picture?**

Also, thank you for all you are doing for the American sportsman. Every year it seems like our "rights" are getting harder and harder to keep involving hunting and firearms ownership. I have been in law enforcement over twenty years, and when we speak out for protecting our "rights" we are labeled "activists" or potential threats to society by the liberal media. Again, thank you for not being afraid to speak out on your beliefs. Best of Wishes, *Al Lavender lavender@uffdaonline.net*

A That cross-dominant eye deal can be a real pisser. All my friends have either gone to a lefty bow setup or gone instinctive, practicing hard-core training the right eye to become the archery eye by closing the left eye during extended practice sessions. It can work. We the people salute you for serving and protecting our American Dream, my friend. Challenge everyone you know to join the NRA and their state hunting orgs and learn to fight for our God-given rights. It's the only hope in the abysmal cultural war against us!! Godspeed.

Q7 **Hey Nuge. This upcoming deer season will be my second ever, and I thought you may be able to give a green hunter some advice. What's your opinion on Scent-lok 3-D clothing? Also, I'm thinking about using groundblinds (natural or commercially made), since I feel more comfortable on the ground. Is this a good idea, or should I bite my lip and pray to the gods of the wild to help me deal w/ the advantage of a treestand?** *J.B, Iowa* **P.S. I'll be switching broadheads this season too. Magnus 100 grain two-blade from now on! Your book kicks ass!**

A Thanx and welcome to our Spirit of the Wild Blood Brother hunting campfire, JB. Groundblinds are great!! AmeriStep, GameTracker, Double Bull, so many will do fine. My favorite is the Invisiblind (800-247-6788 x295 or *www.invisiblind.com*).

A solid twelve-foot ladderstand like my fave NorthStarr (877-302-7827) will give ya a secure, safe confidence and git ya up for height advantage without scaring the bejeezuz out of ya!! You will luv the NugeBlade. If there were a deadlier head, I'd use it! Best of luck.

Q8 **Each deer season I go out to the UP of MI to hunt deer. The 160-acre property is one quarter swamp, one quarter hardwoods and half open fields. We plant corn on the majority of the fields that we then sell as deer feed. The remaining we have rye and clover. Over the past few years we have been trying to enhance the land to grow bigger bucks. We see many bucks, but the majority of them are spikes and forks. Where should we put our efforts to get these bucks to the next level? Is it genetics in the herd on our land that is preventing bigger racks?**

A The mighty UP certainly has genetics as good as anywhere in America, I'm sure. B&C monsters are killed there with regularity. It is universally agreed that good ol' Ma Nature controls the deer herd in the xtreme wilderness of the UP, and that Old Man Winter kills more deer there than hunters ever could. That being said, it sounds like you're doing all the right things to optimize your herd quality. If you can afford to, leave the corn and other crops up for the deer to utilize throughout the harsh winter months. It is also agreed that if whitetail deer have constant access to quality feed at least until Christmas, they will do just fine into spring. There is a killer wildlife feed supplement I believe in by the name of Buck Grub that I would consider on your sacred huntgrounds. Feed it as much as you can throughout the year for enhanced health and stamina, assuring a genetically predisposed buck will attain his potential. But nutrition and genetics can only bring a buck to max antler fruition if he grows to be at least four years old. Preferably, five or six. That means demanding discipline by all your hunters to let immature bucks walk. That is never easy when a handsome three-year-old ten-pointer gives us a shot. But ya gotta let 'em grow. Join the Quality Deer Management Association for all the details and good luck.

Q9 **Ted, I have rocked out to your tunes for years. Just the other day I heard an interview with you on the Robin and Maynard show (KZOK 102.5 Seattle). I just had to check out your website and find out if I could ask you a question. Well here it is:**

How can we expect to keep a balance of nature by controlling the population of wild creatures while not controlling our own population? It is plain mathematics. The planet stays the same size, people population multiplies, space required for animals is depleted. In Washington state, seals are killed to protect the salmon, land currently for cougar habitat is becoming urban

10-point whitetail, Michigan, 1997

sprawl, blah blah blah. I could go on, but you get my point.

I get tired of hearing people complain about the traffic, urban sprawl, crime, etc. when they just pump out a few kids. Do they not see they have contributed to the problem? I can't help the fact that I am part of the population. I was born beyond my control. But I can do my part by not procreating.

Anyway, I guess my point is, how can the balance of nature be kept if the most destructive of all creatures is the one that there is no regulation on population? Your input would be appreciated. Thanks, *Bob*

A You're correct, Bob. Balance demands control on all growth. Global statistics corroborate that America's human population growth rate is the least obtrusive on the planet, and as a conscientious nation, it does not surprise me that we have shown leadership in this critical quality of life issue. That being said, each and

Scimitar horned oryx, Samples Ranch, Texas, 2001

every citizen of this great nation has a moral duty to be more attuned and involved in environmental activism now more than ever. You will discover the truth, that the hunting, fishing and trapping grass roots orgs across the land have always been in the forefront of ecosystem conservation, and of course that critical wildlife habitat we so deeply cherish is the sole producer of our life giving air, soil and water quality. I for one have immense faith in my fellow Americans to do the right thing. Safeguarding wild ground by recycling urban brown zones is paramount to saving Ma Nature's precious renewable resource productivity. Join RMEF, NWTF, Delta Waterfowl and many of the other progressive habitat-saving hunting orgs to be an asset to this forward motion.

Q10 **I was wondering what your thoughts were on the Native American fish-spearing season here in Wisconsin. I read in an article that this one guy was totally against it. He said he wondered what Ted Nugent would say about the spearing. I personally don't care one way or another. But I do know a lot of the caucasians think it's unfair. They seem to think that the Native Americans should stop doing something that they have been doing for hundreds of years. I'm sure he is not even aware of the situation. Thank you.**

A Oh I'm aware of it, alrighty. If it has to do with the great outdoors or the American Dream, I assure you I am aware of it. Renewable resources must be valued. The surplus must be managed for utility, therefore I support all legal methodologies that provide fair opportunity for all "we the people" to harvest our renewable resources. That would include bag limits no matter whether it is fly fishing, snagging or spearfishing. Ya can't grill it 'til ya kill it. The Indian fish and game use isn't really about how they harvest, but rather, no matter who is harvesting, about how much based on a simple scientific sustain yield/productivity equation. I say have at it, as long as the resource is not damaged and the sacred harvest is utilized with respect and without waste. That is the Native American ethic that I was raised on and it remains a self-evident truth today. I do care; you should too.

Q11 Hello Ted Nugent!! I've been a HUGE fan of yours for years!!! I LOVE the work you did with the Amboy Dukes and your solo career! I'm also a drummer and I've been playing for twenty-five years now. I LOVE playing along to "Dog Eat Dog" from *Free-For-All!* I'm also getting the call from the Spirit of the Wild to go bowhunting, but I have no one to go hunting with!! Nobody I know likes to bow hunt! Can you believe that!! So I've been looking at 3D shooting and target shooting and I came across your website and took a look at Renegade Bows. I can see why you use them! I'm also interested in the Non-Typical XL, but I also have other brochures from other bow companies and I'm pulling out my hair! My cash flow isn't all that great and a couple of Pro Shops said I can put a bow on layaway so maybe I can get a Non-Typical XL!! I just wish I could go hunting!! I wish you also lived close by so I could go hunting with you! Could I use the Non-Typical for 3D and target shooting? I also read *Bowhunting World,* is that a good publication? Your help would be greatly appreciated! What else would you recommend on choosing a bow? Stick with one company? I sure hope to hear from you when you get some time, Ted. God bless you and your family, and keep up the good work with the outdoors. And Music!! Bowhunting Rules! Regards, *Jeff Wissing, Milwaukee, WI*

5x5 bull elk, Missouri, 1997

A Cool Jeff! We welcome you to the great Spirit of the Wild Blood Brother campfire of the Great Outdoor lifestyle. You WILL be moved! Renegade bows are my favorite, but there are no bad bows made in America today. You will discover that archery is all about touch, feel and spirit. You must try many bows to find your baby. I do strongly suggest you get a lightweight, graceful, easy-to-draw bow that fits you properly. Being a resident of the great bowhunting state of WI, I'd recommend you contact RAC directly as Bill Weisner and the RAC tribe truly care and really know their stuff. Your best bet is to join the WI Bowhunters Association, as they can really steer you straight for the ultimate bowhunting ops. *Bowhunting World* is a great magazine, as are so many others. We think our *Ted Nugent Adventure Outdoors* is the best there is. Good luck, good rockin', and good hunting to you and yours. Let me know how your mystical flight of the arrow goes. Blood Brothers, Ted

Q12 **Ted, I first want to thank you for all you do to protect the God-given rights and way of life for myself and other sportsmen. I've read *God, Guns, & Rock 'n' Roll* twice, and still go back to some of my favorite chapters during that long summer wait for fall hunting. I've actually given two copies to friends as gifts, and we ALWAYS tune-in to your visits with "The Bob & Tom Show" (WFBQ, Indianapolis). I enjoyed reading about your snow goose hunt (seventy in one day!) and I want to do my part to help manage the snow goose population while having the time of my life beyond the pavement. Is there a place or a guide that you could recommend as close to Indianapolis as possible? Also, am I OK with my Remington 870 Express or would it be wise to invest in a semi-auto for fowl? Thanks Guitarboy, *Brad Morris Indianapolis, IN***

Waterfowling, Michigan, 1995

A Thanx Brad. Is this hunting lifestyle the greatest or what! Did I mention YOWZA? There are more and more states offering xpanded snowgoose seasons. Go to the various states' DNR or F&W websites to discover seasons and dates. Your 870 oughtta do the job just fine as long as you pattern your gun with the various gooseloads you plan on using. Good luck. Kill 'em & grill 'em.

Chief Gonzo

Q13 **Ted, I speak for the city of Clinton, Iowa, when I say you are the single greatest performer American Rock 'n' Roll has ever had, or will ever see! You left me and my town bleeding red, white and blue on July 3rd at Riverboat days. THANK YOU from all of us in Clinton, Iowa! Now to my question: While performing *Great White Buffalo* you wear an Indian headdress. I was wondering if it's from any certain tribe, and if so what might it symbolize? Thank GOD we have a Rock 'n' Roll hero we can still look up to!** *Lee Dose, Clinton, IA*

A Thanx much, Lee. My bands always create the most xciting rock there is. They are the best! My song *Great White Buffalo* celebrates mankind's connection with the Great Spirit of the land and a deep, soulful respect for all of God's amazing gifts of creation. Though my mom and dad and great men like Fred Bear passed it on to me, they were actually carrying on the acknowledgment of our resource stewardship responsibilities to the earth, wind and fire, tooth, fang and claw reality of Nature by living the ultimate hands-on conservation lifestyle of hunting, fishing and trapping. This aboriginal lifestyle is alive and well in America today, and the lyrics and attitude of my song point out the lessons of abuse as man disconnected with the buffalo as a symbol of all life-giving renewable resources. Powerful medicine indeed! Though the actual war bonnet I wear on stage is not official Indian regalia, it surely represents my reverence for my Red brothers and the lessons learned from their history and spiritual subsistence. I have shared wonderful Blood Brother campfires with many tribes around the nation, and the *Great White Buffalo* is our soundtrack for returning to Nature as healer. Heal on!

Axis doe, YO Ranch, Texas, 2003

Q14 Ted, Love your *Spirit of the Wild* TV show! My question is, I am pretty new to big-game hunting and in Wisconsin the firearm season starts November 23rd after the rut. Is using a .30-06 with a 3-9x40 scope in Northern Wisconsin the best method of hunting for that time of the season? Thanks in advance. *Mark*

A The '06 rocks, Mark! And a 3x9 scope is a great all around choice. The only determining factor will always be, how good do you shoot it? As long as you're accurate and comfortable with that set-up, you should have back-straps sizzling as we speak! Good luck.

Q15 I had a chance to attend YMCA camp with my son and his class from school. The camp is in our home town of Napoleon, MI, on Stoney Lake. They had some great lessons on the Environment and Native Americans. The unfortunate part is in the lessons, they left the impression that hunters hurt the environment. I tried to explain the difference between Hunters and Poachers, plus the good that hunters do in taking care of the environment. I know there is information out there that shows this. I have read much of this from you. Could you please help me in locating this information, so I may return to the camp with the correct information that they may teach. I believe (and hope) that their misleading message is just due to improper information. I thank you in advance for your help and hope that with the proper information, they can continue to teach of the earth and environment but not beat up those that fight so hard to protect and honor it. Thank You, *Robert E. Gillow*

A Good stuff, Robert. It is imperative that each and every one of us who know the truth constantly monitor our daily lives to be sure the truth is respected. In 2003, for anyone, especially at a YMCA camp for God's sake, claims to be unaware of the phenomenal success story of wildlife management by the hunting, fishing and trapping community is absolutely inexcusable. You would have to be living under a rock, braindead or just rotten to the core to spew such nonsense. Every wildlife agency and organization will have unlimited information and evidence why there are more deer, turkey, geese, bear and mountain lions in America today than ever in recorded history. Read my books *God, Guns, & Rock 'n' Roll and Kill It & Grill It,* plus the fourteen years back issues of my *Ted Nugent Adventure Outdoors* magazines (800-343-4868) or contact Ducks Unlimited, Safari Club International, Rocky Mountain Elk Foundation, National Wild Turkey Federation or any number of conservation groups for the exciting details. Then stand up and deliver the truth wherever you go. In this cultural war of vulgar denial against truth, it is more important than ever to stand up against "feel-good" PC lies. God bless & Godspeed

Q16 Ted, I watch your *Spirit of the Wild* shows every chance I get. I hunt in Marcellus, MI, on about 350 acres of private land in Cass County. My question to you is, the deer racks tend to be small; some three- , four- , five- , six-point bucks, and some small eights. Now, the property across the dirt road has big eleven- to twelve-point bucks. How is the best way to lure them back to my area? I have clover, wheat, corn, acorns, etc., swamps to bed down in, hills, down tree tops, thick cover. I just can't figure it out. I have bowhunted for about the last eight years. Learning everything I can as well as studying the deers' movements. At one time I had twenty young

The beast is dead--long live the beast! Pollington's Buckpole Ranch, Michigan, 2003

deer and does all around me. Not one buck ever made it into the area. Even in the middle of November. Maybe you have a suggestion to what else I should try. Thanks, *Rich McGrew*

A Frustrating as hell, isn't it Rich! I know the feeling. It sounds like you're doing everything right, and even so, sometimes the old bucks have simply picked out a historical area for a hideout for reasons we will never know. I'll bet the property across the road has more outrageous thickets and hellholes of nasty puckerbrush that the bucks just feel safer in. If you timber off a center core of your land to allow sunlight to regenerate thick ground growth, in about five years you could draw them in. Start teasing them with BuckGrub year round and I bet you will see an upgrade of horn encounters. Good luck.

Black buck antelope, YO Ranch, Texas, 2003

Q17 **Ted, I have a small farm in Missouri that is overrun with deer. For safety, I only allow six hunters at a time in the woods. Most everyone limits out (three deer), and two of us bowhunt and are permitted six more deer, but we seldom can fill all of the tags. So now to the question, short of not planting my crops and burning the forest, how do I control these deer that keep dropping twins and triplets? Thank you in advance for any suggestion you may have. *Carl L. Hunsicker***

A This is an easy one Carl. I'll be right there! Seriously, with average hunting pressure on ideal habitat, it will be impossible to balance your herd adequately each year. What you need to do is get hardcore about killing more does. It sounds like you need to really hammer the female deer. I'd love to help, but short of bringing in the WhackMaster Mr. FixIt OrkinMan Nuge, you gotta recruit some guys who are ready to really hammer 'em. I'd suggest inviting some youth groups to increase the

Ted and Richard Matott, Kamp for Kids, 1995

doe harvest while providing exciting quality outdoor time for the younguns. Our TNUSA MO tribe could help set that up. You should be a TNUSA member and establish a good communication with your fellow MO members to get the job done. Call 800-343-4868 for this overnight upgrade! Good luck.

Q18 Hi. I watch your show *Spirit of the Wild* . . . I enjoy what you have to say . . . I just started shooting the BowTech bow and wanted your opinion on it . . . I used to shoot Golden Eagle but got talked into the Bowtech . . . was just wondering if you have heard anything negative or positive about this new bow. Thanks very much, *Rick Dammerich*

A The BowTech line of bows are killer for sure, Rick. So are the Golden Eagle bows. I believe that every bow manufacturer in America today makes superb quality archery tackle and you cannot go wrong with any of them. The trick is getting your hands on a bow set-up that FEELS perfect for your personal touch. I cannot emphasize strongly enough how important that "touch" is. Shoot as many different bows as you can so you know which one is best for you. Good luck!

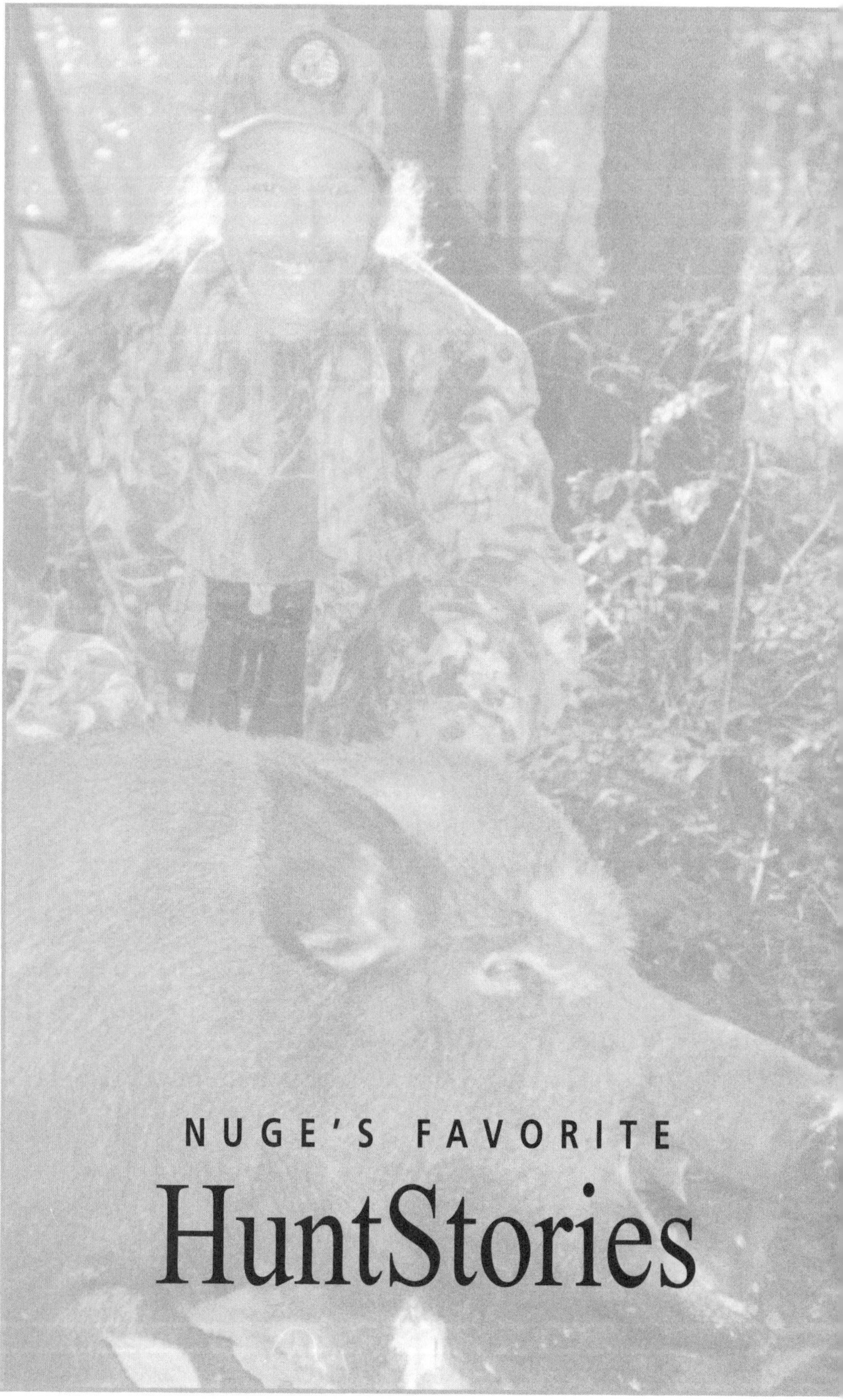

NUGE'S FAVORITE

HuntStories

☆   Difficult to impossible BLOOD TRAIL.

☆☆   Difficult, but readily followable BLOOD TRAIL.

☆☆☆   Apparent BLOOD TRAIL can be followed in walking mode.

☆☆☆☆   Major artery severed, BLOOD TRAIL obvious.

☆☆☆☆☆ Stevie Wonder could follow this BLOOD TRAIL!

NOTE: XX75 is a model of Easton aluminum arrow.

Zwickey, Bear Razorhead, Satellite Titan, Nugent Blade, Muzzy, Bodkin, MA-3, MA-2, Bowlo, Rothar Snuffer, Barrie Royal & Grande, Pearson Deadhead, Howard Hill, Thunderhead, Razorback 4 & 5, Hoyt Chuck-It and Bow-Bullet are hunting arrowheads, called broadheads.

Bear Take Down, Kodiak, Hunter Magnum, Jennings, Oneida Screaming Eagle (OSE), Oneida Nugent WhackMaster and Gonzo Safari are bows.

1

EQUIPMENT: Bear Super Kodiak recurve at fifty-pounds, Bear 8 arrow bow quiver, thirty-one-inches, fiberglass Micro-Flite #10 arrows, Bear Razorheads with inserts-filed.

ANIMAL: Barbirousa Ram a.k.a. Ramboulet, at two hundred pounds, heavy wool, three curls

HIT: Forty yards, running, through center of neck (jugular), went fifty yards

My hunting time was very limited in these years because my Rock 'n' Roll was overwhelming. I had not killed a whitetail yet and was constantly learning. I discovered Louie's hunting operation literally in my backyard of Lower Michigan and was willing to give it a whack. Louie Riggerillo, the owner/operator, had serious reservations about the bow and arrow, but was reluctantly willing to give it a try. When I showed up with hair down to my ass and the attitude to go with it, boy was he pissed. He begrudgingly took me to the hunting area with his Smith & Wesson model 29 strapped on (he was sure he'd have to kill an arrow-poked animal) and we began glassing game. We saw whitetails, fallow, sika, elk, red stag, bison, goats, Corsican rams, hogs, Barbirousas and Mauna Kea sheep everywhere and I was psyched.

Not understanding bowhunting (and not liking this bowhunter), Louie haphazardly approached the game to within one hundred yards and said to "go at it." Thanks a lot. Louie was big, fat and slow and I was long, lean and moved like greased lightning. So I made off into a ravine towards a single, triple curl, Barbo ram. Louie stayed back and watched through his binoculars as I ran out of cover at fifty yards. As I contemplated the shot from a prone position, the ram sensed danger and started trotting left to right. As I rose to one knee he kicked it into high gear. I snap-shot instinctively at him as he was running full tilt. I had always shot Howard Hill-Fred Bear style with my long-bows and recurves, and that lovely Micro-Flite shaft swooped perfectly, to intercept the dirty white ram, like it was on a mission of mercy. The arrow sliced thru the neck like it wasn't even there and I immediately saw the spray of jugular blood coloring the wool. The ram piled up, drained, after a short fifty yards.

The conclusions here are obvious. The jugular vein is the big-daddy of blood flow. It's not the target of choice under most circumstances, but deadly every time. I actually over-led my target, but I'll take it.

Louie and I became friends and he was one of the greatest guys I've ever known. I learned a lot about the wild from him. He was a master hunter. I told him if he'd quit listening to that Country & Western bullshit and cranked up the Rock 'n' Roll, he could kill like that too! Louie passed away in '87, but he got his share of hunting in. He was and exceptional rifle and pistol shot, an A-1 gunsmith, and one of the best hunters ever. His wife, Kathy, and daughter, Angelic, are close family friends and we share many wonderful memories of Big Louie. I'll bet he's on the Blood Trail right now! ☆☆☆☆

2

EQUIPMENT: Bear Super Kodiak fifty pounds, Micro-Flite #10 arrows, Bear Razorheads with inserts-filed
ANIMAL: Spanish Goat–red, at 125 pounds
HIT: Walking away a three-quarter angle downhill at twenty yards, entered over right shoulder-base of neck (jugular), went twenty-five yards

Louie was becoming a big fan of this bow and arrow stuff. Having just witnessed his second bow kill, he claimed they died faster than a rifle of .44-mag kill. And right he was, considering the jugular vein hits I made. I always filed my Bear Razorheads with a ten-inch fine mill bastard file, using the ferule as the file guide. This gave the old green heads a coarse, microscopically serrated edge. They were, and still are, murder.

We saw a lone goat go over a slight rise in the woods. After a sprint to close the range, I duck-walked up behind him, peeked over the rise with an arrow nocked, saw him, and let fly. The hit was actually a bit high, but I'll take it! Zingo! He never knew what hit him. Again, he was high and dry when we got to him twenty-five yards down the hill. Louie was starting to think he could actually overlook my ponytail. The Blood Trail was a beauty. When a razor-sharp broadhead slices clean thru the neck, taking the jugular dead center, you will have the most instant, humane kill possible. The blood flow was maximum. ☆☆☆☆☆

3

EQUIPMENT: Bear Super Kodiak 50-pounds, Aluminum arrows,
Bear Razorheads with inserts-filed
ANIMAL: Corsican Ram, full curl, beige coat
HIT: 120 yards, broadside, one quarter turn left to right, low, went thirty yards

I know, I know! And we're only starting. Yes, I'm back at Louie's, and yes, I know, 120 yards is ridiculous. But you have to realize, I was the ONLY twenty-one-year-old white American on the planet that didn't smoke pot or do LSD. I never did. I admit I was/am different. And I didn't drink either, nor smoke. I'm only telling you this so you realize I was considered weird. I more than made/make up for it with my lust for life.

We had been glassing this beautiful ram since daylight and six hours later we couldn't get near him. We were half-heartedly walking toward a high hill over a pond where we had last seen the group of sheep go, hours before. Suddenly he appeared, like a picture, silhouetted on the skyline, looking down at us from 120 yards. Louie commented that the old boy was wise, but he could be had with a rifle. I always did a lot of flight shooting, and not that there is any excuse for ever trying such a shot, I drew back, raised a little, raised a little bit more, felt good, and touched off. I can close my eyes any time I want to see that arrow arch way, way up there, looking better by the inch, slow motion and all, and watching it slice the belly, right below the rib cage.

By the time the arrow got there, we had our binoculars on him in disbelief. He immediately dropped his head and you could see him fall to the ground. He took one step and stumbled. He barely staggered another twenty-five yards, falling. When we got to him, he was dead. Louie wanted to adopt me. ✩✩✩✩

4

EQUIPMENT: Bear Super Kodiak 50-pounds, Aluminum arrows,
Bear Razorback with inserts-filed
ANIMAL: White Fallow Deer, about two hundred pounds
HIT: Double-lung, forty yards running, went fifty yards

My first BLOOD TRAIL in the snow was a revelation. I thought I'd found the meaning of life! It was beautiful. If you have never BLOOD TRAILED on snow, you have not lived.

The ground was white, the deer was white, and I bought a white intern suit, for camo, so I was white too. I didn't even sing any James Brown songs that day. I put white Mask-It tape on the front of my bow, and I was ready to rock. These Fallow deer were running in a group of about thirty. Louie and my brother, Johnny, had circled the same famous 120-yard Corsican hill. I waited on the sparsely treed gully. These deer came cruisin' from left to right and the big buck exposed himself at the last second at forty yards. I drew and released in one motion and drilled him perfectly behind the shoulder. A pass-thru double-lunger that a surgeon shouldn't surpass. Luck? I guess. Nah, I was hot. I might add that this was the fourth hunt at Louie's in as many months and my fourth arrow shot there! I love that part. After I shot this nice buck, the red-on-white Blood Trail exploded before my eyes. I saw this animal expire in fifty yards, so my first "work" trailing job was still ahead of me. ☆☆☆☆

EQUIPMENT: Bear Super Kodiak 50-pounds, Aluminum arrows, Bear Razorback with inserts-filed
ANIMAL: European Red Stag, 2 by 3, about five hundred pounds
HIT: Frontal neck at thirty-five yards, severed vertebrae, dropped instantly!

This was all we needed to see after the first four kills. An animal the size of an elk dropped in his tracks with one arrow. Johnny again had circled behind the thicket, making his way slow and easy, putting no pressure on the stag. Figuring something wasn't quite right, the big bull trotted straight for my spot. Finally noticing me at thirty-five yards, he stopped and faced me directly. This was not a great position for a shot, but not all bad either. The arrow hit hard, with a resounding WHACK! When he fell so fast and hard, I was surprised as hell, and immediately ran up to him and put another arrow through his heart.

Still no tracking job, but valuable lessons were being accumulated. By the way, though game preserves or game ranches are enclosed by game-proof fences, both Louie and I never allowed a fence to come into play, or even saw one during any of our hunts. Had I just wanted a kill, I surely would have got down the '06 and made it easy. Louie had lots and lots of animals and I had lots and lots of energy, sneakiness and desire. I figure I was just born about two hundred years late.

EQUIPMENT: Bear Super Kodiak 50-pounds, Aluminum arrows, Bear Razorheads with inserts-filed
ANIMAL: Wild Black Russian Boar, about three hundred pounds
HIT: Double-lung, broadside, twenty yards, went two hundred yards

These animals are supposed to have real Austrian boar blood in them, and I was going to let it out. They had all the visible characteristics of European hogs: slim withers, deep chest, long black coarse hair, long straight tail, high forehead, long face and snout, a very un-American attitude, and that famous armor plate over the shoulder and ribs. This heavy-duty cartilage can definitely stop an arrow right now, as I was to learn on future hunts. I had been warned repeatedly to avoid this shield and explained to, in detail, how important it was to get behind it.

My shot was calculated, since we had plenty of time to get ready. We saw the four hogs on the ridge of a small one hundred-yard draw just as the sun came up. Luckily we were dressed warm, as a light snow was accumulating. They took what seemed forever to get in range, probably twenty minutes. I had a nice, easy-feeling, twenty-yard shot at the big dude with white tusks showing about three inches as he rooted. The arrow passed through at the last rib, missing the hard stuff, cutting lungs and liver. He bolted out of sight, and we took up my first BLOOD TRAIL straight away. And a fine BLOOD TRAIL it was.

Even with the snow covering it a bit, we followed it down the ridge, through a line of trees and found the old boy finished two hundred yards in the woods. Picture perfect. I was definitely lucky to have had such a technically perfect hit and BLOOD TRAIL. I wanted to hit all my animals like that, just for the trailing job.

In the heated excitement of the shot, it's always difficult to be certain of arrow placement. My turkey-barred natural feathers on the yellow fiberglass arrows were not highly visible. I believe bright fletch, nocks and cresting are great aids in calling your hits. So far I had not been tested by any of my post-hit situations. But I was sure enjoying all this beginner's luck. The Michigan whitetails continued to give me the slip, but I was bowhunting big game and doing a fine job. A guy could do this full time. ☆☆☆☆

7

EQUIPMENT: Bear Super Kodiak at 55-pounds, Aluminum arrows, Bear Razorheads with inserts-filed
ANIMAL: White Angora Goat, about 150 pounds
HIT: Angling away, three-quarter shot, twenty-five yards, enter last right rib, exit forward left shoulder, went one hundred yards

I had seen this long-haired goat before and he had a fine spread of horns. I hadn't come to specifically kill this animal, but I saw him following a trail leaving a meadow into the woods where there were a lot of blow-downs and tree-top brush. We had failed to get in range of anything all day, and after six to eight hours of hunting, I wanted to try for what appeared to be the biggest, best-looking goat on the place. I put these long legs in motion and covered a big circle a half-mile down wind and out of sight of the two goats that were traveling together. I made a wide loop and got into a tangle of downed tree trunks just paces off the main trail.

As the goats appeared out of the broken terrain, I saw that they were on a different trail. They bobbed in and out of vision as I took advantage and stalked my way to intersect them. I had good cover and wind all the way and as I got to a pile of brush, they were just walking away. I sent an arrow through the big one, although a little far back. It looked worse than it was because the arrow entered just behind the last rib and cut diagonally, completely through, exiting the off-left shoulder, forward of the ball joint. He took off like a cat on fire before expiring after one hundred yards. I had a great BLOOD TRAIL the whole way, with a double-lung hit. The Bear Razorhead left its "X." ☆☆☆☆

8

EQUIPMENT: Bear Super Kodiak Magnum at 55-pounds, Aluminum arrows, Bear Razorheads with inserts-filed
ANIMAL: Mauna Kea Sheep, about 130 pounds, 7/9 curl
HIT: Twenty yards, mid-ship-, big artery, went forty yards

The Mauna Kea sheep is from the Hawaiian island of the same name. A typical curled-horn sheep, he has heavy dark wool with a slight off-color saddle. I was still-hunting a familiar grove of young trees with a steady north wind in my face when I saw this Mauna Kea ram with a mixed group of Corsican, Mouflon and Barbirousa sheep. They were out in the open, in a low meadow just out of the trees, grazing a quarter-mile away. I was in full camouflage for the first time, with face paint as well. It was shortly after sunrise and I watched for a half-hour while they fed paralleling the wood lot. As they disappeared below a crest, I snuck through the edge of the timber. The rise they had disappeared behind met a finger of trees and undergrowth. I saw them working in my direction and snuck as far out into the finger as I could. I moved real slow to intercept them. Without taking my eyes off the sheep, this all took awhile. The last one walked by at twenty yards. It was the dark Mauna Kea and I was sure one of the others would detect me. I think I held my breath the whole time, and as he looked the other way to groom himself, I sent the arrow through him. I had worked myself up to a nervous wreck waiting to shoot and hit him dead-center for what I thought was a gut shot. He bolted and vanished into a ravine with the others, but the BLOOD TRAIL was a wonderful thing. It was just like a jugular hit because I severed the main artery that leaves the heart traveling into the femoral. He went just forty yards. ☆☆☆☆

9

EQUIPMENT: Bear Kodiak, Aluminum arrows, Bear Razorheads
ANIMAL: Wild Boar, about two hundred pounds
HIT: Behind left shoulder-stuck in right, running, went 150 yards

Some people like to go shopping, to the movies, art galleries, plays, and stuff like that. Me, I like huntin'. I've got to be outdoors at least seventy-five percent of the time. So with a fresh quiver of new aluminum arrows, I'm "off to see the wizard." I specifically wanted another black boar for the wall and that great hickory smoked meat.

We saw some small black hogs bedded down in the bottom of a draw, but they spooked at our approach. We saw a band of five to six mixed feral hogs rooting along the edge of the meadow by an apple orchard, so we worked our way toward them without any cover. I climbed up on a blowdown and all hell broke loose. Hogs came boiling out every which way, grunting and carrying on. John had his .44 out, cocked, locked, and ready to rock and I drew on a nice black boar charging out to my left. He squirted out of a jumble of limbs at only five feet.

Like a coiled spring, I snapped the arrow back and did a fine job of drilling him behind the left shoulder. About a third of the arrow was sticking out of his left side as he kicked in the afterburners and covered the one hundred yards across the meadow without losing a beat. John was white, as still more pigs kept emerging from the tangle. I'll bet there were twenty hogs in there, all shapes and sizes. It was really exciting. I had a ringside elevated view of the whole thing and some of those pigs ran within feet of John and me. I saw the hit hog vanish into broken ground beyond the open meadow one hundred yards away. After laughing, relaxing, and cleaning our pants we began looking for blood. Now here was my first panicky and confusing BLOOD TRAIL.

I had watched the path of departure and clearly saw the end of the silver arrow with white crest protruding from the kill-zone, but we could not find any blood. I didn't even want to go to the last spot I saw the hog until I could find some blood. Still, we didn't find blood until we got to the edge of the meadow where I had last seen him. And that took some doing because it all looks different from up close. The two hundred-pounder started bleeding from the lungs through his mouth and nose, but not until he covered all one hundred yards.

Remember this. Mark the hit spot. Then mark the last spot you see him. The boar only went another easy BLOOD TRAIL fifty yards, but I was worried there for a while. The arrow penetrated all the good stuff, but stuck hard into the off shoulder leaving no blood from the entrance hole. ✰

10

EQUIPMENT: Bear Kodiak Magnum at 55-pounds, Aluminum arrows, Bear Razorheads
ANIMAL: Black and White Spanish Goat
HIT: Forty yards, base of tail-spine, dropped

Goats, goats, everywhere goats! White ones, brown ones, black ones, and one with long horns and a black-and-white mottled coat. I wanted him. I remember following these guys as they meandered over hill and dale for about two hours.

I was losing my patience. Where were these goats going anyhow? It was wet after a light rain overnight and I actually GI belly-crawled through that slop to get close. There were a lot of eyes to evade, and at forty yards, one goat nailed me. As I slowly rose to one, then both knees, half the herd was looking right at me. I didn't even notice the forty yards that separated us, an advantage to instinctive shooting. I figured I should shoot now even though my goat was still facing straight away. I tried for the asshole, as I'd heard it's a good hit, and let fly. With a solid KARACK, the black-and-white goat dropped like a sack of potatoes and everybody else split. Only the Bear Razorhead had penetrated, but I had hit the tail bone of the spinal column and finished him with a heart shot. No BLOOD TRAIL today, but I'll still take it.

11

EQUIPMENT: Bear Kodiak Magnum at 55-pounds, Aluminum arrows, and S&W Model 29 .44 Magnum
ANIMAL: Wild Boar, about 250 pounds
HIT: Haunch-charged

I had owned my Smith & Wesson model 29, 6 1/2-inch for a year or so and shot it all the time. I rotated Remington 240-grain Hollow Points and Soft Points and they all hit the same. I carried the big gun in a shoulder holster all the time and felt confident in my shooting ability. My brother, Johnny, and I had spent the morning target shooting and we even killed two rabbits with the .44, he with a six-inch Python .357. Did I mention he's a crack shot, too?

We had been walking silently for a half hour when we suddenly blundered into three big black boars over a rise at thirty-five yards. They saw us as we saw them and we all froze. The wind was good and I was able to pull an arrow out of the bow quiver, nock it, and draw before the trio turned to depart. They didn't seem overly alarmed and I got off a shot at the biggest one as he spun. My shot was not good and as the other two bolted left, the haunch-hit big boy headed down hill to the right. We ran to the edge of the gully and watched him high-tail it away, way off to the far woods. I was pissed. We had little blood, but had a good visual line of his run to follow.

I had never heard of waiting before following a hit animal, so we actually hurried. Tracks and blood led us to that famous one-acre tangle. We were still twenty-five yards away when he came for us. I dropped my bow, drew the .44, and thumbed the hammer. By the time I had the orange front ramp of his bulk, he was a mere ten feet away. Adrenaline-city, folks! The kaboom of the Smith was followed by one plowing hog nosing into the turf. The 240-grain soft point hit him just over the right eye and brained the porker outright. Johnny had the Python up and cocked, but it was over.

Now that's what I call fun! While everybody else is out there ruining their minds and bodies with drugs and booze, the Nugent boys are shopping for Pork the American way. Is this great or what!?! My brother and I were truly moved by the whole thing. It was over so fast. We still talk about that one today, twenty-five years later.

The arrow had hit in one of the worst places. The haunch, or shallow area between the stomach and hams, has only the artery. Nothing else. You miss that and you will probably lose your animal. It happens. ☆

12

EQUIPMENT: Saunders Crossbow 75-pounds, Aluminum arrows,
Bear Razorheads
ANIMAL: Wild Boar, about three hundred pounds
HIT: Shoulder only, tow to three inches penetration

Having a bad hit on the previous hog had nothing to do with my choosing a crossbow. I got one and was interested in it from a historical perspective. Shooting bolts at home was impressive because of the consistently tight groups out to fifty yards. Johnny and I figured we could really do some damage with this baby. We had been told about a big old honker of a hog that was always by himself. He was mottled black and brown, a crossbreed that weighed over three hundred pounds. A crossbreed with a crossbow. No problem.

To make a long story short, from thirty yards I hit him square in the shoulder broadside after a long stalk. We couldn't believe our eyes when only two to three inches of bolt had penetrated. The pig didn't take too kindly to it either. He spun on impact and ran about fifty yards crossways.

At this point, he must have seen me or Johnny, forty yards to my left. He actually took off between us. He then swapped ends and headed directly towards me. Here comes the disoriented express! The shootout at the pork chop corral! My .44 went off first, then Johnny's Python, then my .44, then the Python. He crashed hard like it was all over, but just as quickly, he headed for John. Bang, bang, down again and up, headed for me. He was real close now and we fired two quick shots, double action. He died at my feet, full of holes. We each had one round left in the cylinder and it appeared he had five holes in him. There was no way to be sure, but he was dead. We really enjoyed that. We were willing to wait awhile before we tried it again. The crossbolt (arrow) had hit the heavy cartilage at the shoulder and barely penetrated to the broadhead. No damage had been done; but he was looking to do a little damage of his own. Once again the hippies were preaching peace and love and the Nugent brothers were blowing away charging hogs with large-caliber handguns.

13

EQUIPMENT: Bear Super Kodiak, at 57-pounds, Aluminum arrows, Bear Razorheads
ANIMAL: Rocky Mountain Elk
HIT: Forty-five yards, neck and lungs, went two hundred yards

Elk are big, tough animals. They also have big lungs. I had been glassing this herd for two hours as they hung out in the shadows of the forest edge. Spike bull, six cows, four calves and grandpa 6 x 6. He would chase the spike now and then to a distance he thought appropriate for a subordinate, and would then just stand there like "Mr. Boss Man." I knew twenty-four eyes, ears and nostrils would make for a chancy approach, so I waited. Finally the old cow slowly moved down the coulee and each animal picked their way, nibbling here and there behind her. The bull was the last in line and provided me my chance to make a move.

As changes in terrain allowed, I carefully went from blind spot to blind spot, slowly reducing the one hundred yards that kept me out of bow range. As sometimes happens, a ridgeline consumed the herd and I made as quiet a dash as possible to the last crest. As I peeked over the escarpment, the old big boy was at forty-five yards facing away. As soon as my eyeballs slipped into view, he turned and looked back. My nocked arrow was snapped to anchor and I released straight into the center of his neck. I don't know why, but I ducked down below the rim, nocked another arrow and rose back up, 1-2-3.

All eyes were my way and the bull was now broadside, arrow in neck with his head hung low. Arrow number two went high in the ribs, a certain lung shot, and that's when they all decided to vamoose. With a cloud of dust and a hearty "hi-ho-silver," they were out of there. I lost sight of them right away and sat back down to relax. Right! I was on fire. I ran to the next high point and saw nothing, but I heard a moan. Sounded like a 6 x 6 elk dying to me. There was good blood going over the hogback and after the next two hundred yards, he lay dead, with the razorhead separating the neck vertebrae and both lungs were skewered. ☆☆☆

14

EQUIPMENT: Bear Super Kodiak at 57-pounds, Cedar arrows,
Bowlo Four-blade, Broadhead
ANIMAL: Barbido ram two hundred pounds
HIT: Liver at thirty yards, went a quarter mile

I still had a wonderful mess of cedar shafts at home. They were from Bear Archery with yellow fletch and a red line crest. The Bowlo heads were plastic feruled and threaded to screw onto wooden arrows. The broadheads were difficult to sharpen because of the fixed bleeder blade. They were a very pointed and deadly looking head. I was going to try 'em out.

It was a hazy, almost foggy morning for summer, and I like that for stalking. The sun was barely up when we saw three good double-curl rams being engulfed by the haze on a distant hillside. Having the wind in our favor, my brother John and I pussy-footed up and down hills to see how close we could get. Thank goodness for the fog, for as we rounded a knob on the side hill, the sheep were just ahead, peacefully grazing. We decided that John would backtrack to the other side of the knob and ease into distant view of the game. Hopefully they would spot John and follow their own backtrail to where I would be awaitin'. It took Johnny fifteen minutes and that's when they turned and headed to my right, downhill. I was kneeling and had to pivot in order to shoot off my left shoulder.

As if on cue, the largest of the trio paused at thirty yards as I came to full draw and shot. The arrow vanished into the off-white wool one third of the way back and I saw it sail behind the ram on the far side. He sprung like a buckin' bronco and the three of them raced off downhill. A visible patch of crimson blood grew on his side as the liver-hit animal fell once, then twice. He covered nearly two hundred yards before I lost sight of him, but the apparent blood gave me high hopes. Johnny joined me and we slowly walked the ample BLOOD TRAIL to the downed ram just beyond the two hundred-yard mark. Liver blood is the deepest red of all. ☆☆☆☆

15

EQUIPMENT: Bear Hunter 60-pounds, Aluminum arrows, Razorheads
ANIMAL: Corsican Ram at one hundred pounds, forty yards
HIT: Shoulder penetration, went five yards

I had a new bow now, very similar to the Super Kodiak. It was my dad's, given to him by Fred Bear on a deer hunt in Grayling, Michigan. My dad represented a

Swedish steel company that supplied Bear with tempered spring steel for the auxiliary bleeder blade inserts on their razorheads. Small world. The bow had a factory camo job and I shot it well. It was a little stronger than my bow and I sensed the increase in power in a faster, flatter shooting arrow.

The smallish Corsican ram was broadside at forty yards, feeding, when I gave him a dose of razor-tipped aluminum square in the shoulder. Combined with the stronger bow and his smaller size, the arrow went through both shoulder bones and protruded equidistant on either side of the animal. All he did was lunge once, walk a few feet, and fall over. He tried to get back up, but never made it. I finished him with a heart shot. ✩✩✩✩

►16

EQUIPMENT: Super Bear Magnum 48-inch at 55-pounds,
Aluminum arrows, Razorheads
ANIMAL: Wild Boar, about two hundred pounds
HIT: Heart at forty yards, went seventy-five yards

Again I had a new weapon to try in Bear's famous close-quarters mini-bow, the Super Kodiak Magnum. I shot with my fingers, no glove, and the short bow did pinch a little. It was a cute little bugger and I loved it. The black-and-white color was good looking too.

We were after hogs again with vivid memories of the last charge that had to be stopped with handguns. All that quickly faded away when at forty yards (maybe we didn't want to get any closer!), I nailed a good black boar, perfect, real low, right in the pocket. The arrow was thru him like butter and he scrambled to cover the last seventy-five yards of his life as fast as he could. Even though we saw him fall and die, we took up the BLOOD TRAIL just because it was such a beautiful thing. It was a perfect heart shot with a clean X-hole right through the center. Blood flow was optimum. ✩✩✩✩

17

EQUIPMENT: Bear Super Kodiak at 50-pounds, Aluminum arrows,
Bodkin three-blade
ANIMAL: White Spanish Goat, about 150 pounds
HIT: Double-lung, went one hundred yards

I had a single, old, wide, three-blade, black Bodkin broadhead that I had killed lots of small game with as a kid, and now that I understood the importance of sharpening your heads, I wanted to see it work on bigger game. I used a file on the three blades 'til it felt serious. We saw a good white billy hanging around the water hole all by himself. He was at the base of a small knob just standing there bored to death. Literally. I figured I was just the guy to bring a little excitement into his life, brief though it was to be. It was overcast and the wind was right for me to use the knob as cover for my approach. From the top of the rise I had a clean thirty-five-yard shot and put the arrow right thru the good stuff. The pump station. The boiler room. Where he lives. A pass-thru double-lunger is always a wonderful thing. He got the hell out of there, pronto Tonto, and we swam the Red River of life one hundred yards to a fine dead goat. The big three-blade made the biggest hole I'd seen yet and was probably the inspiration for the great Rothar Snuffer. ☆☆☆☆

18

EQUIPMENT: Bear Super Kodiak at 50-pounds, Howard Hill two-blade, Aluminum arrows
ANIMAL: Feral Hog, about 150 pounds
HIT: Liver and between the eyes, fifty yards

Other than Fred Bear, my other great bowhunting hero was Howard Hill. Though I never got to become friends with him like I did Fred, I admired his pioneering impact on the sport. I got a hold of Hunting the Hard Way and got some of the famous two-blade Hill heads. They filed up to a keen edge and I filled my quiver full of silver aluminum arrows with heavy long-tail turkey feathers I got from Hill Archery in Alabama.

All the hogs I'd killed so far were basically black. I saw a small sounder with a light brown keeper and made my move. At fifty yards, I sent a good-looking arrow thru him, maybe a little far back, but still confident I at least got fresh liver out of the deal. He lunged over a rise and out of sight. Not two minutes had passed as I topped the rise and luckily had another arrow nocked and ready for the charge uphill of one angry hog. My reflexive shot at ten yards put the famous two-blade penetration specialist broadhead just left of the right eye and into the brain. ☆☆☆☆

19

EQUIPMENT: Bear Super Kodiak at 50-pounds, Aluminum arrows, Bear Razorheads
ANIMAL: Wild Boar, about 225 pounds
HIT: Spine and Heart at thirty yards

It was just another nice, clear Michigan summer morning, on its way to a hot sunny day. My kind of conditions for a little pork outing. With a lone black hog in the distance, wind was checked and a stalk commenced. You always expect the worst from boar. My thirty-yard arrow hit high and dropped him in his tracks. I sprinted to him and put the coup de grace thru the heart.

20

EQUIPMENT: Bear Super Kodiak at 50-pounds,
Aluminum arrows, Bear Razorheads
ANIMAL: Black Spanish Goat, 125 pounds
HIT: Lungs at twenty-five yards, went fifty yards

Let's see, I had a pair of white goats, a blonde Angora, a black-and-white one and a red one. There was a herd of about fifteen picking their way through the north woods. A solid black one was the biggest. Because they were moving along, I kept way out of sight and waited for some cover at an ambush or stalk location. When it came, I zinged a clean kill, twenty-five yards, double-lunger right thru him, square behind the shoulder. I was really "picking the spot" to shoot at now, and it paid off. The herd scattered, but the BLOOD TRAIL led me fifty yards to a fine black goat. ☆☆☆☆

21

EQUIPMENT: Bear Super Kodiak at 50-pounds,
Aluminum arrows, Bear Razorheads
ANIMAL: Whitetail Doe, 150 pounds
HIT: Spine at twenty yards

I truly had grand expectations come the fall of 1971. I knew I could shoot and I'd learned a lot about getting ready for the shot. Of course, no whitetail is a game preserve goat, but all of my scouting gave me confidence for success. I got into my favorite fenceline as usual at 3 p.m., and waited for the evening to come. The deer that fed in the alfalfa field were to the south.

At 5 p.m., a doe and two yearlings materialized at fifty yards in the open. After a sweat-inducing, nerve-wracking wait, I was ready to shoot at twenty yards. Her head went down, my arrow came back and wham! I knocked her down with a broken spine. Without missing a beat I sent another one thru her ribs and had my first bow-killed whitetail. I gutted her and ran all the way home to call dad, brothers, uncles, and friends.

22

EQUIPMENT: Bear Take-Down Recurve at 53-pounds,
Aluminum arrows, Bear Razorheads
ANIMAL: Wild Boar, two hundred pounds
HIT: Ham-Femoral Artery, forty yards, went forty yards

Nothing like a wild boar hunt in between Rock 'n' Roll concerts to keep the spirits in line and the nerves on edge, I always say. I had a new Bear take-down recurve with 53-pound limbs that I just had to try out. I was using aluminum arrows almost all the time now and really had the sharpening of my razorheads down pat. I executed a good slow stalk on a lone, rooting hog and made a poor, inaccurate shot in the ass.

As soon as the arrow left the bow I felt I had blown it and was sure when I saw it hit. That hog took off like greased lightning and I disheartenedly approached the area of the hit. I was greeted by the calling card of the BLOOD TRAIL gods with a great trail of red. The pig had only made it another forty yards with the big femoral artery severed. ☆☆☆☆

 23

EQUIPMENT: Bear Super Kodiak 50-pounds, Fiberglass green arrows,
Bear Razorheads
ANIMAL: American Bison
HIT: Double-lung pass thru at sixty yards, went one hundred yards

Every time I have hunted and have seen buffalo, I've been moved by their sheer size. This size, combined with the historically pivotal role they played in the life of the original bowhunters, beckoned me to a different time and place. A private ranch in Michigan had these majestic animals and I was amazed to hunt one. There were four small bulls, only nine hundred-pounders! Only. Get down. Jeff, his brother, Mark, and I were at first surprised that we couldn't find them. But when we did, the fun began.

The huge animals appeared at ease, almost lazy in an open meadow. We made the mistake of casually exposing ourselves as they came to attention and they thundered off and out of sight. We walked another mile and found them once again standing in a clearing. This time I attempted a sneak, while Jeff and Mark worked around opposite sides. The buffalo weren't going for it and started to get restless.

I closed to sixty yards when they broke into a trot. They looked big and I instinctively pulled back, got a momentary sight picture and arched a long shot that hit just behind the churning shoulder of the largest animal. The arrow went through and hung for a second by the fletch on the far side. With both lungs punctured, he made it one hundred yards, stopped, laid down, and died. They have big bodies, big lungs, and big BLOOD TRAILS. Fantastic eating. ☆☆☆☆

 24

EQUIPMENT: Bear Take-Down at 53-pounds,
Fiberglass green arrows, Razorheads
ANIMAL: Corsican Ram, 125 pounds
HIT: Lungs at forty-five yards, went one hundred yards

This was a typical stalk. Utilizing cover and wind gave me a forty-five yard broadside shot at a standing multi-colored ram. The arrow entered the center of the lungs and exited the far side. A dead run of one hundred yards resulted in a clean kill and a primo BLOOD TRAIL. ☆☆☆☆

 25

EQUIPMENT: Bear Take-Down at 53-pounds,
Fiberglass green arrows, Razorheads
ANIMAL: Barbirousa Ram, two hundred pounds, three curl
HIT: Gut shot, lungs at thirty-five yards

This ram almost became a lost animal, and if it wasn't for their relaxed disposition, it would have been. I got a reasonable walking shot at thirty-five yards but hit badly, right through the guts. The arrow passed thru and the animal hunched up and slowly walked away. I did the unorthodox and ran up to thirty-five yards again and zipped him thru both lungs. He stopped and stood before collapsing quickly. ☆

 26

EQUIPMENT: Bear Take-Down at 53-pounds, Fiberglass green arrows,
Broadhead, Zwicky Eskimo two-blade
ANIMAL: Black Wild Boar at 250 pounds
HIT: Rear end at thirty yards

This kill is interesting because it was going-away shot right up the butt at thirty yards. The big wide broadhead penetrated all the way to the nock, severing lots of good stuff, and he bled out the front, back, nose and mouth. He only ran fifty yards before dying. ☆☆☆☆

27

EQUIPMENT: Bear Take-Down, 53-pounds, Aluminum arrows, Razorheads
ANIMAL: Mule Deer
HIT: Jugular at fifty yards, went twenty-five yards

Now we're getting serious here. A bowhunt to Colorado for mule deer, no less. I had left Jerry Byrum's camp to still-hunt behind the hills, when I encountered a lone deer out ahead a ways. I thought he was alone, but one minute he looked like a bald doe, the next I saw spikes. I had no binoculars with me at the time, so I just kept my distance for a good hour. Finally, I was sure I had seen horns and it was now or never as I made my way to within fifty yards of the browsing animal.

As it lifted its head, I let loose a long shot and heard a slicing as I saw the arrow go for the neck. The deer ran hellfire off the mountainside into a cut and I ran up to where it had been. What a treat to find blood everywhere. Another jugular hit; I love that. I followed a head-high BLOOD TRAIL for twenty-five yards over the first rise and found my big Muley doe dead. There must have been two deer. ☆☆☆☆

28

EQUIPMENT: Bear Take-Down Recurve at 60-pounds,
Bear aluminum 8.6 mm arrows, Zwickey Broadhead
ANIMAL: Wild Boar at two hundred pounds
HIT: Ribs at ten yards, knocked down

This has only happened to me a few times and I never understand it completely. A spine, neck or tail-bone (all vertebrae hits) will paralyze an animal and knock it right off its feet. But when I get the same reaction from a chest shot, I'm baffled. I've got to figure that a rib is jolted off at the spine, separating enough to cause paralysis. Anyhow, I saw this nice black boar easin' in and out of these broken mounds, and I headed for a rendezvous point up ahead.

I guessed well, because he walked thru a little opening at ten yards and I was ready with the fastest shot of my life. Again, using a razor-sharp, wide Zwickey Eskimo Delta, I hit hard behind the shoulder and blew this old boy down for the count. I couldn't believe my eyes. He thrashed about like he'd been spined, but the arrow wasn't where a spine should be. Being unsure of the hit, I quickly sliced another one through the heart to finish him.

29

EQUIPMENT: Bear Take-Down Recurve at 60-pounds,
Bear aluminum 8.6 mm arrows, Zwickey Broadhead
ANIMAL: Whitetail Doe at 175 pounds
HIT: Double-lung at fifteen yards, went seventy-five yards

Getting cocked and locked and ready to rock on a big-game animal is ninety percent of the task at hand. Getting to this full-draw mode, "condition-one," on a whitetail is the ultimate. For so many years I'd done my homework and put myself in the right place at the right time, only to be nailed by some mystical whitetail deer before I could get to full draw. But this time I did it. It is a great benefit to my killing ability when I have a surprise encounter and just pull back and let go. I never miss under those circumstances. It's the long, drawn-out, psychotic waits that turn me into a pile of worthless human debris, when I take my time and miss. I'm a real prick for days afterward.

But this time it wasn't too long, or too abrupt. I was barely moving parallel to a hay field border fence line when she exposed herself thru a small opening at fourteen yards across the brush line. I eased up, slow motion, and got off the shot before she knew what hit her. It looked good and I took up an o.k. BLOOD TRAIL, slow, but right away. She followed the fence row then out across it at the corner. I lost blood a couple of times, but I needed the test. After seventy-five yards, she was all done. ☆☆

30

EQUIPMENT: Jennings-T Hunter, 60-pounds, Bear aluminum 8.6 mm arrows,
Bear Razorheads four-blade
ANIMAL: Whitetail Doe at 140 pounds
HIT: Twenty-five yards, over left shoulder, exit low right shoulder,
lungs, heart, went forty yards

I abandoned my standard locations this afternoon, opting to explore the big timer from where most of the deer emerged each night. Trails were obvious, so I picked a good set-up, and looked for a climbable tree. Being part ape, I squirreled up a skinny little maple, way up into the top, swaying with the wind. I felt a little goofy, but I liked the view, so I stayed put. Just before dark, a lone deer appeared, meandering slowly down the trail towards my flagpole. I believe my movement in the flimsy branches again diverted my mind just enough from my shooting to allow me to get off a smooth arrow. Without the overt concentration on the release, my target panic did not surface, and the hard downward angle shot was perfect right over the left shoulder, passing thru both lungs and the top of the heart, exiting low behind the right leg. She swapped ends and trotted for forty yards and died. ✰✰✰✰

31

EQUIPMENT: Bear Take-Down Recurve at 60-pounds,
Bear aluminum 8.6 mm arrows
ANIMAL: Mule Deer Buck, twenty-eight inch, 4 x 4
HIT: Center artery, twenty yards running, went forty yards

Jerry Byrum was one hell of a guide. Not only a great individual, but dedicated and super-hard working for his hunters. Ron Chamberlain had introduced me to Jerry's outfit in 1973 and I was back for more. We were setting up a small sneak drive of a quackie lot with about twelve hunters.

As I positioned myself as an end-stander, three beautiful, velvet-racked bucks broke out of a small finger of aspens. The two biggest ones, real big, went up behind me, but a real dandy twenty-eight-inch 4x4 ran headlong, crossing in front of me. It was another classic, no-think, snap-shot, and though not great arrow placement, I severed the big artery mid-ship and he painted the vegetation red. He was a bona-fide trophy deer and I was elated. ✰✰✰✰

32

MY FIRST WHITETAIL BUCK
EQUIPMENT: Bear Take-Down Recurve at 60-pounds,
Bear aluminum 8.6 mm arrows
ANIMAL: Whitetail Buck, eight-point at 180 pounds
HIT: Shoulder at forty yards, went one hundred yards

I was long overdue. So far as I could tell, my success rate was one deer per thousand hours of hunting. Something had to change. And 1975 was going to be the year. April brought me my first Michigan turkey permit and a nice gobbler. I had returned to Grand Junction, Colorado, with Ron Chamberlain and the boys to bowhunt mule deer with Jerry Byrum.

September 10 saw my Bear Take Down Recurve send a Razorhead through the vitals of a beautiful twenty-eight-inch 4 x 4 muley, and I was on cloud nine! Big time! Things were looking up. Am I getting' even here or what? I couldn't wait for the October home season to arrive.

The first week was stock. Plenty of deer seen and even had some close calls.

Now it was one month to the day since my Colorado muley. October 10. Black, drizzly, and ducky. So, naturally I loaded up the Bronco with decoys, shotgun and chest waders for a little waterfowling. Dawn was a little ways off as I started the truck down the driveway for the big swamp. I didn't make it. I stopped, thought for a second, saw the weird east wind pushing mist at my windshield, and said, "Nah, this is deer huntin' weather!" I swapped camo, painted up my face real quick, and grabbed the Bear. The conditions were my favorite. It was misty, wet, dark, and stalky, with a steady east wind.

Ten minutes later I crossed the fourth fence row into a hay field edge on my way to a brushy oak ridge. Even in the fog I could see shapes in the field approaching. I was exposed in the field, but the three deer kept coming. I eased to one knee, nocked an arrow and picked out the lead doe at thirty-five yards. Right over her back. They darted away, but only for twenty or so yards and then they stopped. Again they cut across my front, but now with a larger deer bringing up the rear. The three doe trotted briskly across the forty yards. Now I could see antler as number four walked deliberately on their trail.

My arrow was nocked and I was cocked, locked, and ready to rock, doc, as he moved perfectly broadside. Instinctively, I anchored and released. The aluminum arrow with the Bear Razorhead slightly arched the forty yards, SMACKO-WACKO, right square behind the shoulder. With little noticeable reaction, he turned ninety degrees and headed kiddie-corner across the big field. Twenty-forty-sixty-eighty-one hundred yards and over he goes. Bingo! Still! Don't ask me why, but I immediately sat down and stared at him lying over there in a heap. Goofy. Then I picked up the BLOOD TRAIL and peeked at him, then the blood, him, then the blood! I guess my psyche just wasn't accepting the scene yet. Half way to him I figured, "What the hell am I doin'? He's dead Nuge, go get him!"

I charged over to him, knowing only that I saw headgear when I shot. I grabbed his rack and counted twelve points and thought I was gonna die! A twelve-pointer! Holy Guacamole! Eight points with four-inchy kickers. A buck! DEAD! Mine! Oh, the glory of it all. I be-bopped all the way home in nothing flat. I called my dad, uncle, brothers, buddies and neighbors. They all thought I was nuts. It was wonderful. It's always wonderful. I strapped that beautiful animal to the top of my truck and showed him off to everybody. My first whitetail buck with the bow and arrow. I'll never forget it.

That was hundreds of deer ago, and this past season, twenty-five years later, I went just as nuts. It's always a thrill. For every deer killed, you spend sometimes hundreds of hours hunting, experiencing many exciting encounters. When you ultimately make that hard-earned clean kill, you should take it for all you can. I cherish all those moments. Embrace those sensations, and let them drive you. Tooth, Fang and Claw! The call of the wild! Hear it. Do it. Whack 'em! ☆☆☆☆

33

EQUIPMENT: Bear Take-Down Recurve at 60-pounds,
Bear aluminum 8.6 mm arrows
ANIMAL: Whitetail Doe, 150 pounds
HIT: Lungs at twenty yards, went sixty yards

Meanwhile the world had gone compound bonzoid, but I had no part of it. So far. I climbed a tree and drilled a nice fat doe at twenty yards, just like the doctor ordered. The old stick bow gave complete penetration and I had a great BLOOD TRAIL for sixty yards to another fine whitetail. ☆☆☆☆

34

EQUIPMENT: Bear Take-Down Recurve at 60-pounds,
Bear aluminum 8.6 mm arrows
ANIMAL: Whitetail Doe, 135 pounds
HIT: Lungs at thirty yards, went seventy yards

Rock 'n' Roll could possibly save many critters if the pace keeps up. I was busy as hell, but not for deer season. I have lots of good treestands and a nice doe strolled by at thirty yards for a clear double-lunging. The arrow stayed in the deer for a few yards, but dropped out the exit hole and produced a good BLOOD TRAIL. I followed for seventy yards and there she was. ☆☆☆

35

EQUIPMENT: Bear Take-Down at 53-pounds, Bear aluminum 8.6 mm arrows,
MA-3 three-blade, small
ANIMAL: Whitetail Doe, average size
HIT: Heart at twenty-five yards, went twenty-five yards

I used the file on the MA-3 heads and attained a keen edge. Another favorite treestand produced at twenty-five-yard broadside shot at an average size doe and I put the Y right thru her heart. She stumbled away like she was stoned and lost all her blood in twenty-five yards. I've never seen this kind of reaction before.

Studies describe this "stoned" effect as a euphoric state brought on by the shock of blood loss. The brain actually denies pain, as the animal loses consciousness and expires. This type of shock happens within seconds of a significant interruption to the circulatory system, a.k.a. a well-placed, super-sharp broadhead. ☆☆☆☆

36

EQUIPMENT: Jennings Super T at 60-pounds, XX75, 2117,
Bear aluminum 8.6 mm arrows, Bear Razorheads
ANIMAL: Alaska Yukon Moose
HIT: Last rib, big artery, liver, lungs at forty yards, went seventy-five yards

1977 was the year I finally switched from the stick bow to the compound. It's funny, too, because I had begun to experience a bit of target panic with my recurve and was scared of its ramifications. There were times that I absolutely could not release smoothly on target. I would freeze above my point of aim and could not bring my bow hand down onto the bullseye. At other times I couldn't miss. It was very frustrating. Even as I departed for my dream hunt in Alaska, I was unsure of myself. I had killed a grand B&C barren ground caribou at 150 yards with my SW.44 and had won my guide George Faerber's confidence. I had also missed two enormous bull moose in the seventy-inch class at forty and fifty yards.

This day we had glassed a smaller bull working his way down the gravel riverbed and had moved down to intercept him. I expected him to pass my alder thicket location at twenty yards, but he turned early. As I steered clear of the brush, he covered some ground and gave me a forty-yard, three-quarters angling away shot and it helped that I only had time to pivot, turn and shoot. The Bear Razorhead-tipped Easton XX75 2117 caught him mid-stride just forward of the left hip, severing the big artery and penetrating the liver and into the right lung. He quickly covered his last seventy-five yards to the bend in the creek before dying. ☆☆☆☆

37

EQUIPMENT: Jennings Super T at 60-pounds, XX75, 2117,
Bear aluminum 8.6 mm arrows, Bear Razorheads
ANIMAL: Whitetail Doe
HIT: Both shoulders at twenty yards, went fifty yards

This target panic malady was going to drive me nuts. I had, in the first week of October's archery season, missed good shots at six different bucks. One nice ten-pointer stuck around while I helplessly whipped my bow arm and a quiver full of arrows (eight shots!) at him, leaving me shattered in my treestand. Finally, deep in the big timber, high in a young oak tree, a lone doe took a good arrow thru both shoulders and lungs for a clean kill. She traveled another fifty yards with lots of blood and both front legs were broken. ☆☆☆☆

38

EQUIPMENT: Jennings Super T at 60-pounds, XX75, 2117,
Bear aluminum 8.6 arrows, Bear Razorheads
ANIMAL: Whitetail Doe
HIT: Double-lung at twenty-five yards, went fifty yards

After missing lots of deer later in the season, I connected on another doe at twenty-five yards and zipped her real nice thru both lungs for a repeat kill. ☆☆☆☆

39

EQUIPMENT: Jennings Super T at 60-pounds, XX75, 2117,
Bear aluminum 8.6 mm arrows, Bear Razorheads
ANIMAL: Whitetail Doe at 180 pounds
HIT: Spine at five yards

This deer came directly below a treestand in a fence row. The shot was the straightest down-body twist I've ever made. The Bear Razorhead broke her back and, like all spine-shot animals when breaking occurs, she hit the deck semi-paralyzed and was completely disabled. Knowing the position of the low-lying heart is important for a finishing arrow.

40

EQUIPMENT: Jennings Super T at 60-pounds, Bear aluminum 8.6 mm arrows,
Bear Razorheads
ANIMAL: American Bison at 2,200 pounds, #1 Burkette Trophy Book
HIT: Double-lung at sixty yards

I had handgun- and rifle-hunted the famous YO Ranch of Texas with the Schreiners before, but this was to be my first bowhunt there. We rode out on horse-back at sun-up, over the harsh, rocky Texas terrain. After an hour of riding up and down the gullies and thru the brush-choked draws, we saw a small band of six buffalo, some laying down and some up feeding on the sparse grasses. Wind was steady in my favor and as we glassed from one third of a mile away, I planned a stalk.

Not knowing how used to people these big boys were, I stealthfully eased my way into range using all the cover I could find. After a long forty-five-minute stalk, I was crouched behind the last bit of puckerbrush available at forty yards. The obvious herd bull was quite a bit larger than the other animals and he was laying chewing his cud and angling slightly away from the herd. I don't like laying-down shots, because an animal of this size is actually squashing his heart and reducing the apparent size of his vitals.

From a one-knee position, I drew the Jennings and tried to shoot just above the ground line. Unfortunately, I hit just in front of him and we had a mini-stampede on our hands. The animals were not aware of my presence and they bolted a short distance into thicker cover and filed into a rocky draw. I hauled ass on foot to the forward edge of the draw and spooked the herd. As the biggest bull lunged, quartering away at a fast trot, I swung with him and touched one off at sixty yards. Just like my last buffalo kill, the arrow flew true and sliced mid-body behind the right shoulder and passed thru both lungs. He let out a big woof and ran one hundred yards to the nearest thicket.

I met Walter and Tom Huser with my horse and carefully approached on horseback. The big bull was still on his feet. He had almost had it, breathing labored with evident blood at the nose and mouth. From the saddle, I nocked another arrow and put it two inches from the first shot. He fell right there and by the time we dismounted and approached the fallen monarch, he was dead. ✰✰✰✰

41

EQUIPMENT: Jennings Super T at 85-pound, XX75, 2117, Bear aluminum 8.6 mm arrows, Bear Razorheads, four-blade
ANIMAL: Warthog, Sudan, Africa
HIT: Forty-five yards running, hit behind left ear, brain

Each day had its frustrations. These folks just didn't get the challenge of bowhunting. We were returning from a long day, way out in the outback, when I saw a trio of big warthogs, about one-quarter mile ahead. I made them stop the Land Rover, and instructed them to back out of the area and give me a while to try for the ugly, wonderful beasts. I glassed them moving in and out of the scrub, and made a semicircle upwind. I thought I had stalked undetected up to forty yards, but as they lifted their heads, I nocked an arrow. Immediately the threesome erected their scrawny tails, and began their stiff-legged trot. I swung on the nose of the biggest, lead hog, and touched 'er off. The arrow THUNKED right into his head, directly behind the left ear, and slammed him to the ground. He kicked and spun for a moment, but it was over. ✰

42

EQUIPMENT: Jennings Super T at 85-pounds, XX75, 2117,
Bear aluminum 8.6 mm arrows, Bear Razorheads
ANIMAL: Dik-Dik Antelope, thirty pounds
HIT: Lengthwise, went fifty yards

Going to Alaska in '77 was a dream come true, but the really exotic hunting fantasy was Africa, the Dark Continent. After extensive inquiries with Bob Eastman of Game Tracker, who had been with the same safari outfit previously, I decided come hell or high water, I was going to give it a shot. This was to be a full-fledged, old-style, big-time tent safari out in the bowels of deep Africa. I could write volumes just on my preparation and equipment. I will continue to keep it brief and will detail the kills only.

My first kill in Africa with the bow was a tiny little antelope called the Dik-Dik. At only twenty-five pounds, this is considered to be the world's smallest member of the antelope family. Dik-Dik were everywhere and it reminded me of hunting rabbits. The heavy 85-pound Jennings flashed a Razorhead that went lengthwise thru the little bugger, stem to stern, and cut up everything he had. He still covered fifty yards and needed to be trailed. ☆☆☆☆

43

EQUIPMENT: Jennings Super T at 85-pound, XX75, 2117,
Bear aluminum 8.6 mm arrows, Bear Razorheads
ANIMAL: Dik-Dik Antelope
HIT: Back of the head at fifty yards, running

Another Dik-Dik at fifty yards, running again, this time shot right in the back of the head and knocked head over heels.

44

EQUIPMENT: Jennings Super T 85-pound, Aluminum arrows, XX75, 2117,
30-inch, 4 four-inch vanes, Bear Razorheads with insert
ANIMAL: Dik-Dik Antelope at twenty-five pounds
HIT: Double-lung at thirty yards

On my first safari into the wilds of the big country of the Sudan, Africa, in 1978, game was at an all-time high, prior to the ridiculous wanton slaughter at the hands of the natives, shortly after they received their so-called independence. Dik-Dik were running all over the place, along with most of the other teeming wildlife species. The professional Portuguese hunters in charge of the safari company had noted that they had never seen such an abundance of wildlife in their twenty years of operation. Good. I like that. Makes for some pretty intense bowhunting.

Unfortunately, the safari staff was inexperienced at guiding bowhunters, and it was an exercise in frustration for me. With game in view at nearly all times, opportunity after opportunity for good stalks was ideal. But between the language barrier and their reputation for stubbornness, I failed to redirect their approach with bowhunting's specific demands in mind. After a couple of days killing good trophies with the rifle, I convinced the guides to let me wander a ways from camp on my own for some serious bowhunting.

My first encounter was with this diminutive little critter. As I stalked the broken line of bush above camp, I would see Dik-Dik darting in and out of the thorn scrub ahead of me. Using my best whitetail tactics, I was able to move in on a lone male browsing along in thick cover. Finally a small clearing opened up for a thirty yard quartering away shot, and I drew and released, hitting him square behind the right shoulder, passing thru and out the other side. No mean feat, but the right stuff, passing thru the lungs, and breaking out the left shoulder upon exiting.

The little antelope sprung forward in a leap, and fell over dead. The lunge had taken him out of sight, but the blood was apparent thru the scrub, and he lay there motionless at the base of the brushes. They are amazing animals, of course because of their size, but also because of their numbers and rabbit-like actions. They are handsome little animals, deer brown, with a darker saddle across the backstraps, with two- to three-inch straight horns, miniature in every way. Oh yeah, and real tasty too. ✩✩✩✩

 45

EQUIPMENT: Jennings Super-T 85-pound, Aluminum arrows, XX75, 2117, 30-inch, 4 four-inch vanes, Bear Razorheads with insert
ANIMAL: Dik-Dik Antelope
HIT: Body length at forty yards, went fifty yards

A slight stir riveted my attention to a branch tangle, thirty yards ahead. It was difficult going in the thick, thorny African bush, always snagging on the merciless five-inch dagger-like thorns of these "wait a minute" briar bushes. The movement materialized into a nice black-horned trophy male Dik-Dik. I didn't think I would be able to get off a shot in the confining vegetation, but luckily broke free without giving away my position. When I finally came to full draw, the little bugger was a good forty yards away, walking swiftly in and out of impenetrable bush.

With nervous calculation, I was able to discern a body-sized hole in front of him as he turned slightly to his right. I sent a 2117 with my trusty Bear Razorhead into that hole just as he entered it, catching him in the right ham. I could see the shaft zing out the other side, like it never slowed down, and the Dik-Dik vanished. The deadly broadhead had traversed the length of the two-foot body, slicing everything in its path, even shattering the far shoulder. Amazingly, the spooky little antelope traveled fifty yards. The BLOOD TRAIL was equally amazing. There was no blood left in him, because it was all on the ground! ☆☆☆☆

46

EQUIPMENT: Jennings Super-T 85-pound, Aluminum arrows, XX75, 2117, 30-inch, 4 four-inch vanes, Bear Razorheads with insert
ANIMAL: Dik-Dik Antelope
HIT: Neck at fifty yards running

Sometimes, all too often, I let my guard down, and pay the tortuous price. Here I was in the Sudan, Africa, in obviously phenomenal game country, casually bopping along like I was on a stroll thru Central Park. Sure as hell, I blundered in on a band of Dik-Dik antelope at close range, caught flat-footed! They scattered as I slipped an arrow onto the string and I cursed myself for not paying attention. I kept my eyes on all I could, in hopes of getting off a shot, and followed a darker animal thru the scrub, came to full draw, and touched 'er off as it broke clear at fifty yards running.

It was beautiful! That's what makes bowhunting so damn special, watching that shaft fly thru the air from you to the target. It almost seems like slow motion, especially on longer shots, with a little arc in the arrow's path. Neat. Anyhow, that arrow flew true, intersecting with the departing antelope, almost miraculously, right thru his neck. He rolled. I saw him kick once as I ran over to him, impervious to the scratching thorns tearing at my flesh en route. It is shots like this that come from those beginning years with the long bow, snap-shooting, instinctively, like throwing a ball. In fact, I am at my deadliest when I shoot quickly. No time to complicate things. Just do it. ☆☆☆☆

47

EQUIPMENT: Jennings Super-T 85-pound, Aluminum arrows, XX75, 2117, 30-inch, 4 four-inch vanes, Bear Razorheads with insert
ANIMAL: Dik-Dik Antelope
HIT: Throat thru the length of the body at ten yards

Some days we would drive around for hours, just viewing the grandiose spectacle that is Africa. Looking back, I realize how lucky I was to experience this great, wild land, before the locals viciously abused and raped the wilderness. Ever wonder how the desertification has occurred? How about the fact that these human populations have expanded, so out of control for so long, and the simple fact, that because they live a basically prehistoric lifestyle, THEY HAVE BURNED EVERY LAST STITCH OF VEGETATION FOR HEAT AND COOKING!!!! It's unbelievable, but true. Everywhere I went in this country, I saw people cut, carry, stack and burn wood. Logs, branches, sticks, everything, and the "browseline" just keep getting further and further out. With the elimination of erosion-controlling vegetation, in creeps the desert. Maps of their continent-devouring phenomenon correlate this man-made alteration to its disastrous toll on lives and land.

And then, of course, upon getting their independence, the ensuing horror stories are well documented. Bands of tribesmen, armed with AK-47 assault rifles, drove around the bush, with nothing better to do than hose down entire herds of plains game, anything that moved, with an unlimited cache of communist-supplied 7.62 x 39 mm ammo. Thanks a lot, boondockers. It has been often repeated in that great land, and it saddens me. I've got life-threatening horror stories of my own I can tell, at the hands of viciously corrupt, self-appointed "officials." Talk about clowns. But I've already gone too far, and that human topic should be a book unto itself, I suppose, I mean, Idi Amin was right next door, and I know he has some grisly human Blood Trails of his own. What a pud.

So, anyhow, we were driving around, really enjoying ourselves, seeing all kinds of wonderful critters. The majestic Roan antelope was a primary specie of the Sudan. White-eared Cob, Lesser Kudu, Cape buffalo by the thousands. Fantastic.

We had covered a lot of ground this morning and were returning to camp, when I saw trophy-sized Dik-Dik melt into the river's edge far up ahead. I told the guide to go ahead, that I would walk the rest of the way to camp, and hopefully whack a little something on the way. The Range Rover circled out and away, as I slipped into the tree line along the winding river course. I was at peak awareness as I crept along, stalking the known Dik-Dik, as well as the probable other potential targets that lay ahead. I was wondering where the heck the little fella was after covering the first one hundred yards, when he appeared walking directly towards me on the very trail I was on. I already had an arrow nocked, ready to go. He just kept coming, with his head down and bobbing. Fifty, forty, thirty, twenty yards! All right already!

I held on him with only the frontal chest-spot possible, and released when he was a scant ten yards in from of me. The arrow zipped right under his nose, disappeared into his throat, passed all the way through him, and exited his crotch. There was no BLOOD TRAIL, but instead, a blood puddle, because he just did about two complete somersaults, kicked once and died. The outfitter claimed he would be the new Roland Ward world record because of the length, and circumference of his two shiny, black, pointed horns. Big deal. He may or may not be a record-book contender, but he was a small target, killed swiftly and humanely, one on one, in the wilds of old Africa, with my bow and arrow. I carried him back to camp, and I will take these life-accelerating memories to my grave. Not to mention the belly-full of delicious steaks I took to bed with me that night! I LOVE THIS! ✩✩✩✩

48

EQUIPMENT: Jennings Super-T bow, Aluminum arrows, XX75, 2117, 30-inch, 4 four-inch vanes, Bear Razorheads, two-blade
ANIMAL: Alaskan Bull Moose
HIT: Fifty-five yards up hill, broadside, double-lung, pass thru, ran fifty-five yards

I was back with George Faerber, in the wilds of wonderful Alaska. We were camped in a beautiful tundra valley. My shooting was still erratic, but I was determined to relax and try for the huge Alaska Yukon Moose. These are massive animals, regularly going over one thousand pounds, with old mature bulls exceeding 1,500 pounds. I like 'em. We had glassed a real keeper high on the mountain about two miles from camp. He appeared to push the sixty-inch mark thru the spotting scope, so we began our trek across the valley. The spongy lichens are always a lot of fun negotiating, and few hours later we labored up the steep, spruce-infested hillside, approaching the distant ridge the bull was on. We could only hope the big boy remained. Half way up the incline, fifty-five yards distant, loomed the huge form of the world's largest deer. His head was invisible behind a large fir, but his body was big. George cautioned me that he wasn't sure if he was a keeper, as he glassed the animal. I instinctively nocked an arrow and asked if it was a bull. George said yes, it is, but small in the antler department. As the bull turned away from the tree, I saw his Mulligan rack, picked a spot on this mid chest, and released the arrow, second nature. It was beautiful! The arch of the orange shaft was a thing of beauty, floating from me to him, connecting dead center, tight behind the shoulder, slicing in on side and out the other. Red-white foamy blood appeared immediately and the bull bucked as he spun to crash straight for us. I heard George rack a round into his .375 as this huge beast, wild-eyed and mowing down every-thing in his path, came charging head on. I yelled that he was deader than hell, just didn't know it yet! Don't shoot! We literally dove for cover out of his way, as he slammed to the ground at our feet. Not a twitch. DEAD. He had not lived for five seconds following the hit. ✩✩✩✩✩

49

EQUIPMENT: Jennings Super-T Hunter at 85-pound, Aluminum arrows, XX75, 2117, 30-inch, 4 four-inch vanes, Bear Razorheads four-blade, two arrows
ANIMAL: African Cape Buffalo at two thousand pounds
HIT: Liver, lung, femoral artery, at fifty yards and seventy-five yards

These bastards are cool. Anything that can backtrack, lay in wait and ambush the hunter, then stomp him into a foaming puddle of snot, hair and blood is my kind of beast. My first big bad Cape didn't read the book and died real reasonable like. Good boy. The guides and trackers were impressed, I was high as a kite, and quite relieved. Days passed, and now we came upon a large herd in the distance. After a long circle, we poked our noses out of the tangle of thorns, only to have the whole wad break rank and scoot. I pulled free of the dagger-like thorns and picked out a decent bull vacating the premises, simultaneously nocking and anchoring my arrow, and instincting the arch of a 2117 from my 85-pound Jennings to intersect with the massive rump of the black locomotive. My lead was a tad behind the fifty yards, but still the thirty-inch arrow buried to the feathers just rear of the rib cage. SHAZAM! Nice shot, Nuge babe. He did not change pace at all, and my follow-up shot was on its way in three seconds. This arrow was a beauty, too, landing squarely in the right hip as he and the herd rounded the heavier scrub brush, penetrating to the vanes. The Portuguese guide slapped me on the back, and the trackers were smiling. Me too. We gathered our wits and gear, returning to the vehicles. Fortunado, my professional white hunter, and I picked up the trail at the point of impact, discovering an ample BLOOD TRAIL. We took it to the thickest, most impenetrable brush zone I have ever seen in my life, and contemplated the situation. Here was THE classic big-game danger scenario. A mortally wounded Gonzo Beast from Hell, in hell itself. Visibility was nil. I entered first, insisting that if a killing shot must be made, I must be the shooter. I left my bow in the truck, rammed a tubular round up the snout of the big .460 Weatherby, and began my move. Fortunado would be a close second, also carrying his big .460, safety off, followed by a trained shooter, ditto. It was hairy! You want high!?! You probably don't want it this high. I couldn't see ten feet in any direction. Cute. Half the time, all our effort was just pushing limbs and vines out of our way. I could not believe an animal the size of a Cape Buffalo could move thru here! Amazing. After a breathless, scratch-mastering, sweat-pouring hour and one hundred yards, we were waist-deep in wet slop, near panic. All at once I glanced to my right, and not five yards to my side was McSlam the Wonder Truck, ready to crush ass! I spun so damn fast and slapped the trigger, howitzering a 500-grain solid up his nose, thru the brain and into outer space, that it was a blur. I swore I saw blood in his eyes, but Fortunado said he was already dead. Safeties were returned to "on" and the magnificent monster was admired for all the formidability the good Lord designed into him. My first arrow killed him, and my second arrow killed him. Liver, lungs, and the big femoral artery were all history.

The BLOOD TRAIL only gets a ☆☆☆ rating because of all the water involved. But the excitement is beyond a rating. Something like a twelve-diaper rating! ☆☆☆

50

EQUIPMENT: Jennings Super T at 85-pound, Aluminum arrows, XX75, 2117, 30-inch, 4 four-inch vanes, Bear Razorheads
ANIMAL: Cape Buffalo
HIT: Artery at the top of the heart at twenty-five yards

Now here was Africa's "bad boy." The almighty Cape Buffalo. A ton-and-a-half of danger and fury. I had read everything I could get my hands on about Africa and the big Cape Buffalo in particular. I constantly reminded my gun bearer to stick close by with my equally big and mean 460 Weatherby. I was taking no chances.

This first buffalo was shot from twenty-five sweaty yards, and I hit perfectly. The arrow hit straight broadside, real low, actually cutting the back hind of the foreleg, burying into the flesh and shooting right back out as fast as it went in. You would have thought the hit was too low, but it actually severed two inches of the big artery right off the top of the heart. That big boy started gushing blood like nothing I've ever seen, as he swung to look at what the "twang and slice" was all about. All I could do was gawk at the visible blood flow and he took but a few steps and keeled over!!! Guess that was the first Rock 'n' Roll experience he had ever had. I was in love. ☆☆☆☆

51

EQUIPMENT: Oneida Eagle at 60-pound, Aluminum arrows, XX75, 2117, 30-inch, 4 four-inch vanes, Bear Razorheads - no inserts
ANIMAL: Whitetail Buck, seven point.
HIT: Center of the hip

This is one of my all-time favorite bow kills because it satiated a built-up frustration. I had sat in my favorite tree blind for over a dozen afternoons, off and on, and had seen bucks through the thick stuff more often than not.

My cousins, Brad, Chris, and Joe, from Pennsylvania, were hunting with me and anticipation was running high. The rut was coming on strong and I had placed everyone in red-hot killer tree blinds all around the ridge of the swamp.

My set covered a draw leading out of a large tract of marsh grass, cattails, alder thickets and impenetrable puckerbrush. It was only twenty or so minutes 'til shootin' light would fade and here comes a buck, like walkin' smoke. He was coming down my eighteen-yard trail, just like the doctor ordered, when I felt the breeze hit the back of my neck. He stopped and was screened, as usual, by some brush. We had our mandatory frozen stand-off and then he spun and bolted back into the swamp.

At fifty yards, he stopped with only his right hip showing out of a patch of popple saplings. There was a tall, narrow window clear to his hip, and I really thought I could make the shot. I turned, drew and released. The arrow flew PERFECTLY through the top of the window and hit squarely in the center of his hip. I knew that this was a proven deadly shot and watched the buck ritualistically explode down the bottom of the ridge-line towards Joe's stand two hundred yards away. Crash-boom-bang-stumble-silence! It sounded like he made it half way and hopefully was down for the count.

We all went home and called George and Bryan and the six of us hauled lanterns and flashlights back to a three-star BLOOD TRAIL. The pretty high seven-pointer had not read the rule book, as usual, and had run uphill away from the swamp, water, and thick stuff with a severed femoral artery. Even the BLOOD TRAIL was not typical for this hit. It was on again, off again, with most of the blood in the deer's cavity. This is the only femoral hit I've seen that wasn't a four-star BLOOD TRAIL. He died swiftly after a seventy-yard run.

52

EQUIPMENT: Oneida 60-pound, Aluminum arrows, XX75, 2117, 30-inch, 4 four-inch vanes, Zwickey, two-blade Delta
ANIMAL: Whitetail Buck, six point
HIT: Jugular at twenty yards, went 125 yards

I prefer a reasonably low treestand of fifteen feet, but I know the advantage of being way up there (twenty to thirty feet). On this cold fall afternoon, I was twenty-five feet up in one of my favorite borderline oaks, overlooking a cut cornfield at timberline. I watched a good eight-point feeding with uncharacteristic calm on spilled kernels at two hundred yards for twenty minutes, when a smaller buck came out of the thorn apples at the half way mark.

He was a small deer of only 130 pounds and he catty-cornered a straight line for me. He turned slightly and paralleled the tree line at twenty yards when I began my draw. I swung too far forward and instead of hitting behind the right shoulder, I watched the big Zwickey slice into him forward of the shoulder bone. He whirled in an instant and my game-tracker line fed out like I had a marlin on. The sprayed blood was visible from the wide two blade cut the jugular real nice-like and I had a classic four-star BLOOD TRAIL all the way. ☆☆☆☆

53

EQUIPMENT: Oneida Eagle 55-pound, Aluminum arrows, XX75, 2113, Hoyt Bow Bullet
ANIMAL: Whitetail Doe
HIT: Lungs at forty yards, went two hundred yards

Doug Walker and I had just wrapped up a pleasant and memorable deer hunt with Fred Bear at Grousehaven and were now in Marion, Michigan, at my friend Claude's deer camp. I was up twenty-five feet in my favorite big pine tree over-looking a clover field bordering a wood lot and marsh.

Does and fawn began filtering into the field early, at 4:30, just a half hour after I got there. I waited 'til seven deer were somewhat at ease within fifty yards and picked the biggest doe in the bunch. The arrow hit a little high, but as she raced for the woods, I saw the growing red patch on her hide. The game-tracker string played out for two hundred yards and all was quiet. ☆☆☆

54

EQUIPMENT: Oneida Eagle 55-pound, Aluminum arrows, 2117, XX75, 30-inch, 4 four-inch vanes, Bear Razorheads
ANIMAL: Whitetail Doe
HIT: Heart at ten yards, went fifty yards

This was another textbook, close-range kill at ten yards. The 160-pound doe was walking broadside when I whacked her low behind the right leg, exiting low behind the left leg. She only traveled fifty yards with a nice Bear Razorhead X through her heart. ☆☆☆☆

55

EQUIPMENT: Oneida Eagle 60-pound, Aluminum arrows, 2117, XX75, 30-inch, 4 four-inch vanes, Bear Razorheads - no insert
ANIMAL: Whitetail Buck, seven-point
HIT: Double-lung, running at forty-five yards, went seventy-five yards

This is one of my favorite bow kills. I thought I wouldn't have a chance to hunt this day because of a shopping trip with Sasha and Toby. But we made it home with an hour of shooting light left, so I headed behind the house into the pine trees.

I climbed a sixteen-foot Texas tripod seat and saw a buck beyond the pines eating berries off the autumn olive bushes before I could even sit down. At seventy yards I could see a small seven-point rack, but figured he wouldn't have time to get close before dark. So I climbed down to sneak through the pines, taking advantage of the gusting wind to cover my stalk.

As I ran out of cover at the last row of pines, I couldn't see him. There was one thick tree between me and the bush line and here he came. He wasn't on a fast, dead, run, but moved right to left at a good run at forty-five yards. I had only one hole to shoot through; it was now or never. I swung the white shaft with him and followed through as I released.

There's nothing more beautiful than watching an arching arrow intersect with a running deer perfectly behind the shoulder. I got Sasha and Toby, and the three of us followed blood for seventy-five yards to a fine fat seven-point buck. ☆☆☆

56

EQUIPMENT: Oneida Eagle 55-pound, Aluminum arrows, XX75, 2213, 30-inch, 4 four-inch vanes, Hoyt Bow Bullet
ANIMAL: Whitetail Doe
HIT: Double-lung at twenty-five yards, went eighty yards

The trail had been there forever, cutting a fence row between two tillable fields, no matter what was planted. Every year I'd see it and vow to do something about it, someday. Wednesday morning I built a sixteen-foot ladder stand, camouflaged it and set it up against a choke cherry tree amongst the tangles of the old fence line, just twenty-five yards north of the run. I cut a few branches for clearance but left up plenty of cover to shield me from view.

Thursday morning before daylight, I climbed aboard and couldn't wait to see what might happen. I wasn't long in waiting, for twenty minutes after the sky pinked in the east, four full-grown does ambled my way from the south along the corn field. The lead deer was the biggest and she stopped at the mouth of the run, acting like she knew I was there. She was already broadside when the Bow Bullet caught her behind the left shoulder and came out in a flash. Again I had a game-tracker spool attached and watched the line zing out for about eighty yards. I got the top of the heart and both lungs for a red string-white string. ☆☆☆☆

57

EQUIPMENT: Jennings Super T Hunter 75-pound, Aluminum arrows,
2117, 30-inch, 4 four-inch vanes, Bear Razorheads
ANIMAL: American Bison, two thousand pounds
HIT: Broadside at thirty-five yards, double-lung, traveled one hundred yards

Bison is delicious. Next to nyala and elk, it is some of the best-tasting meat to be found. I was ready for another.

A slight snow covering had fallen the previous night, and it truly felt like a hunting dawn. I love that. You have not lived 'til you experience a new day IN THE WILD, with the pre-dawn pink glow highlighting the shimmering reflection of a broken ground snow field. This is a vision like no other.

I was bundled up good, warm even in the sub-zero air, leaning against a big oak tree, watching the small band of wooly tanks in the valley below. Every encounter with these majestic creatures leaves me in awe of their beauty, history, and sheer size. I love 'em. Steam circled their heads, mine too, and they leisurely strolled across the open before me.

I wore white snow camo, and picked my steps from cover to cover, cutting the distance between us from two hundred to one hundred yards, then seventy-five to forty-five. This is exciting. I had no more cover, so carefully prepared for the shot. I was kneeling in a crouch, and I kept my arms tight to my bulky insulated body to appear as a lump of snow. The biggest bull was last in line, and it was truly amazing to be so close to them as they angled along the hummock off my left shoulder, bringing the procession thirty-five yards away.

I let the herd bull pass me an extra ten yards, for the perfect forward angle into the boiler room, and picked a little spot on the huge side. The Bear Razorhead tipped arrow zipped in all the way to the nock, with only the turkey-barred feathers protruding. The other animals did not react till the big bull lunged past them at a slow trot. They all thundered one hundred yards or so then slowed to a walk, with the mortally-hit bull stopping, staggering, turning in a tight circle, and falling over to move no more.

The BLOOD TRAIL on the pure white snow was a pair of straight red lines to the fallen monarch. The rest of the herd took off as I approached from the tree line. I circled the beautiful, heavy-haired buffalo, feeling a sense of kinship that must be unique to the American Indian, early settlers, and those of us fortunate enough to sample this sensual, blessed connection.

Knowing that the increasing bison herds in this country are a direct result of compassionate, thinking conservationists like Teddy Roosevelt and other visionary hunters, I felt proud to be part of the equation. The complete equation being: man, earth, beast, bows, arrows, garlic, and butter! If you ever get the opportunity to bowhunt the American Bison, go for it. It's cool. ☆☆☆☆☆

58

EQUIPMENT: Oneida Eagle 60-pound, Aluminum arrows,
XX75 2216, 30-inch, 4 four-inch vanes, Zwickey two-blade
ANIMAL: Whitetail Spike, 150 pounds
HIT: High on right shoulder, exit low left, double-lung at twenty yards

It was cold, late October, just a day or two before Halloween. This is prime hunting time around the country. The Midwest rut is cooking, and woods-wise hunters are at it for every daylight hour they can.

Sunset was still three hours away as I pulled my bow up into the huge white oak. I barely removed the tow string when I saw the deer approaching from the east, twenty yards out. I straddled the big limb like a pony and carefully, but quickly, nocked an arrow. I had to twist my body around to take the shot, hard off my left shoulder.

Second-growth oak and maple saplings grew like weeds all around my perch, and at the height of twenty-two feet, I was worried that no opening would be found. My peripheral vision discovered a hole one step ahead of the small buck, the nock came back to the corner of my mouth, and deer shoulder and arrow joined in the hole with a loud CRACK!

The buck was slammed to the ground, but was instantly up and gone. The death run lasted only seconds, and I heard the unmistakable crash where I was sure the buck had piled up. There was a skiff of snow already on the ground, and now more white stuff was beginning to fall. I picked up the apparent BLOOD TRAIL, with plenty of kicked-up dirt and forest-floor debris for an easy spoor to follow. A short forty-five yards later, I gutted the handsome buck and prepared for the drag out to the Bronco, and a dinner of fresh liver, heart, and onions. Thank you Lord! ☆☆☆☆

59

EQUIPMENT: Oneida Eagle 60-pound, Aluminum arrows, 2117,
30-inch, 4 four-inch vanes, Bear Razorheads–no insert
ANIMAL: Whitetail Buck, seven-point
HIT: Double-lung at twenty-eight yards, went seventy yards

I could watch the heavy traffic on I-94 and hear the big semis roar by on a lot of my sets. I actually came to prefer the blinds nearer the highway. The deer seemed to be lulled into a reduced awareness as they traveled their routes amongst the continual flow of traffic. It was November 1st, George's birthday and a traditionally killer date. I was twelve feet up on one of Bryan Schupbach's homemade ladder stands along the south edge of a marsh grass area, leading to high ground and the oak woods. This would be the first time I used this set in this location and felt it was a typical roll of the dice.

I approached the stand from the east end to steer clear of the deer's anticipated approach route. It paid off. Only forty-five minutes after daylight I saw two figures approaching from out of the north sawgrass. The lead deer stepped onto hard ground and paused behind a large oak tree just long enough for me to make those last-second preparations for the draw. I could see that the second deer was lingering in the thick stuff and definitely had horns. I was surprised when the lead deer emerged from behind the tree and produced a head full of horns too.

I like surprises that make me shoot quickly, and I did just that. He was slow, walkin' broadside at twenty-eight yards, when I yanked the 2117 back to my lip and let 'er rock. The arrow entered textbook perfect, completely penetrating directly behind the left shoulder. He ran out of there lickity split and I watched him fall seventy yards down the line. I recovered, sniffed the coated arrow, and strolled through the sawgrass to one dead buck. ☆☆☆☆

60

EQUIPMENT: Oneida Eagle 55-pound, Aluminum arrows, XX75, 2413, 30-inch, 4 four-inch vanes, Hoyt Bow Bullet
ANIMAL: Whitetail Doe, 175 pounds
HIT: Double-lung at fifteen yards, went forty yards

This was a big 175-pound doe that took a textbook shot right square behind the left shoulder clear through and out the right side. It deflated both lungs and she only went forty yards with a four-star BLOOD TRAIL. ☆☆☆☆

61

EQUIPMENT: Oneida 65-pound, Aluminum arrows, 2413, Hoyt Bow Bullet
ANIMAL: Michigan Black Bear at 650 pounds, P&Y 20
HIT: Heart, forty feet up a tree at seventeen yards

Gosh, I love bear hunting. I had been on a few cross-country bear-hound races before and knew this was a specialized hunt for only the hardest, athletic hunter. I'm not talking about driving the pick-up around the roads. I'm talking about crashing through the thickest, nastiest, most impenetrable hell-holes that only a chased bear will run mile after ass kickin' mile with the pack of hounds. There is nothing in this world like the motivation and drive of five or six hard runnin', baying hounds to bring out the last ounce of log-jam climbing energy from a hunter.

We had already run and bayed a small bear that morning for a good eight-mile run. We let him go and now had a big track and a pack of hounds gone out of earshot. At this point there's one best thing to do and Matt Gettler and his dad, Norm, agreed that it was time to hit the woods towards the last howl we had heard.

Michigan's vast Upper Peninsula can go for many miles without crossing roads or any other man-made conveniences, and we knew what we could be in for. True to form, we nearly killed ourselves cruisin' through the wilderness. After a blind three miles of pure hell, we thought we heard a hound due north and crossed another beaver pond. The dogs got louder and we felt confident the chase had either treed or cornered the bear.

After sweating and stumbling into the din of howling hounds, my eyes peered through the colorful maple foliage at a major wad of black beast forty feet up a large tree. The chaos of the dogs actually seemed to calm me as I nocked a 2413 and found a hole to shoot thru. A dead-center chest hit thru the heart and ten seconds later the giant whomped to the ground, stone dead.

I had my first Michigan Black Bear and it was a trophy of a lifetime. The Gettlers, their fine hounds, and Dale and Lucy Gray of Michigan's Gonzo Bear Camp had produced a twenty-inch P&Y black bear, equal to the quality of their camp and service. This BLOOD TRAIL, a five-star! ✫✫✫✫✫

62

EQUIPMENT: Jennings T Hunter at 60-pound, Aluminum arrows, 2117, 30-inch, 4 four-inch vanes, Bear Razorheads
ANIMAL: Whitetail Doe
HIT: Double-lung and big artery at fifteen yards, went ten yards

The big, flooded beaver marsh valley encompasses a good one hundred acres. It is surrounded by big Michigan timber and thick cover consisting of tangles of alders and willows. Grouse and woodcock thrive in this ideal habitat, and the deer use the entire area for a secure bedding ground. It lies to the south of the oak ridges, sloping up to pines and some open grass zones. Most of my stands are located in this travel corridor, theoretically, hoping to catch the deer moving up in the after-noon and down in the early morning hours. Sounds good and has actually paid off on occasion. A real dandy eight-pointer taken with my .270 is still a glowing memory. This fall day was cool and overcast, and I was settled in a fifteen-foot treestand, facing west, anticipating a southerly approach. This would be ideal for a right-handed shooter, setting up a handy off-the-left-shoulder draw for me. The slight southwest breeze was perfect. Two deer were like ghosts, back in the forest about two hundred yards distant when I first saw them. My bow, with an arrow nocked, hung from a hook at eye level. My seat was above knee level, to minimize my movement in standing for the shot. A sitting shot is not bad, but when possible, I prefer to stand. I eased up, grasping the Jennings, and setting the bottom limb in my thigh pants pocket, sewn there just to hold the bow in shooting position, waiting. The forty-five minutes it took these two yearling does to get to me were fascinating, exciting, and nerve racking all together. Their grace and beauty as they fed along on acorns and stuff was the essence of the thrill of the hunt. My binoculars revealed their delicate features, and their uncanny alertness. A big, bushy-tailed fox squirrel joined them at one point, and the three of them shared a snack of mast. One doe sniffed at the squirrel a mere inch or two from the little critter's face. Yes, cute is in the wild. Their random path eventually meandered my way, and put them a short fifteen yards upwind of my perch, for one of the most ideal maximum-percentage shots we could ever ask for. Even as I made the decision to draw, the target doe stretched her neck to look off into the distance on her back trail. My fingers touched that home lock position in the corner of my mouth, and from the corner of my eye I saw second deer lift her head and look directly at me. But it was too late to give a warning, because the arrow was already in and out of the doe's chest, just above center, sticking hard into the ground beyond. Number two exploded to the south, as the foamy blood saturated the hit animal's side. She buckled for an instant, then drunkenly sauntered a short ten yards before collapsing, dead without a twitch within seconds. The filed Bear Razorhead had sliced the aorta above the heart, and X'd both lungs. Instant death. ☆☆☆☆☆

63

EQUIPMENT: Oneida 55-pound, Aluminum arrows, 2413, 30-inch, 4 four-inch vanes, Hoyt Bow Bullet
ANIMAL: Whitetail Buck, 160 pounds
HIT: Double-lung at forty yards, went seventy-five yards

We had a great camp full of bowhunters up for a weekend in the big timber of the North country. Taxidermist Mark Ditzel and his assistant, John Dean Schvetee, Dale and Lucy Gray and I were in all the hot treestands for the second morning with a beautiful fresh two-inch snowfall to add to the great hunting conditions. Daylight was barely breaking when three small deer slowly moved across the edge of my clearing, picking up acorns along the way. As they passed only twenty yards from me, I could see that all three were button bucks.

Deer number four was bringing up the rear at a distance, and even through the light snowfall I could see antlers and a much larger body. He stayed another twenty yards beyond the three fawns' trail and stopped to look things over. I slowly cut the game-tracker string off my arrowhead for the long forty-yard shot, picked a spot and let fly just as he turned his head to continue. Slammo! The Hoyt Bow Bullet broadhead sliced in and out right behind the shoulder and off he went. I watched him cover seventy-five yards and fall. ☆☆☆☆

64

EQUIPMENT: OSE 50-pound, Aluminum arrows, 2213, 30-inch,
4 four-inch vanes, Hoyt Bow Bullet
ANIMAL: Whitetail Doe
HIT: Double-lung at twenty yards, went fifty yards

This doe showed up on a difficult rear approach and gave my nerves another test. At twenty yards she finally dropped her head long enough for me to draw and zap her good. The game-tracker string reeled out for fifty yards, but the BLOOD TRAIL was easier to follow than the string. ☆☆☆☆

65

EQUIPMENT: Oneida Screaming Eagle, 70-pound, Aluminum arrows,
XX75 2413, 30-inch, 4 four-inch vanes, Bear Razorheads, two-blade
ANIMAL: Spanish goat, 140 pounds
HIT: Thirty-five yards, point of right shoulder, pass thru, double-lung

Jeff Roe is one hell of a bowhunter and friend. One of the last of the good guys. Preparing the Damn Yankee recording in Northern California gave me opportunities to run around the hills and desert with him. Shemane, Jeff and I were looking for goats, and were about to learn a valuable lesson in survival. I'm a survival nut. Not in theory or planning so much, but rather in common-sense preparedness. On the street, in the business world, career, or just plain staying alive and fighting the odds, I INSIST on staying alive to my maximum capabilities, to be with my family, state my piece, and go hunting. Period. So here we were, 110 scorching degrees, cooking under the midday sun, looking for goats. Cool. We saw several a mile away, so now we were slowly heading to the distant mountaintop to make a move on them. Jeff's Bronco inched its way the last possible distance on the rim, and we decided to continue on foot, descending the hard slope to the creek in the deep valley below. This is where they were headed, so us too. We knew it was dangerously hot, but somehow in the excitement of the chase, completely failed to load up with water and emergency rations for our descent. Maybe it was the proximity of the vehicle, full of food and drinks, not realizing the extent of the walk ahead. Whatever is was, we blew it. I took a long swig of mineral water as we left the truck, but we packed nothing on us. And it was seriously hot. We carefully slid on our butts, working our way straight down. One hundred yards, two hundred yards, one-half mile later we were absolutely pooped, and drenched in sweat. We slumped against a boulder, breathing hard, glassing for goats, still unaware of the gravity of our situation. We squatted for twenty minutes, when a burp and grunt to our left got Shemane's attention. She figured it was me, and I'm too deaf to even hear it, so we looked thru the stunted trees and thick brushy vegetation in the direction she pointed out. At once, the black-and-white form of a big billy goat materialized amongst many bodies, thirty-five yards sidehill. Shemane picked up her camera as I readied my bow, our shoulders touching from the narrow view to the animals. A second later I whispered, "Are you on him?" Shemane said, "GO!" I drew back, nudging her as I released the arrow, its path on video, straight into the shoulder of the big goat. Critters exploded. We looked at each other, smiled, and reveled in the spontaneity of the event. Shemane did great, and luck worked out. Now the adrenaline of the moment picked us up, taking the ample BLOOD TRAIL, further downhill, fifty yards to one very dead goat. Pictures taken and skinning done, we were exhausted. The impact of the realization of just what lay ahead was overwhelming.

We looked far up the mountain, knowing we did not have the power to make it. The heat had taken its toll, and our failure to carry water had us drained of energy. We breathed hard as we painfully took each laborious step up the steep, difficult slope. Barely fifty feet were climbed before we had to flop down beneath leafy branches for refuge from the sun. It was a long ways up to the Bronco, and fear added to our dilemma. Jeff carried Shemane's heavy camera gear, and both of them were done. It must have been the extra water I had consumed hours earlier, for I instructed them to remain under the tree while I slowly made my way to the vehicle for food and water. To make a long story short, I did trudge up, barely making it, feeling a sensation of depletion like I never have before or since. As I literally crawled the last few yards to slump against the truck, I realized how stupid a person can be. BE PREPARED. I fortified myself with water and fruit, then returned to Jeff and Shemane with supplies for them. It all worked out fine, but was much too close for comfort. The fanny pack I so religiously carried on all of my hunts before will NEVER be left again.

Here is an outline of what we should always have on hand:
- waterproof matches
- toilet paper
- water purification tablets
- plastic sheeting

- canteen
- tea bags
- diarrhea pills
- spare socks
- a good WhackMaster knife
- space blanket
- aspirin
- a S&W M29 .44 mag plus twenty to forty rounds of ammo

- candles
- tin cup
- needle and thread
- sunscreen
- compass
- beef and chicken bouillon cubes
- candy bars

 66

EQUIPMENT: Jennings T Hunter at 60-pounds, Aluminum arrows, 2217, Bear Razorheads
ANIMAL: Fallow Deer, 175 pounds
HIT: Double-lung, running at sixty yards

This was one of those shots. A white deer on snow running by as fast as he could with about thirty other deer. I swung out from behind a large oak tree and snap-shot like a recurve. I watched as the long shot arched and penetrated right through the ribs. ☆☆☆☆

 67

EQUIPMENT: OSE 55-pound, Aluminum arrows, 2213, 30-inch, 4-four-inch vanes, Bear Razorheads
ANIMAL: Javelina
HIT: Double-lung at twenty yards, went fifty yards

We were hunting outside Glove, Arizona, with Tim and Ted Spradling during Doug Walker's Bowhunter's Jamboree. Tim and Ted lived in the area, so they knew likely spots to find the pigs. My buddy, Bob Blevins, and some of his GI buddies had joined us. In the gusting wind, the nine of us slowly worked our half-circle army down the slope toward the seven or eight javelina, munching on cactus.

With all that humanity, the hogs got wary and started to move off and almost on cue, it seemed, everyone started "varmint calling." The squalling caused the pigs to dart in confusion, offering a few moving shots when a lone animal trotted up the ravine to my end-line position. As he walked past on a downward angle at twenty yards, I laced him clean behind the shoulders. The arrow shot thru and into the ravine and the javelina piled up after fifty yards. ☆☆☆☆

68

EQUIPMENT: 65-pound Oneida bow, Aluminum arrows, XX75 2413, 30-inch, four four-inch vanes, Satellite Titan four-blade
ANIMAL: Whitetail Buck, seven-point, 150 pounds
HIT: Stalked, twenty yards, double-lung, ran twenty-five yards

Being a part of the wild is the main thrust of hunting, especially with the bow and arrow. If we don't blend, we don't fit. I certainly relish every moment in a treestand or ground blind, but the ultimate is still hunting, stalking big game.

It was kinda dank, with a slight mist in the air, as I knelt beside a big beech tree, taking in the world around me. It was silent. Even my wounded Rock 'n' Roll ears can work at their optimum capabilities under these peaceful conditions. I was tuned in. A good five-ten minutes would be spent at each little crouch stop, keeping a minimum profile, trying my best to vanish in the understory. I wore standard military-type woodland camo, with a tree-bark cap, and had a slight beard to reduce my face shine. The real secret is stealth. SLOW! QUIET! UNOBTRUSIVE! I would scour every inch of terrain in advance of each step. Keeping low to the ground is important. Staying close to large trees and broken cover helps hide any movement. A very special level of awareness has the hunter. It is the ultimate high. You can feel the earth rotate. The hours of glory in this place are life. And now I felt the presence of a large critter.

The ridgeline sloped down to my left into a twenty-some acre alder marsh. From there came the tawny shape of a big deer. With its head down browsing, I secretly slid an arrow onto the string and peered thru the ferns. A pretty little seven-point rack came up, and he picked his way up the line. I was crouched tight to ground and cautiously eased myself forward, knowing I had to cut the sixty yards in half in this thick cover for that high-percentage shot I needed. Only when his head was down in the vegetation, or covered by timber would I slink ahead. He was in no hurry, and therefore, neither was I. The sleek buck would pause to groom his backside, and I felt privileged to be in his domain. The torment of biting mosquitoes was tolerable in his presence. I was high. He disappeared momentarily behind some brush, and I secured my release on the string, and started to tense up. As his nose came into view at twenty yards, I touched the nock to the corner of my mouth, picked a spot low behind the shoulder, and watched the buck flinch as the arrow passed thru his heart. A brief dash of two seconds, and he piled up stone dead. Beautiful! ☆☆☆☆

69

EQUIPMENT: Oneida Eagle, 65-pound, Aluminum arrows, XX75 2413, 30-inch, 4 four-inch vanes, Bear Razorheads, two-blade
ANIMAL: Catalina Goat, 125 pounds
HIT: Fifteen yards, stalked, broadside, double-lung, pass thru

Scott Walker and I were spending the weekend with Stan Swart, kicking back in the hills outside Livermore, California, again. It is frustrating as hell when I am locked into recording or touring, eliminating any chance at a bona-fide, extended big-game bowhunt. If it were not for these private hunting grounds across the country, I'd go nuts! We had just finished a mid-morning snack of cheese and crackers and cold pop, and sat glassing the canyons and ridges around us. One moment, the south slope was critterless, the next, there stood a long-horned, dirty white goat, nibbling brush. He was three hundred yards off, on a side hill, even with us, but two mountaintops away. So down and up we go, hoping the wind would stay in our faces. An hour later, we huffed up the steep slope, just short of where the landmarks indicated our goat was last seen feeding. Scott had his camcorder, and stayed close behind, hopeful for a video opportunity. We felt close as we stepped carefully along the rock- and shale-strewn hillside. It is a good thing we were optimistic and slow, because, abruptly, the tips of thirty-six-inch wide horns bobbed twenty-five yards ahead, peeking above the vegetation. We crouched backwards, into a small screen of scrub, started the camera, and nocked my arrow. Everything was right. A good breeze in our faces, shadows away from the rising sun, and a near-perfect blind of leafy bush, replete with a convenient, eye and goat-level shooting window yet! With Scott tight over my left shoulder, the billy fed step by step closer, exposing his deep chest and trophy sweeping horns. Apprehensive, I readied as he came directly on, worried I would have a difficult, frontal shot. Bingo! At fifteen yards he turned towards a different bush, I drew, anchored, and released for a dreamy dumper of a shot. The picked spot at the shoulder consumed my white fletched shaft perfectly, lacing him. He butt-spun and trotted right past us thru the brush that concealed us, almost running us down. He cut straight down the steep valley slope, up the other side and vanished amongst the rocks. The BLOOD TRAIL was primo, and we followed it quickly, for thirty seconds, to a precipice, overlooking a deep gorge. On the far side, wavering, he clung to an outcropping of boulders at seventy-five yards. With the camera rolling, second nature nocked another arrow, aimed high, felt good, and we took in the long flight of the arching arrow, hitting the billy, right square in the head, nocking him crashing down the mountainside. All was quiet. Scott loved it almost as much as I did! It was spectacular. Even the goat thought so. How could you ask for more? Would you believe Scott mistakenly erased the whole thing!!! Oh well, we'll just have to do it again! Hey Scott, let's go bowhunting! ☆☆☆☆

 # 70 & 71

EQUIPMENT: Oneida Screaming Eagle, 75#, Aluminum arrows,
X-C Caliber fluted 2212, Hoyt Chuck-It 85 grain
ANIMAL: Two Corsican Rams
HIT: Both double-lung, seventy-five and eighty yards

Stan Swart, at the Bow & Bore ranch in Livermore, California, has Disneyland beat all to hell. I mean, what fun is the Captain Cook ride if you can't shoot the hippopotami?? So my kick is to join Stan and Jeff Roe and the boys, take Toby and some of his friends, and head up to Northern California for a little hill climbing and adventure. This particular weekend was typically hot and dry, and Toby and I had recently had an incredible time teaming up on a gorgeous big Catalina goat and a Texas Dall sheep. Toby is an incredible shot. Atsa my boy! I was going it solo late in the morning, with the sun getting up with the temperature. Beautiful, full-curl, trophy Corsican rams could be seen at long range all the time, but they were impossible to stalk. I had gotten lucky in the past on ambushes and taken some beauties, but a certain light, cream-colored sheep was calling me. Two hours were spent sitting on a promontory, glassing the band of eight sheep, way out there in the open at a half-mile, grazing. It appeared hopeless. AH, for the .270! All of a sudden, they vanished! They were wide open, then gone in an instant. I concluded that there must be a cut, ravine, or some break way up there, so I hit it at a dead run. As I neared the ground they were last seen feeding on, I could tell that a huge ravine did in fact cut the hillsides in half. I crawled on my belly to the precipice and peered over the edge to see the band working their way up the opposite slope. It was a long poke. But my cream ram was in the lead, and side-hilling at about seventy-five yards. I nocked one of Carl Lekavitch's 2212 lightweight fluted shaft, with a light 85-grain Chuck-It, envisioned my long-range sight picture of one thousand of seventy-five-yard target and game shots, and willed the Scott release to let 'er go. You have to see it some-time to believe it! The incredible sight of that long arching path from you to the target is like no other thing in life. Especially at this moment, when the arrow zeroed in perfectly behind the ram's shoulder, for a dream double-lung pass-thru!! Even at that distance, I could see the red on his chest as he stumbled in reverse, and fell over dead in ten steps. The other rams jumped and stared, and it was then that I saw the other light-coated full-curl trophy above my fallen prize. I had another round on and ready to go as I added another ten yards on my sight picture, let go, and reveled in the repeat arrow trajectory, impaling the second ram identically as I did the first! KOWABUNGA!!! This animal topped the high rise with the others, then fell over dead as well. Both expired in less than ten seconds each, for the ultimate in quick, humane kills. It does not get any better than this. We celebrated with hot, roasted ribs at the campfire that night. ✰✰✰✰

72

EQUIPMENT: Jennings T 60-pounds, Aluminum arrows, 2117,
Bear Razorheads
ANIMAL: Whitetail Buck
HIT: Double-lung at thirty yards

I was hunting at John Cunningham's farm before he started bowhunting.
I clawed up into a big oak tree next to a big marsh area when this deer walked by
at thirty yards. ☆☆☆

73

EQUIPMENT: 50-pounds, Aluminum arrows, 2213 Satellite Titan Bear
Whitetail Compound
ANIMAL: Wild Hog, 250 pounds
HIT: Shoulder at twenty-five yards, went thirty-five yards

Ken DeRocka of Sherwin Industries and I were testing the new carbon and
stainless steel Satellite Titan four-blade at Buck Fuller's Florida ranch. Buck's son,
Jay, had showed me a thick-as-hell palmetto tangle where the hogs sometimes fed,
so I eased along a trail, watching for snakes and pigs.

A black form twitched through the undergrowth and I made out the head of a
big porker. As it came into view past the leaves, I drew back a borrowed Pop
Creeson's signed Bear Bow and zipped a 2213, tipped with the new Titan head,
clear through that fat booger perfect behind the shoulder. The hog exploded out of
there but only went thirty-five yards. ☆☆☆☆

74

EQUIPMENT: Bear Whitetail Compound, Aluminum arrows,
2214, Satellite Titan Four-blade
ANIMAL: Wild Hog, 150 pounds
HIT: Shoulder

On the second day of huntin' with the Fullers, I spied a dark-red hog feeding along
a grove of trees, in and out of the vegetation. After a good one hundred-yard stalk,
I put a Satellite Titan four-blade square into his shoulder and blew him off his feet.

This is a very rare occurrence: Though the shot was two inches left of perfect
into what appeared to be the "impenetrable" shoulder bone, something must have

snapped, because the hog fell over just like a spine hit. All I can figure is that a rib must have been shattered off the spine, causing a spinal disruption. Does this make any sense to any doctors out there?

One gets a bit regimented at times after accumulating years of kills via disciplined procedures and stand sites. Once in a while, one feels the urge to wander at will and find new locations of game activity. In my home state of Michigan, we're loaded with millions of acres of state and Federal land open to public hunting. Even in the '90s, a guy can escape the legion of bowhunters afield and discover hotspots all for himself. I've logged many enjoyable hunts on these public lands and seen and bagged lots of deer. I'm sure I'll do more of the same in the future. Maybe I could write a book titles, Misses! Of course, it would take forever to write about each one!

75

EQUIPMENT: Oneida Screaming Eagle, 65-pounds, Aluminum arrows, XX75 2413, Bear Razorheads
ANIMAL: Whitetail Buck at 140 pounds
HIT: Forty yards broadside, one lung and liver

George Nicholls had once again honored me with his best tree set, and I was ready. I don't believe it is possible to sit in his sets without a damn good chance for a shot at a buck. This guy is one of the all-time masters.

The northwest wind came directly from the I-94 freeway, with semis and morning rush-hour traffic splashing by at high speeds. The mature corn to my rear left and the swampy woodlot to my right front represented the "from & to" of the local deer herd's movement pattern. A dozen majestic whitetails melted in and out of the broken brush and fence rows in the first twenty minutes of daylight, and now a lone deer faded amongst the thornapple scrub near the highway.

My Zeiss binoculars revealed his small rack, and he moved west to east along the right of way, a good 150 yards out. He came to the fence row my tree was in, and instead of continuing into the woods, he took a sharp right and headed straight for me. I wonder if George had these guys trained!?! So anyhow, here he comes, slow but sure, nibbling here and there, taking his merry old time. This is one point that hunters must come to grips with; critters are in absolutely no hurry whatsoever. So we must learn to relax (yea, sure), and let them proceed at will. Always prepare for the shot in advance, be ready for anything, but expect nothing! At one point this buck stopped at a low spot in the fence, faced it and appeared to be ready to cross. I readied to draw, but then he dropped his head and began to approach me again. At the forty-five-yard mark, he veered right and cut diagonally across the fallow field in front of me. I was already standing with the bow in position, and when he barely passed me at forty-ish yards, I burned a hole in his heart with my eye and sent the arrow off. Forty yards is a long shot to a degree, and I was off a bit, with the arrow hitting slightly right of mid-lung, exiting a bit back. He bolted headlong into the fence row, jumped, stood in the corn a second, then took off at a walk. The BLOOD TRAIL was good, with bright-red liver blood, and I took it about two hundred yards to a wooded gully. I was stalking the BLOOD TRAIL cautiously, alert, with an arrow nocked. All at once he erupted from the saw grass, and as he jumped the fence at twenty-five yards, my second arrow sunk deep into his hip, putting him down for good. ☆☆☆

 # 76 & 77

EQUIPMENT: Oneida Screaming Eagle, 78-pounds, Aluminum arrows, Bear Razorheads - no insert
ANIMAL: The Non-Conformist Wildebeest Man
HIT: **#1:** Double-lung at ten yards
        #2: Heart at eighteen yards, went seventy-five yards

I thought whitetails were spooky. C'mon. Get in here! Twenty-four eyeballs were a lot to be careful of, and these big critters were definitely on their utmost alert. Five good-size blue wildebeest were already in close, a mere ten yards in front and below me. But the bonzo man was still hanging back there, waiting, watching. I was sixteen feet up in a gnarled, skinny, pickery tree, reasonably comfortable in a five-way crotch. Frozen still. Cocked, locked, and ready to rock!

The biggest of the bulls was now exercising his dominance over the entire herd, and boldly waded right into the muddy waterhole beneath me. As he quartered away to stare down a submissive, lesser bull, I drew back to anchor in one fluid motion. I could see the white Rothar three blade as I touched the release to my mouth, and I let 'er rip. Talk about party time! Crash, bang, splash! Wildebeest running everywhere. And the big one had the most beautiful white fletching showing barely behind his shoulder as he thundered off into the heavy African bush. Bingo! Just what the doctor ordered. I wanted one of these big antelope in a big way, and it looked like I got him.

After only ten minutes of waiting, more familiar African game began to materialize from the tangle down below. Darkness was setting in, so I felt compelled to investigate the trail of the herd's departure. I had watched intently as the arrowed animal followed the running herd, so I had a good feeling for direction. However, true to form, another African animal defied the blood-letting capability of a deadly razor-sharp broad-head. With no apparent blood sign to coincide with the witnessed arrow strike, the ensuing darkness left me no alternative than to head back to camp. I knew he was dead.

Even though the animal had both lungs sliced, and a broken shoulder, the professional tracker and I walked a solid mile to the downed animal. And we weren't the first to find him either. The huge eight-hundred-pound antelope had been partly devoured by the resident predators. He was a beauty though. Twenty-six inch horns put him well up in the SCI record book for bow-killed blue wildebeest. I was thrilled to say the least, but somewhat disappointed about having to leave him overnight like that. No Blood Trail whatsoever. Zilch. If it weren't for the uncanny, almost miracle-like tracking capabilities of the tracker, I would have had a hell of a time finding this trophy.

The blue wildebeest came hard for me. I had seen herds of these impressive animals every day during my first South African bowhunting safari in 1988. With the goal of establishing exclusive bowhunting grounds for Archers Africa, I had the run of 30,000 acres all to myself. Am I the luckiest guy in the world or what? Some of this amazing game seemed to be impossible to get within bow-range of. But I was learning.

Determined to kill one of these boys outright, and tip 'em right over, I concentrated my efforts upon my return in '89 to the high-percentage stomping grounds. Again, this particular waterhole looked like the winner. The first two afternoons were filled with excitement, as a continuous procession of fascinating big and small game filed thru the bush, and usually right into the hole. I whacked impala, warthog, duiker, and saw each of nearly all thirty-six species from this one set. Now, the moment of truth.

In the distance, barely discernable thru the screen of impenetrable thorn scrub, a pair of good-size bulls were step-by-step, cautiously working their way towards me. And I was ready this time. Extra ready. I was shooting a solid 75-pounds, and this time my payload was the slicemaster supreme, an old Bear Razorhead, no insert, filed and honed to a deadly edge. I was focused on his heart, low in the chest. The two wary bulls took their merry old time getting into range. That always makes it extra hard on me. The waiting game. But I was determined, and as the bigger bull nudged the smaller, I snap-shot, holding extra low, putting that old broadhead PERFECT, dead center thru the ticker at eighteen yards.

I couldn't have been more sure of myself as I climbed down with the setting sun. Where he crossed the main trail, I found a wonderful splash of crimson blood. Just like back in America! It was getting dark as usual, and I almost panicked when I couldn't find any more blood after only fifty yards. I had a hunch, and circled a heavy scrub area to find the giant deader than hell. He hadn't traveled twenty-five more yards and lived more than five seconds, I'm sure. The Bear Razorhead had passed clean thru the chest cavity, severing the top ventricles right off the heart. A near-instant death.

Bottom line is, after all these years of bowhunting, I'm convinced that the ultimate killer broadhead is a properly sharpened two-blade with a leading knife edge. You have heard it all before I'm sure. I must repeat that any strong, sharp broadhead, on a GOOD FLYING ARROW, will kill most anything cleanly. There seems to be a million on the market these days. But when it comes to big, hard-to-kill game, or just to getting that extra edge for a clean kill, I have seen what I know to be the best. I feel I have taken the best penetrating attributes of the old Bear and Zwickey and put them together in my new Nugent WhackMaster. Slice 'em and dice 'em. When I hit the game trails of the world, the WhackMaster is going to do some Master Whackin'! Elk, caribou, stag, buffalo, zebra, moose, bear and, of course, one of my favorites, the African Blue Wildebeest.

78

EQUIPMENT: Oneida Screaming Eagle 78-pounds, Aluminum arrows, X-C Caliber fluted 2212, Bear Razorheads, Hoyt Bow Bullet, four-blade
ANIMAL: Waterbuck
HIT: Severed neck vertebrae at forty-seven yards

The African Waterbuck is a strong, tough, solid, six-hundred-pound antelope. He has more girth and muscle than an elk and his skin is a good inch thick, twice that of an elk. We all know how tough elk are. Well, waterbuck are tougher. This big one-horn granddaddy was seen now and again within sight of the huge Baobab tree. This massive tree is thousands of years old, and as I settled into the house-like branches thirty feet off the ground, I could only imagine the vast numbers of wildlife that had crossed in its shadows during its tenure. Now if only my time would witness but a brief sample. My wife, Shemane, shared this perch with me this morning, and now we waited.

As occasionally happens, patience waned and thoughts of video footage gave way to breakfast plans. We gathered our gear after only a few hours of waiting and lowered the video camera to the ground. No sooner had the unit touched down, off dashed three waterbuck cows about forty yards out. With our vantage-point view, I'll never know how they got that far undetected, but I was pissed. We laughed at out lack of patience and it was then that I saw the one-horn. He stared at the cows that had stopped seventy-five yards distant and I eased a 2212 fluted arrow with a two-blade Bear out of the quiver. He was forty-seven yards out with only his head showing. One step ahead of him was a mere body-length clearing before he would again be swallowed up by thorn brush.

Now I waited, as his first move would necessitate a snap-shot, if anything. All along I had told all the other bowhunters in camp the importance of silent equipment and how a squeaky draw would ruin a shot. Well, as he took one step into the open,

I drew my 78-pound Oneida Screaming Eagle with an audible squeak. The moleskin had come off the rest, and at the sound, the huge bull froze smack-dab in the clearing. I love that part. The arrow flashed across the distance and the bull had already jerked to dodge into the bush when the Bear Razorhead sliced just forward of the shoulder ball and disappeared completely through the animal. At once has was slammed to the ground like Hulk Hogan had hit him off the ropes. He was part-way up and right back down, up, down, up, down.

I couldn't believe my eyes! Could one break the back or neck of an animal this size? I didn't think so. He flip-flopped away for forty to fifty more yards, so I quickly, but carefully, climbed down out of the big Baobab, knowing all too well that it ain't over 'til it's over. And that means, he ain't mine 'til he's here and his guts are there! I eased my way through the confusing vegetation, now at an all-time thickness because of abundant rainfall, and I picked up his obvious spoor.

After eight-five to ninety yards, I saw his head weaving above the grass at fifty-five yards. I hit the dirt GI fashion and pushed my bow ahead of me. At forty yards, I peeked over the grass, nocked a 2213 XX75 with a 145-grain Hoyt Bow Bullet four blade and aimed low through the grass to where I figured the good stuff was. At impact, I heard the beautiful whoomph and his head jerked and fell. I cautiously approached his motionless form, and now he was mine. The first hit had been a pass-thru with the little two-blade Bear actually severing two neck vertebrae as only a two-blade could have done. The BLOOD TRAIL was negligible 'til the very end, but the four-blade coup de grace had opened him up perfectly. I would rate this a one-star BLOOD TRAIL. What a trophy. ☆

79

EQUIPMENT: Aluminum arrows, 2213, XX75, Hoyt Bow Bullet, 145 gr., four-blade
ANIMAL: Impala, eighty pounds
HIT: Neck vertebrae and jugular at forty-two yards

My first bow kill of Archers Africa '89 came on a misty, dewy, uncharacteristic South African April morning. The dampness facilitated good still-hunting and I had game in sight all morning long. Duiker, warthog, tsesebee, zebra, baboon, reedbuck, wildebeest, steenbok, kudu and impalla by the hundreds. As I slowly rounded a big patch of trees, a lone impalla paralleled me at forty yards. He was small at eighty pounds, with only immature fourteen-inch horns, but on my first day out, tender steaks for camp were in order. He stopped as I stopped, but only stared for a minute before continuing to walk on a slight angle away. I already had an all-white 2213 XX75 with a Hoyt Bow Bullet 145-grain four-blade ready to rock, and as he crossed at forty-two yards, I put it dead center thru his neck. The arrow just kept on going as he piled up in a heap. The big four-blade hole had severed the tender neck vertebrae and sliced the jugular in half. By the time ten seconds were up, I was standing over him, and he was stone dead. The WhackMaster returns. ☆☆☆☆

➤ 80 & 81

EQUIPMENT: Screaming Eagle 78-pounds, Aluminum arrows, Easton 2213, XX75, Hoyt Bow Bullet
ANIMAL: Two Gemsbok
HIT **#1:** Shoulder, went eighty yards
#2: Double-lung at eighteen yards

Being the manager for Ted Nugent's Archers Africa, thirty thousand acres of exclusive bowhunting grounds, puts me in a very interesting and new position. My hunting time has always been sacred and very personal. Now, instead of hunting on my own, finding my own spots and whackin' and stackin' 'em, I have to consider the best possible hunting conditions and locations for all my paying hunters. At first I was concerned if I would be generous enough to share my hot spots, but I soon learned that Africa is one immense, unlimited hot spot and no fifty hunters could cover them all. So upon our arrival into camp on April 5th, I felt a whole new excitement in the role of guide and professional hunter, setting each hunter up in a prime area. My two hundred marked trees and stand sites from '88 were now treestands and blinds, and anticipation was running high. A friend from Detroit wanted a Gemsbok in the worst way, so we set him up in a hay bale ground blind at their favorite waterhole. He spent over a week there, sometimes all day long, but didn't get one. He saw them regularly and even had shots, but not until he had to leave for home did I move into that area.

Like a good marine, I had to adapt and change tactics. Dick had seen the herd approach the water in the distance, on many occasions from the same general direction, so one midday, Rocco and I scouted and circled the area and found a concentration of tracks about one hundred yards off the periphery in a sandy area. It appeared to be a staging zone. The animals hung around before exposing themselves in the vicinity of the waterhole. My handy dandy Ted Nugent-American Rock 'n' Roll Bowhunter-Gut Piles-Rus-Slice 'em-Dice 'em-Whack 'em-Stack 'em-Bone Ripper-Filet Master-Custom-Hi-Performance-Killer-Elite-Hi-Tech-Backstrap-Legal-Victorionox-Pocket-Gonzo Hunting Knife came out, glistening in the hot, afternoon, South African, blazing sunshine and I commenced to set up a forked tree twenty-five yards downwind of the open crossing area.

The next morning at 7:30 or so, I walked in, climbed up, hung my bow and quiver from a nail, put my cooler and canteen in a crotch of the tree and settled in for the Gemsbok Boogie. In only thirty minutes, a good one hundred-pound warthog strolled right on down the trail. Beautiful. Having whacked nineteen warthogs in '88, I decided to keep things peaceful in hopes of a Gemsbok parade. After all, I wanted one of those elusive, beautiful, five hundred-pound, scimitar-horned oryx in a bad way, too. I had only another thirty-minute wait and from the north, the magnificent grey, black and white antelope melted out of the scrub, heading right for me! Hallelujah! Praise the Lord and pass the broadheads! This is it.

My bow hung advantageously in front of my face with an Easton 2213 XX75 Hoyt Bow Bullet nocked, locked, cocked and ready to rock, doc. As it passed my position at thirty yards, I canted my 78-pound Screaming Eagle and touched 'er off. The arrow passed thru perfectly, center body, just behind the shoulder. The Gemsbok only flinched and kept walking, circling away from the waterhole and into the dense scrub. I thought I saw it fall or lie down behind a large bush at about eighty yards, so I put another arrow on the string and settled back, took a big swig of bottled water, a bite of sandwich and grinned from ear to ear. Here's where it really gets interesting.

Forty-five minutes later, I was about ready to abandon ship and go get my Gemsbok, when I saw five more about two hundred yards to the south. They cautiously worked their way towards me with the largest bull in the lead by forty yards. Both bull and cow Gemsbok have large horns, with the cow's being longer, but the bull's reaching more mass.

I was ready when this big 'ol boy looked away at eighteen yards and I whacked him perfect, low behind the shoulder, a true pocket shot if I've ever made one. Off he crashed, the arrow falling out and the bull disappearing in the trees.

Here's what happened! Making a very, very long story short, the first Gemsbok, a thirty-six inch cow, new SCI #1 bow and arrow, left no BLOOD TRAIL!! Not a drop. It had been double-lunged with almost no blood! ☆

Gemsbok number two went seven miles, left two splashes of blood, and our main tracker, Freddy, a black, master tracker, stayed on him, following tracks and hunches for seven hours to where I finally had to .44 mag him in the neck at one hundred yards, and a second time with the .44 S&W at 140 yards in the neck before bringing him to bag. Unbelievable!!!

Here are the insane details of the hit. Invisible to the naked eye, like a whitetail ducking and spinning from an arrow, the big bull Gemsbok had thrust his leg either at the moment of impact or just prior, forcing the forward angle of the arrow rearward with his left front elbow, causing the arrow to miss all the vitals and end up in the guts, even though as I looked at the dead animal on the ground, the four-blade arrow hole was perfect right in the pocket, low, behind the shoulder.

I truly believe there are some occasional circumstances where ideal conditions can be negated by uncontrollable possibilities. I was glad to have recovered this beautiful antelope with Freddy's expert tracking and my handgun marksmanship. Even so, I will forever be dismayed.

 # 82

EQUIPMENT: Oneida Screaming Eagle at 75-pounds,
Aluminum arrows XX75 2413, Barrie three-blade Grande
ANIMAL: Warthog, three hundred pounds
HIT: Thirty-five yard, broadside, double-lung and artery

Waterholes in Africa are life itself. A day ensconced in a ground blind or treestand will beat the hell out of all the TV wildlife specials combined. Every animal, insect, and bird that is part of the constant drama is a spectacle to behold. The baboons are the smartest, and will not come in no matter how well you are concealed. Kudu have nerves that dwarf a whitetail's, if you can believe that! Zebra and wildebeest are uncanny in their alertness, and warthogs and impalla will not tolerate the slightest inconsistency. A scraped shirtsleeve or minute squeak of the arrow on the rest will spook any of these critters that have been existing with large predators for time immemorial.

As they approached the area surrounding the water, they were on red-alert, code-three! This ambush arrangement necessitates complete preparedness on the archer's part, as our blinds are usually and should be within a thirty-five-yard zone of our anticipated shot zone. Silent clothing and gear is number one. Keeping the shooting area off the left shoulder for right-hand shooters, with the bow at ready, is essential. Face camo will help, along with good dull coloration of all equipment and clothing.

Now, I was comfortable in my circle of thick reeds on a slightly elevated bank, rimming a small mudhole. It was hot. Always is. No bugs really. Just wonderfully peaceful. Quiet. Well, quiet by bush standards, with the constant cawing and singing of the millions of dove, grouse and other birds, punctuated by the call of the baboon and squeaks of distant monkeys. This is my kind of music.

Small bands of impalla had been visiting the left end of the water all morning, but none that I wanted to take. They gave me the opportunity to watch and learn, which is the essence of hunting anyhow. Being a part. I maneuvered my bow into shooting position a few times, just to practice my moves. A couple of small rams tempted my trigger finger, but I restrained myself, having already shot some good mature specimens with the meat larder in good shape.

A rustle across the opening caught my attention, when three very large, grey, muddy warthog boars emerged from the surrounding cover. The first one was enormous. Big in body, tall, bold, and with great tusks over twelve inches each. I committed myself. With the bow in my hand, an arrow on the string, I lifted slowly as the trio cautiously moved towards water. The big, wide three-blade Barrie Grande broadhead was obvious at the end of my 2413.

Robert and Bruce are dedicated bowhunters and family folks who have a well-respected, tried and true design here, and I was putting them to the ultimate test on hard-to-kill, tuff African game. And here I go!

The big boy took but a sip of water, while the other two gulped. The target hog turned to leave, and at the apex of his spin, I anchored, picked that spot, and watched the shaft arc across the expanse of thirty-five yards to connect dead center behind the shoulder. I knew immediately what I had done when the entire chest turned red with blood, the beast spun twice, and fell over dead. In a cloud of dust, his bachelor buddies scrambled off in their unique erect-tail run. The Barrie head had sliced in one side and out the other, taken the mass of artery off the top of the heart, destroyed both lungs, and bled out the warthog in seconds. Cool as hell. He didn't go five feet! The slaughterhouses of the world have NEVER killed so efficiently as this. Bowhunting is the coolest. ☆☆☆☆☆

83

EQUIPMENT: Oneida Screaming Eagle at 75-pounds, Aluminum arrows, XX75 2413, Zwickey
ANIMAL: Southern Impalla, one hundred pounds
HIT: Quarter frontal, shoulder, jugular, at thirty yards, went forty yards

Often times, I find myself literally strolling, slowly, thru hunting terrain. Not really still-hunting per se, but just taking it all in, enjoying being there. Enjoying being.

When I do commit myself to a serious still-hunt/stalking maneuver, it takes on the intensity of an athletic event for me. You have to concentrate with all you've got. Add the heat of the African sun or the cold of a Midwestern Nor'wester, and it can gratifyingly drain a guy. I like that.

So, I had put about four hours of diligent creeping amongst the scented scrub of the African bush since daylight, and now felt like a leisurely stroll back to camp headquarters and some warthog sausage and eggs with the family. Even at this pace, the hunter within has a wonderful, proud level of awareness that I thrive on. With every change in topography and new view of terrain, I eagle-eyed for game. Each and every step one takes in the wild produces a new corridor of vision, exposing new angles of observation and, therefore, potentially revealing hidden objects. Your eyes are having an orgy.

It was on just one such occasion that I stepped up a slight embankment. With every inch I rose, a fresh panorama greeted me. I paused, sensing with the hunter's sixth sense, and took it all in. Not content to gaze upon the expanse of thorn scrub with my naked eyes, I shouldered my bow, and brought the Zeiss 10X40 binoculars to my face. Immediately, I identified the tawny brown hide of game, just inside the thicker thorn clump. I looked hard, and finally distinguished the shape of impala, staring straight back into my face, at about thirty yards.

No doubt, I had not yet been identified, and the intrusion was tolerated because of the safety of their cover. If they could think, they were thinking that I couldn't possibly have seen them yet. Surprise, surprise Mr. Steak!!

Knowing that any miscalculated move could send them fleeing, I slowly lowered the binoculars, trading them for the bow and an arrow from the quiver. I hadn't really made my mind up for the shot yet. There was seemingly way too much crap between us. But the last thing my brain registered was a baseball-size hole right at the ram's shoulder. Even without the glass, I could now see the ram and the hole. Plenty of room! I'm sure the only part of me visible to the animals was my head and shoulders, and I kept as much movement as possible below the line of sight.

They didn't move. I focused everything on the small window thru the brush, and let 'er rip. The big 2413 slid beautifully into the hole and whacked hard into the ram's shoulder. At once, the area virtually exploded with bounding impala, tearing off helter-skelter in every direction. I had seen three or four in the bunch, but the cover hid more than twenty-five animals. They were gone in an instant. It is truly amazing how critters vanish so quickly.

I felt real good about the shot, took a swig from my canteen, and slowly approached the scene of impact. There was real good blood, and I knew I had sliced a major artery for sure. There is no mistaking it. I did not wait, but rather, briskly took up the spoor, zig-zagging thru nasty, scratching thorn scrub for forty yards, to a beautiful, graceful, long horned Southern Impalla.

The arrow had passed thru the ram, severing the bottom of the big jugular vein, just forward of the shoulder joint, catching the front tip of the right lung. ☆☆☆☆☆

84

EQUIPMENT: Screaming Eagle at 78-pounds, Aluminum arrows, 2212, 4-blade Satellite Titan, 125-grain Broadhead
ANIMAL: Impala, 130 pounds
HIT: Femoral artery, running at one hundred yards

The African Southern Impala is a beautiful, graceful antelope weighing around one hundred pounds for a mature specimen. They are very much like our pronghorn antelope in stature, actions, and physique. Having killed a good number of these animals in varying sets of circumstances, I had come to appreciate the relative ease of dispatching compared to the larger, bullet-proof species of the region. This particular kill occurred after a long stalk, a long fifty-five-yard shot, and a resultant hit in the rear left ham. My 78-pound Screaming Eagle, 2212 fluted 29-inch arrow and four-blade Satellite Titan, 125-grain broadhead killed him in seconds after a dead run of one hundred yards. A severed femoral artery, always a wonderful BLOOD TRAIL, bagged a beautiful twenty-one inch trophy. ☆☆☆☆

85

EQUIPMENT: Screaming Eagle at 78-pounds. Aluminum arrows, 2212,4-blade Satellite Titan, 125-grain Broadhead
ANIMAL: Nyala
HIT: Paunch

African folklore has it that God touched the brown face of the Nyala bull and left white finger marks on Africa's most beautiful antelope. Though all the animals are truly a wonder and beautiful, I have to agree with the legend. At around four hundred pounds, with two-foot spiraling horns, chocolate hide with cream lateral stripes over the saddle and a luxurious mane, the Nyala is beauty to behold. The females are smaller with a plain reddish-tan body and their numbers are high and growing at Archer's Africa. They like the thick growth along the river courses and reed beds, and I believe they are the ideal bow-and-arrow game animal in all of Africa.

A pair of good bulls were seen from the distance, and from thirty yards I made a poor hit. Classically too far back and a bit high on the walking shot. I get sick when that happens, but I wisely left the area following the shot before taking the spoor. Just after dark, with barely visible shooting light, our ranch owner and professional hunter and I had a fleeting glimpse of the ghost and his .270 put him down. The BLOOD TRAIL was scarce and difficult, with only a splotch here and there, but once again, the talents of Africa's pros did the job. The foregone conclusion of this book and all experienced hunters is that a vital hit is the only good hit and everything else is bad. Practice, discipline yourself, and strive to make that double-lung shot. ☆

There is so much you experience in the hunting world. It's damn near religious at times. I relish the pursuit, learning equipment stuff, animal stuff. The outdoors is so incredible, the kill is climactic, but probably the best part of anything in life is the connections made with special people. You learn real early in life to weed out and eliminate the assholes right away, and embrace the good people. No question, I've been blessed to have had Fred Bear as a dear (or is that deer?) friend for so many years. And there are others. Claude Pollington and George Nicholls take a back seat to nobody when it comes to bowhunting deer and sharing a spirit of life that makes it all worthwhile. George Nicholls, a Jackson County resident, with his wonderful wife, Lois, has successfully bowhunted whitetails for over fifty-two years. He actually killed the first buck in Southern Michigan with the bow in 1937. When George talks, I listen.

I've always said that if there is anything good about me at all, it's probably because of my mom and dad, and if I'm any good at all at bowhunting, it's most certainly because of Fred, George, Claude, Bob Munger and so many other great men who I watched and learned from. They all have so much knowledge, you must pay attention.

George started when longbows were all there were. He killed many deer with them, and recurves, and compounds. He makes his own arrows with the big full-cut feathers he burns himself, and has used MA-3s, MA-2s, Zwickey, Bear, Bodkin, Bowlo . . . probably all of 'em. He has settled on the Bear Razorhead without the insert and has used it for forty years.

Claude Pollington has quite possibly killed more whitetail bucks than any living man. A young outdoorsman in his fifties, Claude has hunted all his life and has had incredible opportunities to hunt his large Michigan property, including his year-round hunting in a state-approved enclosure. Having hunted his property a lot with him, I am convinced that the smartest whitetails anywhere live in his enclosed area. They are hunted more and have developed a ghost-like ability to read people's activities. Talk about knowing their own backyard! These deer are uncanny! Claude shoots a 70-pound Oneida Screaming Eagle 2413, XX75, four vanes four inch and Whackmaster two blade. Like George and Fred, he hones them to a razor sharpness, shoots year round, and lives with the deer.

There is that controversy about two versus four blades in some camps. Fred insisted on his insert and others swear by the two blade alone. In my experience overall, I give the nod to two blades. The bottom line is strength, sharpness, and aerodynamics.

 86

EQUIPMENT: Screaming Eagle 60-pound, Aluminum arrows, 2213, Zwickey Broadheads
ANIMAL: Goat, 140 pounds
HIT: Haunch, double-lung

Once again I was slippin' and slidin' down those damn California desert foothills with that wonderful essence of fresh goat in the air. Sweat had spread throughout my clothes and I was losing ground. My son Toby had disappeared a half hour earlier on a distant hillside, and now the mixed group of about twelve goats were slowly working their way on a rim forty yards below me, nearly invisible through the dense brush.

It was a waiting game of hide and seek. My camouflage outfit gave me the upper hand as I nocked a 2213 Zwickey payload for the shot I hoped would come. Time barely moves at moments like this and I eased cautiously around the screening vegetation. With their attention on the intruder to the rear, the big grey-and-black leader moved his troop parallel to my path. When I again caught a glimpse of them, they were seventy-five yards below me where the slope met a grassy plateau.

My wife, Shemane, had followed their and my progress accurately on video and the moment of truth had finally arrived. Though seventy-five yards was definitely a long shot, I had confidence in the set-up after years of honing my long-range shooting. The split second the big two-toned billy separated slightly from the other goats, I drew, anchored, concentrated for the steep downhill angle, and released the 60-pound Screaming Eagle. Whack!! A tad far back, but I immediately saw arterial blood flow on the center haunch with the arrow half way through the animal.

The herd exploded as I nocked arrow number two. The target goat stumbled, yet bolted down and around to my left, running, about to enter the brushy draw, when I squeezed my Scott release and touched off a 2312 X caliber tipped with a Bear Razorhead at ninety yards. That's basically a ridiculous shot in hindsight, but at the time it felt like second nature and I watched the beautiful, romantic arc of the shaft intercept the galloping goat perfectly, right behind the left shoulder, penetrating both lungs, at damn close to one hundred yards!

Now, pay close attention. I shoot upwards of one hundred arrows every day. My twenty-eight, 3-D animal course has targets at five to one hundred yards. I practice incessantly. I do not recommend anyone shooting beyond their own personal range capabilities. How often do you practice? At what ranges? I believe in the National Bowhunter Education Foundation (NBEF) suggestions regarding twenty-five to thirty yards being a reasonable limitation.

I am in good company when it comes to long range PRACTICE and shooting. Howard Hill, Fred Bear, Ben Pearson and many others prepared themselves for extreme conditions and opportunities. Think hard, practice hard, and hunt hard. I do.

This goat was deader than a mackerel within seconds of these two hits. Humanely killed. ☆☆☆☆

87

EQUIPMENT: Oneida Screaming Eagle at 70-pounds, Aluminum arrows, XX75 2213, Zwickey two-blade, small
ANIMAL: Wild Boar, 150 pounds
HIT: Forty yards running flat out, uphill shot, hit behind left ear, instant kill

Up and down, up and down. Sometimes I love it, sometimes I don't. Especially in the California desert in 105°. But it sure is preferred to hanging out at the pool ordering room service! I had a Sagittarius sixteen-arrow quiver loaded, and stalked shirtless, in the expanse of scrubby foothills. My daypack had Gatorade, and my canteen hung from my belt full of ice water.

I was hunting with Scott Walker and Chuck Wagner, looking for sheep, goats and hogs. Of course the animals, being the wiser species, were holed up in some cool, shady ravine somewhere, chuckling at our little hike. Scott had made an astounding forty-five-yard running heart shot on a beautiful Corsican ram earlier in the day, and now we were split up, working our way parallel along the rocky slopes. Someone had tossed some good-size rocks into a brushy draw bottom, and out burst a lone boar, hauling ass over a hogback.

A yell got my attention as the black pig crested the ridge simultaneously with the nocking of my arrow. He was hell bent for leather, running just as fast as a hog can, and I got a foothold in the loose shale of the incline, to pivot with the shooting gallery blur above me. Instinct subconsciously calculated the speed of the animal, angle of the shot, swing of my body, trajectory of the arrow's path, and somehow my finger pressured the Trophy Release, sending the 2213 away.

It all happened as fast as could be, and the shaft connected with a loud THWACK right into the pig's skull, rolling him head over heels, dust flying. A quick squeal, and he rolled down the hillside, dead. The Zwickey two-blade had penetrated the entire skull, slicing the brain, and severing a big vein. YUM YUM!! There would be no bruised, bloody meat on this pork. ✩✩✩✩

88

EQUIPMENT: Oneida Screaming Eagle at 75-pounds, Aluminum arrows, XX75 2213 Muzzy Broadheads
ANIMAL: Warthog, 250 pounds
HIT: three-quarter angle walking away, double-lung at thirty yards

John Mussachia, his son John, and daughter Michelle operate Muzzy Products, and manufacture their fine broadheads of the same name. These are well-constructed, strong, sharp hunting heads with durable replaceable blades, designed to be bad to the bone. I like that. Now we shall see.

I straddled a thick limb, cleared of the annoying little barbs, overlooking a series of well-worn trails. Coming out of the south, through heavy scrub thickets, leading to a small waterhole full of fresh tracks, I knew it would only be a matter of time before some grand African critter showed up. We always think that, don't we! Earlier, I had shot a fine Duiker antelope, and knew we could use some pork for the grill, to feed the hunters and guests in camp this evening.

My bow hung from a small branch before me, an arrow on, and ready. The Muzzy four-blade was impressive looking. Stout. From behind came "a grunt and a huff," and I was caught off guard to see a big warthog boar kick up dust and walk away at twenty-five yards. He had snuck in on my bad ear. The bow was in my hand, the string yanked to my lip, and the spot was picked as the hog hit the thirty-yard mark. My lead and swing were just right.

The four five-inch white Trueflight feathers protruded from the midsection, angling 45° forward into the chest cavity. He huffed again and stiff-legged it out of sight. Instantly I saw him reappear, circling to my other side, and he piled up in a heap, fifty yards out. I followed a real good BLOOD TRAIL in a semicircle to him. The Muzzy head was indeed "bad to the bone," having sliced thru the last rib, taking both lungs and penetrating hard into the off-left shoulder, killing the eleven-inch tusker outright. The head was like new, with no deformity or wear. ✩✩✩✩

89

EQUIPMENT: Oneida Screaming Eagle at 75-pounds, Aluminum arrows, XX75, 2413, Satellite Titan, four-blade
ANIMAL: Warthog, 350 pounds
HIT: Chest hit thru the top of the heart and both lungs at thirty yards, went twenty-five yards

I think sitting in a thorn tree is one of the coolest things a guy could ever want to do. I enjoy still-hunting overall, more than any other form of bowhunting, but to have a bird's eye view of all this African wildlife throughout the day is truly fascinating. Typically, you are blessed with a parade of animals no matter where you set up at Archer's Africa. It's just a matter of patience, good timing, and making the slow, proper moves at exactly the right time. As always, playing the wind and good concealment are imperative. For the bowhunter on his toes, there is never a dull moment.

I had discovered a new mudhole area, with tracks of all different varieties of game in abundance. Even as I first approached, warthogs, impala, and a kudu cow and calf bolted for cover after their midmorning drink. I liked it. A trio of gnarled old briar trees bordered the south end of the waterhole, and deep game trails fingered out from the scrub in nearly every direction. These are the kinds of conditions that give a guy confidence in a stake-out.

The southeast wind would afford me great cover for the major trails. I squatted, reasonably stable, in a thorny crotch, with a good view of the surrounding area. The first visitors were a pair of smallish warthogs from the opposite end of the hole. They casually strolled in together, leisurely switching their tails back and forth, without a care in the world. Just as they neared the water's edge, their heads shot up erect, they swapped ends and dashed off, double-time. The wind had given me away, but I was not surprised. The real potential for a shot was in fact from the zone behind me. I waited patiently.

Monkeys would occasionally squawk in the distance, and different critters could always be seen off a ways. But it was almost two hours before close action began to unfold on the hot trails. A huge old warthog boar showed himself, barely, about one hundred yards off. He was no easy goin' stroller. He hung out in the distance and it was a good half an hour before he carefully continued his approach. This old boy had had his share of predator encounters, and I had my work cut out for me, for sure. Even at ninety yards, I ever so cautiously began my slow, easy-goin' moves to get in position for the shot. I swear, even at that range, fifteen feet up in my tree, my slightest little turn made him stop cold in his tracks! Damn, I hate that. The waiting game with a big, target animal in sight is my nemesis, and he took full advantage of my weakness.

Forty minutes later, after many scrutinizing stops, he was entering the danger zone. I was up, left-shouldering him, arrow nocked, cocked, and well, you know!! My thirty-inch XX75 2413 was solid white, with the stainless Satellite Titan 125-grain four-blade payload ready to rock. This big hog was on full alert, and seemed ready to bolt at any moment. Tuff! So was I. At his next step, still thirty yards off, I eased the string back to the corner of my mouth, looked right thru his forward chest, and turned 'er loose! KER-THA-WHACKO-ZIPPO!!!

I think he actually sensed the release of the arrow, but it didn't matter. At 266 fps, the shaft was in and out before he could even begin to turn. And I might mention, thru all the good stuff, too. A dead-center forward chest hit, slicing clean thru the top of the heart and both lungs. Vundebarr! For such a big, bold, tuff animal, a quick short run of twenty-five yards ended with a crash to the ground, and not even a kick. I saw him pile up in three seconds or less. Talk about the power of the arrow! A dream, perfect, immediate, humane kill. It is times like these, and I have personally witnessed hundreds and hundreds of times, that make me laugh at the fools who claim bows and arrows are inadequate for cleanly killing big game. The term "kiss my ass" comes to mind. ✩✩✩✩

➤90 & 91

EQUIPMENT: Oneida Screaming Eagle at 60-pound, Aluminum arrows, XX75, 2213, Hoyt Chuck-It 90 grain
ANIMAL: Barren Ground Caribou and Arctic Red Fox
HIT   **#1:** Lengthwise, went fifty yards
          #2: Behind the shoulder at twelve yards, trotting

February at Lake Iliamna. Not smart. It was cold. Like about minus 65F. Kurt Lepping and Jimmy Harkins had graciously invited me on this arctic test hunt, in the splendor of a snow-covered heaven on earth. Though modern technology has developed phenomenal heat-retaining garments, this extreme weather could kill you real fast.

I had been the guest speaker at the Alaska Bowhunter's convention and was now out on the tundra for a bit of the real God's country that this wonderful state has to offer. Flying in, over and thru the mountain passes was a spectacle to behold, and cold or no cold, I was ready for a few days of serious survivalist bowhunting. Herds of wintering caribou could be seen from the air all the way to our tiny trapper's cabin on the shore of frozen lake Iliamna. Our two Piper super cubs were loaded with necessary arctic survival gear, and we each had extra clothing of down and thinsulate plus double sleeping bags. The only heat source would be our Coleman two-burner for heating water and liquid food, and a special adapter for thawing the airplane engines prior to starting them. I was reasonably versed on survival techniques under these conditions, and felt added security with these two veteran Alaskan hunters as my companions.

First day out was slow going in the bitter cold after a rude night of trying to sleep, virtually frozen in our bags. We all took off in different directions. I covered about five miles before I encountered my first herd of caribou. I was excited as hell to be in their presence, but at the same time apprehensive because I was so far from camp in Mother Nature's most unforgiving of conditions. Very little stalking cover existed on this rather barren tundra, and I patiently glassed the group of seventy-five or eighty barren ground caribou for a good hour before I made my belly crawl towards them.

The mostly cow, calf and small bull herd was nonchalantly resting and chewing their cuds as I squirmed from miniature bush to small tuft of grass, trying my best to be invisible. I cut the distance down to sixty yards before the first guard cow nailed me. If I had been upright in position for a shot, their range would have been reasonable to the closest small bull, but laying there on my belly with the bow shoved out in front of me made it impossible to even think about a shot.

Instantly, the entire herd was on its feet, some trotting away and some staring a hole right thru this strange snake-like thing sneaking up on them. I quickly nocked a 2413 and picked a smallish bull that had stopped to look back at about seventy yards. The arrow literally skimmed off his backbone, flipping skyward and causing the herd to stampede over the rise away from me. I sat down, seriously considered circling ahead of them, then figured the only prudent thing to do would be to get my ass headed back to camp before dark. A cup of hot Tang sure sounded good right about now. To think of spending a night out here was scary, to say the least.

I got to the cabin just after dark, finding Kurt and Jimmy celebrating Jimmy's small bull. We shared some of that hot Tang, a good hot soup with fried backstrap, and sat around for awhile relishing our good fortune for the opportunity to experience such incredible country and sensations. At one point we heard a slight noise outside the cabin door. I got up to peek out the window, not thinking anything could possibly be out in this desolate zone, and saw a beautiful red fox dash to the left of the steps. I grabbed my bow and got an arrow ready. As the richly furred fox trotted back across in front of the cabin, Kurt swung the door open, I drew back and sent the broadhead clean thru him trotting at twelve yards.

In the full moonlight, I could see blood spraying on the hard-crusted snow as he sprang away over a slight rise. Stuffing my boots on, I ran to the edge to see him laying there, dead. A fox is one small target, especially when moving, but the arrow had sliced him right behind the shoulder for an instant kill. A hell of a bowhunting trophy for sure. We skinned him immediately, knowing that the whole carcass would freeze in only a matter of minutes, for the inside cabin temperature was only twenty or thirty BELOW zero! And that was with the Coleman running full tilt. Overnight it would get double that, and everything would certainly freeze solid. I had on two pairs of polypropylene long johns, goosedown long johns, and two down sleeping bags rated to thirty below each, plus a wool stocking cap and double socks. I was snug, but had ice around my face and beard all night. Unbelievable!

The next morning brought a whole new meaning to wanting to stay in the sack! Nonetheless, we rose to hot tea, coffee, some bacon and eggs, and we were ready to get 'em. Again we headed out in search of game. I crested a large crater-like bowl and saw a group of forty or so caribou heading up the other side in my direction. There was absolutely no cover, so I knelt down with an arrow ready, hoping for the best.

The first damn cow to top the rise nailed me right now and spun, taking the whole bunch with her. I stood and picked out the nearest animal going straight away, looked at a spot in the middle of its ass, and poked it dead center with 2413 and lightweight 90-grain four-blade Chuck-It broadhead. The herd kicked in the afterburners and vanished over the lip of the canyon.

I walked to the spot and found blood sprayed everywhere. Ten yards along was the blood-covered arrow, and the four-star BLOOD TRAIL was wonderful. I glanced ahead and saw the dead cow in a heap after a short fifty-yard run. The arrow had transected the entire length of her body, slicing everything she had to offer. Another quick, humane, one-shot arrow kill that everyone would be proud of. George Trotter of Louisiana designed this great broadhead, and this prototype for Hoyt had performed well. I have to say that the going away straight up the ass shot is deadly as hell as long as you can put your arrow right up the middle. The anus, up the rectal canal, offers very little resistance, and leads to liver, pancreas, major arteries, some lung, heart, and possibly jugular if you shoot enough bow with the slicemaster super-sharp head. ☆☆☆☆

92

EQUIPMENT: Oneida Screaming Eagle at 65-pound, Aluminum arrows, XX75, 2213, Bear Razorheads
ANIMAL: Whitetail Buck, 150 pounds
HIT: Stomach hit at forty-five yards, went ninety yards

I hate gut shots, but I've made a few. A gut-shot animal should be ninety-plus percent recoverable. Literally, from all studies conducted over many years on wounding animals, it is clear that arrow-hit game is realistically ninety-plus percent recoverable. Should be an easy one hundred percent with the proper effort. You see, if an animal's vitals are not penetrated, the clean cut of a sharp broadhead is more than likely to heal over completely. Studies bear this out, including my own personal experience and witness. The worst-case scenario is the gut-shot animal that leaves little or no Blood Trail. I have even seen deer and African game, fully recovered and healed from what appeared to have been paunch hits. It is a matter of just what exactly was severed. If certain organs are not disrupted or cut, the animal will have no complications. They go about feeding and everyday life as if nothing has happened.

On a possible gut hit, the rule is to mark the path of departure of the animal as accurately as possible, and leave for six to twelve hours. No, this is not a pleasant thought, and is why we must strive to be accurate as hell, but as mistake-making humans in an imperfect world, now what? The animal will not travel far, and will lie down if not pressured. They feel sick, just like they always have in the natural world, when NOT shot in the guts. Upon returning to the area after a long wait, a reasonable search will generally turn up the animal. Whether scavengers get to it first or not is matter of your hunting location. Watch for crows, buzzards jays and other birds to pinpoint the downed animal.

This particular gut shot turned out quite different. A group of seven deer had emerged from the forest edge, working their way across a wet meadow. My tree set was inside the alder and popple line on the far side, and now a lone five-point buck was getting in range.

At forty-five yards he turned broadside and passed my position as I drew and released. Either my lead was insufficient or he lunged a bit, because my arrow hit square in the middle of his body. He swapped ends and ran hard for the opposite wood line, and I could see blood flowing from his stomach.

As he entered the trees, I saw thru my binoculars what appeared to be his entrails falling out. OK, so this doesn't sound too good. What does? With a minor attempt at honesty, the human population of this country and the world could admit that this is EXACTLY how a billion chickens are handled each and every day of the year. Gutted hanging. Even compared to daily death in the wild, this kill was average or better.

Anyhow, moralistic judgment and intellect aside, I picked up the ample BLOOD TRAIL at point of impact and followed it easily the ninety yards to the trees where he was piled up dead. Couldn't have lived more than ten seconds. He had literally disemboweled himself. Thanx for the help. Not a pretty death, you say? Please give me a list of pretty deaths. I must have missed something! ☆☆☆☆

93 & 94

EQUIPMENT: Nugent-Oneida Whackmaster 1 XX75 Nugent Whackmaster 2213, Whackmaster two-blade 125, Aluminum arrows
ANIMAL: Two Rabbits (Yes, rabbits! Believe it or not).
HIT #1: Shoulder at twenty-five yards
#2: Chest at thirty yards

Okay! Big deal, some of you might say. But I had just got my very own signature bow, arrow, release and broadhead, and I couldn't wait to get out there and whack something with 'em. It was a warm day for our Michigan winter, with the sun shining strong in the eastern sky. The orchard behind the house is where my son Toby and I cut lots of brush piles all the time for the small game, and once in awhile take the .22 pistols or our bows for some real challenging rabbit hunting.

I was on my own this morning, and slipped thru the tangles looking for some bunnies. I've killed lots of small game with my bow over the years, and get as serious a kick out of it as I do big game. And a lot of hunters are surprised to learn that smaller critters often take just as much killing as full-sizers do. It will still take a razor-sharp broadhead thru the vitals to kill a rabbit just as it would a deer or a moose. The easier part about killing smaller game is the softer and smaller bones that offer so much less resistance. The hard part is that they are so damn small. Some bowmen prefer to use small game arrow stoppers behind their broadheads to impede penetration, keeping the arrow inside the animal for some strange reason. Maybe to help them find the arrow I suppose. My experience has shown me that slice 'em-dice 'em is the only way to go if you want to kill outright.

This particular morning, I saw my first rabbit almost immediately. At twenty-five yards, there isn't much of a target. Picking a spot is more important here than ever. I sent my 2213 Whackmaster XX75 clean thru, right at the shoulder; sailed thru like there was nothing there. This bunny flipped straight up in the air about three feet, did a somersault or two, hit the ground, and took off like a bat outta' hell for twenty feet, then rolled over dead. How nice. The wild part was the blood trail. I wish I had 'em this good on some big-game kills. There was about two inches of fresh snow on the ground and this little guy's BLOOD TRAIL was wonderful. ✩✩✩✩ for sure.

Rabbit number two came out of a tangle of brush just fifteen minutes later. He scampered a short distance ahead, and I was prepared for a running shot just as he stopped thirty yards out. The arrow cut him dead center, again not slowing in the least. This guy took off full speed ahead, and kept right on going until he was out of sight. Very interesting situation.

I couldn't find my arrow for anything, so I started following the blood trail. It was a good one too, showing perfectly on the snow, meandering thru the nastiest of briars and blowdowns. I couldn't believe I was still on it after seventy-five yards, with strong blood the whole way. Remember, a rabbit can cover seventy-five yards in seconds, and within about three minutes, I came upon him sitting and weaving under a picker bush at about forty yards. This arrow had a rubber blunt on it, and I smacked him real good close to the head, probably in the neck, and sent him flying into the weeds. The first hit appeared to be a borderline gut shot, and again proved that only a good hit will get the job done correctly. I wonder if there had not been snow on the ground, if I would have been able to follow this trail. As it was, against the snow cover, I had a good ✩✩✩✩. Big or small, PICK A SPOT.

95

EQUIPMENT: Oneida Screaming Eagle at 65-pounds Aluminum arrows, 2212 fluted, four fletch feathers Hoyt-Chuck-It, four-blade 85 grain
ANIMAL: Whitetail Buck, Spike
HIT: Broadside thru the chest at forty-five yards, went seventy yards

Everything was soaking wet after an all-night fall rainstorm. I had spent the dawn in a treestand overlooking a hot game trail, but felt the wet conditions were too good to pass up for stalking. Two does had already been spooked by my too-fast pace, and I was settling down a bit. The idea was to cover maximum ground with the eyes, and not the feet. I knew that, now if only I could do it!!

A steep rise swelled up out of the sawgrass swamp I stood in, and I single-stepped the edge, at full alert. I knew this area was the prime bedding ground for the local deer coming off the corn and hay fields from the night feeding, so I went ahead and nocked an arrow. Fred Bear always said not to nock an arrow while you hunt, but rather wait until you have game in sight. He was right, of course, but once in a while when I'm hunting spots I know to be super hot, I will nock an arrow, just to be extra ready. And it was a good thing. Just as I snapped the nock onto the string, I saw the buck, up the rise to my left at forty-five yards. At first, I didn't see the spikes, but was mentally prepared to shoot a doe anyhow. Only as I began my draw did I take notice of the little horns.

It was at that same instant that the deer nailed me too, but my arrow was already on its way. He was standing almost broadside, very slightly angling toward me, when the arrow sliced thru his chest, right at the juncture of the ball joint. These ultra-light shafts produced by Advanced Archery in Torrance, California, really sizzle. At 65-pounds, I could use such a light arrow, partly because I use the Bill Scott release that is ultra-forgiving. This combination was chronographed at 260 fps, and the little buck didn't have a prayer in dodging the arrow. It was in and out before he could even react. He erupted at full-tilt boogie for the flooded alders ahead, and I could see the red patch growing at the point of his shoulder as he vanished over the rise.

I always go first to the spot of impact, to look for first blood. There was plenty. The arrow lay beyond his position about twenty yards, soaked with beautiful, bubbly red blood. The first twenty-five or so yards were excellent blood, then it petered out and only showed where he landed from his long bounds. But still ok. The trail was easily discernable thru the wet grass where his flight had splashed the ground cover, free of moisture. I stood on the hill and looked down to the swamp, and could see his path clearly. A spray of blood every ten feet or so on the ground vegetation made it all the more simple to follow, and I walked up on him after a short seventy yards. He had died on the very edge of the flood plain, and lay in about three inches of water. ✰✰✰✰

96

EQUIPMENT: Oneida Screaming Eagle at 65-pounds,
Aluminum arrows, 2413, XX75, four feathers, Bear Razorheads, two-blade
ANIMAL: Whitetail Buck, 160 pounds
HIT: Shoulder

This was an unbelievable kill. It was November 1, 1986, the rut was as hot as it could ever get. The night before, I had made such a pitiful miss on a nice high-racked eight-pointer, that I punished myself by not hunting this morning. Instead, I would spend the day on the range, practicing, so I would not blow my next opportunity. It is very painful. My good friends, Matt, Shawn, and Ross Pollington, were down at the farm for a little hunting. They had had a fun morning, seeing lots of deer, and even managing a few misses between themselves to keep things interesting. It was already almost 11 a.m., so we all decided to hit my archery course behind the barn, thru the orchard. It wasn't very cold, but the wind was actually howling out of the west. I mean HOWLING!!! It had to have been 40 mph, with gusts fifty percent higher. Crosswind shooting was very interesting to say the least.

The first three targets went fine. I couldn't miss the boiler room. It only confused me more. Why couldn't I do that last night on a real deer? Anybody ever say that before? We shot the Delta coyote target along the lane, back against the fence, and again they were all ribbing me how deadly I was on styrofoam. I pulled everybody's arrows from the target, talking loudly, laughing and basically being loud and rowdy. I had my back to the fence row when Ross pointed behind me, yelling for me to look at the deer. Sure as hell, there was a nice, heavy-racked, big-bodied buck, standing in the cut corn field, just twenty yards across the second fencerow, only thirty-five yards out! Ross already had a target arrow at full draw, and I yelled, "Not with a field point!!" I yanked out a hunting arrow, found a hold thru the two fence rows, and nailed that big boy square behind the right shoulder. It threw him to the ground like a Motor City wrestler!! Not only that, but he had only one side to his rack, just like the one I had missed, seven miles away, the night before! But it surely was not him. He was much different looking. Plus, the 2413 had only penetrated a mere five or six inches, even with the ultimate two-blade penetrator. This was due, no doubt, to the incredible wind blowing down the fence row, crosswind to my shot.

We all stood there, absolutely dumbfounded by the sequence of events. It all happened incredibly fast. Seconds after he was blown off his feet, he got back up and wobbled off like he would fall again at any moment. I nocked a second arrow right away, but had no clear hole to him for a follow-up shot. He staggered to his feet and wobbled off before any of us even could come to grips with what had taken place. I knew the arrow had struck right in the hot spot, but was totally confused at what appeared to be a total lack of penetration.

This was, once again, proof that arrow flight is the definitive element in the penetration equation. An unstable, erratically-flying arrow actually causes friction against its own entrance walls, putting on the brakes. There was very little blood in the field, and we spent an exasperating day on hands and knees, desperately searching for the buck. At dark, we were four very tired, frustrated bowhunters. In fact, after my guests headed home the next morning, a local farmer that plants my land for me called with a report of a big buck dead in the fence row behind the pole barn! Upon examination, my suspected hit was confirmed. He had traveled about one mile altogether. He was a good size, 180-pound, two-and-a-half year-old deer in prime condition, except for the loss of one side of his rack. ☆

97

EQUIPMENT: Screaming Eagle at 78-pound, Advanced Archery fluted 2212, Aluminum arrows, Bear Razorheads, no inserts
ANIMAL: Blue Wildebeest
HIT: Heart at twenty to twenty-five yards

This particular kill is a perfect example of these animals' unwillingness to cooperate. Having laced a huge eight hundred-pound blue wildebeest in '88 perfect with a big three-blade 200-grain Rothar Snuffer and NO BLOOD, I was determined to open one of these buggers up. I returned to my comfy little picker-tree for an afternoon vigil, just like a year before. Warthogs came and went, but traffic was greatly reduced due to the increase in available water following heavy rains.

At 5 p.m., with a little over an hour of shooting light remaining, from the south came two big horse-sized antelope. These blue wildebeest have earned a reputation, even with the heavy-caliber rifle hunters, for being just plain tough. The big boy up front was a huge specimen with maybe thirty-inch horns, a truly outsized trophy. His buddy was a respectable 26 1/2-inch and I was cocked, locked and ready to rock, doc, again. Unbelievably, he came to the near edge of the waterhole, step by cautious step, within fifteen to eighteen yards of me. Of course the larger antelope eased to the water's edge, keeping a heavy thorn bush smack dab between my perch and his vitals.

Not being a particularly picky hunter, my decision was easy, as the 26 1/2-incher was wide open at twenty to twenty-five yards. I drew the 78-pound Screaming Eagle twenty-nine inches to my anchor and slapped the release, sending a thirty-inch 2212 fluted shaft tipped with a white Bear Razorhead without insert. I had talked myself into a low hold to hit the heart and at 270 fps, only the feathers showed, protruding from his right armpit, and he kicked and bucked away from the dirt bank. I saw one good red spray of blood as he bolted into the thick scrub and lost sight of him at about eighty yards. I felt good all over. That arrow had found its way home for sure. I smiled real big as I took my time lowering my bow, canteen and binoculars down on my rope.

By the time I had organized my gear, ten or fifteen minutes had gone by and I picked up the first blood at the point of impact. Not much really, because the dry, dusty ground sucks it up quick. I found half of the shaft covered with blood and following his frantic tracks was easy. Again, I was amazed at the lack of blood. There was a small spray every twenty feet or so for one hundred yards, but mostly I was stooping over looking intently at the grass and vegetation. At one hundred yards, I could not find any more blood. I trailed a game-tracker line behind me for good measure, taking no chances.

With the daylight fading, I left the spool at last blood and made a forty-yard circle in line with his flight and after a half-circle camp upon the huge beast, stone dead. The Bear Razorhead had indeed sliced thru the heart and into the far low shoulder. A damn good hit for sure, but I would rate it only a two-star BLOOD TRAIL. Always interesting. ☆☆

98

EQUIPMENT: Oneida Screaming Eagle at 65-pounds, Aluminum arrows, XX75, 2413, Satellite Titan, four-blade, stainless steel
ANIMAL: Black Boar, ninety pounds
HIT: Neck at fifteen yards, went thirty yards

Shemane, my wonderful wife, was following me thru the Florida hell-hole swamps, carrying the big, heavy video camera. We were guests of Buck and Linda Fuller at their ranch, north of Tampa, for another attempt at making movie stars, brief movie stars, out of the local hog population. Jay and Laura Fuller were our A-1 guides and outfitters, along with Flash, the Basset wonder-hound. Though large, two hundred-pound trophy boar were our main goal, the property was so infested with wild hogs that any size animal would be killed for the sake of the land. Hogs are virtual roto-tillers gone amuck, and the open areas were torn to hell. We had been down here before and experienced the action-packed hog hunting, so anticipation was running high.

It was the middle of the afternoon as we strolled into the thick palmetto tangles. Within minutes, ol' Flash was yelping and a bellowing, hot on fresh pig stink. Shemane followed close behind as we maneuvered thru the waist-high vegetation, attempting to shortcut the fleeing hogs. The hound was obviously off running some different hogs, because I could see some body movement in the thicket ahead. Two or three pigs were slowly coming our way from the direction of Flash, so I nocked an arrow and signaled Shemane to be ready. A small red hog, followed by a black one, were just up ahead, unaware of our presence. I could only make out the front leg and neck of the black hog and decided to take him.

At a short fifteen yards, I picked a spot where the leg met the body, and sent the 125-grain Satellite four-blade into that spot. I thought. A resounding squeal erupted from the brush, and pigs scrambled everywhere. I had a game-tracker sting on my arrow, and the line fed out in a whir. After only a few seconds, all was quiet. The game-tracker device, under the right conditions, is a real God-send.

We began to follow the line, with ample blood on the coarse, green leafy vegetation. Thirty yards later we came upon one very dead ninety-pound solid-black wild boar. Not the biggest in the world, but a prime eatin' hog. The arrow had hit just below the ear in the back of the head, cut some major artery, and bled him out clean. I was surprised that he was able to go anywhere, because the hit appeared to be a brain shot. The broadhead had penetrated about six inches, and the BLOOD TRAIL was a winner. The next day we had our traditional barbecued pork roast, and he was the star attraction. There is nothing sweeter than a wild-boar BBQ. ☆☆☆☆

99

EQUIPMENT: Nugent-Oneida WhackMaster at 65-pounds,
Aluminum arrows, 2213, 125-grain WhackMaster Broadheads, two-blade
ANIMAL: Wild Boar, 160 pounds
HIT: Double-lung

The day had been a long one, with a couple of unforgettable silly misses on real trophy animals. Forty yards broadside on a huge Nilgai bull, and twenty yards at a real good javelina had me in a not-so-friendly state of mind. I was trying real hard to figure out why I miss easy, dumper shots like that, when I sensed movement ahead in the thick mesquite brush. I instinctively nocked an arrow, and cautiously stepped into the screen of vegetation. There were a couple of small piglets chasing each other around the bush at twenty-five yards, and I watched them for a moment, knowing a big one or more must be nearby too.

A crash to my left startled me as a large, reddish hog came dashing across in front. In the fading light of late afternoon, I was still sure that this was a reasonably good-sized hog. I swung up and ahead, focusing my eyes on the shoulder area. The white fletching looked good as it vanished dead center into the chest behind the foreleg, with only about four inches of arrow showing. It was silent. I felt good about the shot. It would be dark in a matter of minutes, so I went to the brush the hog had entered. Only a drop of blood could be found, so I marked the spot with a piece of toilet paper and crawled forward, finding very little more blood. Blood is almost impossible to see in low light conditions.

Not having a flashlight with me, I could wait for Mike, my guide, to help, or make a short sweep of the area. I busted thru the nasty, thorny, brush in a fifty-foot arc. Many years of Blood Trailing have taught me that this pattern of a sweep is practical in finding a mortally, double-lung hit animal. The vegetation was unbelievably thick.

I was certain that no so-called animal lovers from the city would ever in their wildest imagination be found in the real wild, where I had spent my day. Especially right now, in the dark, on my hands and knees, nose to the ground, trying to find a big, dangerous wild hog in a tangle from cat-scratch hell!! But I was loving it immensely. And right on schedule, there it was, about forty yards in, on the line of departure into the thicket, deader than hell. The next morning, I returned to the scene of the crime to see the condition of the trail after the night. Very little could be found, but the same tactics would have worked to discover the dead hog. Even with a textbook double-lunger, only tiny splatterings of blood were apparent on the leaves of the scrub. At the spot where the hog was found, however, a virtual pool of blood had poured out. I had seen this same inconsistent pattern on occasion throughout my hunting life, especially on swine, like warthogs in Africa. Sometimes they do, and sometimes they don't. ☆

 # 100

EQUIPMENT: Nugent-Oneida WhackMaster at 65-pounds, Aluminum arrows, 2213, 125-grain WhackMaster Broadheads, two-blade
ANIMAL: Wild Boar, 180 pounds
HIT: Vertebrae and jugular at thirty-five yards

The neat little Texas tripod ladder set-up was okay. I spent a few extra minutes bouncing around on it to relieve the stress and eliminate the squeaks. The position inside the mesquite edge covered me well enough, but more importantly, gave ample shooting room in the area of the water hole.

It was only 5 p.m. on a warm spring day, and I could have used a brief rest after my trek thru damp vegetation for the last three hours. Game seemed to be everywhere on the Kennedy Ranch, and I was pumped. I had missed a large javelina boar at a ridiculous twenty yards from this very stand the day before, so I was hoping to make up for it today. Patience is not a strong point with me, and like a stupid kid, I climbed down after a brief hour. I just wanted to explore the different areas of this game-rich country, and maybe get a whack at one of those incredible Nilgai bulls.

I stalked about, sneaking into every nook and cranny of brush that I could. I found some really dandy whitetail sheds, saw cottontails, armadillos, lots of deer, some distant Nilgai, jack rabbits and hundreds of turkeys. After a couple of hours of this, I figured maybe that tripod was the place to be for those last couple of hours before dark. I circled the section to work my way back, cautiously approaching the waterhole with the wind in my face. Wouldn't you know it! Already at the hole waiting for me were about eight wild hogs, rooting, drinking and wallowing in the mud, twenty yards in front of the stand! Figures.

I kept as much vegetation between them and me as I could, and slowly stalked the hole. At thirty-five yards, I had a small window to shoot thru to the biggest, blackest pig in the group. From my knees, with my bow canted a little more than usual, I fired a WhackMaster two-blade. It struck with a loud KAWHACK! just forward of the shoulder, in the middle of the neck. On wild hogs, oftentimes it appears as though they have no neck, but rather a body connected right to the head. Anyhow, that's where my arrow struck, and blew that hog right into the mud. My two-blade had severed the neck vertebrae and sliced the jugular vein all in one whack. As I walked up to him, he was stone-cold dead.

➤ 101

EQUIPMENT: Nugent-Oneida WhackMaster at 65-pounds,
Aluminum arrows, 2213, 125-grain WhackMaster Broadheads, two-blade
ANIMAL: Wild Board at three hundred pounds
HIT: Chest shot thru the heart

Winter has taken its boredom toll, and you're looking for the great escape. Last season's hunts are still vivid in the mind, but it does little to satisfy the craving to just get out there and wander the wild again. Some late-calendar bowhunts are available, like mountain lion in a bunch of states, exotics in most, Texas and Florida hogs all year, and a choice here and there if you can travel and flex your schedule.

As a combination of everything a hunt should be, wild hogs are great. Though their eyesight is not the greatest, a miscalculated move on the hunter's part will eliminate any chance for pork chops, because they have excellent hearing and olfactory senses. And did I say pork chops? Wild hog ham is one of the best meats you will ever taste. Whether chops, steaks, hams or ground breakfast sausage, it is terrific. A good smoking job will give you prime eating, the likes of which are rare indeed.

Here in my home state of Michigan, deer season winds up on New Year's day, and I, like so many of my bowhunting comrades, actually feel a pang of post-season depression come on in waves the first day of the New Year. (If it weren't for my Whiplash Bash I don't think I would survive at all!) Sure, I still get out the bow and hunt rabbits and hares, but it just isn't the same. Luckily, only a four-hour drive north of Detroit, outside the city of Cheboygan, is the Renegade Ranch. The ranch consists of a large tract of wild, rolling, diverse Michigan terrain. Charley Antoviak and his son Brian manage a top-notch hunting outfit. The beautiful log-cabin lodge sits above a sparkling blue pond, where the hills break into low swamps, and majestic pine forests meet valleys and meadows interspersed with oak, maple, hickory, and beech timber stands. Whitetail, sika and fallow deer, elk, bison, Spanish goats, assorted rams, turkey and my all-time favorite, pork chops on the hoof, running wild, just waiting to do their duty for a hungry bowhunter and his family. Sure beats the hell outa goin' to Kroger's!

Renegade Ranch is famous for its wild European boar. Distinguishable by their long snout, narrow withers, long tail, and nasty disposition, these animals give you plenty of bowhunting excitement at every corner. First off, hogs are never the challenge of a deer. Whitetail deer are the ultimate challenge, and like Fred Bear always said, if you can kill a whitetail, you are ready for any big-game animals with the bow and arrow. Yes, a fence surrounds the property, but more than likely, you will never encounter it in your hunt. For the bowhunter, it represents a real hunt where there is no room for mistakes. You have to make the right judgments in order to get within bow-range, and then, of course, you have to make that accurate, vital shot.

These hogs are tuff, and don't cotton to dumb mistakes. They take a lot of killing, and a poor shot could get you in big trouble. There are some folks out there who don't want to hunt hogs on private preserves. Fine, don't. All hunting is not for all people. In fact, the anti-hunters like to claim it is considered "slob hunting." Not true. I take different game as they come. All game is different, and each species offers a different experience and degree of challenge. I have hunted wild hogs many, many times in free-ranging, wild regions with no fence whatsoever, as well as on game preserves in a number of different states. A wild hog is a wild hog, and I've found no difference in or out of an enclosure. I get a blast out of it either way (and of course they are delicious regardless). It will demand the disciplines that all good bowhunting takes: stealth, adherence to weather and terrain conditions, smart moves, good camo and precise shooting judgment, with proper equipment. I like it, and will always go for it. No Jimmy Dean for the Nugents.

Recently, with ever-increasing regularity, I have put together some very special hunts. We caravan a convoy of smelly bowhunters from around the Midwest for a two-day pig-whacking festival of fun and games like you have never seen! We arrive after daylight for a full day of hunting, four-wheelin' Rock 'n' Rollin', and we have the time of our lives. We have hunted hard and experienced one hundred percent success on hogs and other exotics so far in 1990.

In March, twenty of us descended on Charlie and Brian, complete with Rob Trott and his Great Lakes Outdoors TV crew. We showed just how much fun some guys could have. Good, clean, productive, LEGAL fun. Rob heart-shot his first-ever wild boar, and you could talk with any one of the hunters to hear just how great a time we had. Senator Jim Barcia from Bay City, Michigan, was among the happy hunters who took a trophy boar, along with Gonzo Bear Camp's Dale Gray. Matt and Norm Gettler brought the best bear/boar hounds in the world. It was wild! My three hundred-pound brute came as the camera crew was following Rob and I along a pine grove cut. I'm sure they wanted to be right with me as I made my shot, but I couldn't resist an advance sneak on a band of about five big, black boar, out of their sight. The camera was rolling as I advanced around the hillside for a shot, and on video you can hear the "kathwack!" of my arrow striking thru the high leg bone and into the chest of the biggest of the bunch. The group exploded up the hillside and I trailed them into a ravine in short order. The two-blade WhackMaster had sliced thru bone and penetrated the heart for a quick, humane kill. Just what the doctor ordered.

Year-round hunts can be booked for available species, No kill, No pay. My custom WhackMaster bowhunts include some specialized activities like the Benihana-shrimp school of instant flash-gutting, late-night, rock-out log-cabin, Rock 'n' Roll, hunt-song concerts, and always the heated discussions of what to do with the toxic carcasses of the anti-hunters! Bear bait is all we can think of!!! Important, too, is solid, strong gear. Broadheads will get a workout, and must be razor sharp and durable. Proven heads on our hunts have been: WhackMaster, Rocky Mt. Supreme, Bear, Zwickey, Satellite Titan, Gametracker Double-Cut, Thunderhead 125 and 160, Razorback-4, the new Wasp 3- and 4-blade, and Howard Hill style as well. Of course, the real determining factor is shot placement. Always!

Bottom line is, serious bowhunters keep themselves tuned up year-round. Shoot regularly in hunting-type conditions, the best you can. These off-season hunts are perfect for keeping the pace. If you want to expand your bowhunting calendar, book one of these hunts. It is always best to get good references. Like anything else in this wonderful world of ours, there is the good, the bad, and the ugly! I have found that you can take precautions to ensure a fun, quality hunt every time by insisting on a certain amount of control. Acknowledge that these hunts are different, but that you can expect a fair-chase bowhunt. You will not accept a cornered, fenced situation, nor an assembly line, in-and-out hunt. Take it slow and easy. Patience and self-discipline can make or break the hunt. Ask in advance:

1. How much and how wild is the property on the hunt location and type of terrain.
2. What species of game, at what cost, is available.
3. Deposits and other costs.
4. Rules concerning "first blood."
5. Camp rules (I insist on NO drinking or drugs whatsoever).
6. How many hunters in camp.
7. Maps, lodging, meals, accommodations, etc.

Never be afraid to ask any question and insist on names and numbers for references. Like any hunt, or anything, it will be what you make it.

Bookings can be made thru:

Ted Nugent Sunrize Safaris
4008 West Michigan Avenue
Jackson, Michigan 49202
517-750-9060

Bring your hunting gear, sleeping bag and personal items, plus some practice arrows and judo heads for stump shooting, which is always fun. Meals are delicious and generous, and it will be a special bowhunt I promise you will never forget.

OTHER PERSONALLY RECOMMENDED HOG-HUNTING CAMPS:

- Buck Fuller - Rt. 2 Box 483A, Bushnell, Florida, 33513, 904-793-5325
- YO Ranch - Box 85, Mt. Home, Texas, 78058, 512-640-3222
- Bow-N-Bore Ranch, Stan Swart, Box 2102, Livermore, California, 94550, 408-897-3262
- Steve Haines, 1877 Plaines Rd., Leslie, Michigan, 49251, 517-589-5469
- Tom Nelson, 634 Maple, Grand Ledge, Michigan, 48837, 517-627-3251
- Smyth Ranch, Marcia Smyth, P.O. Box 478, Uvalde, Texas, 78801, 512-278-3848
- Squaw Mountain Ranch, P.O. Box 155, Jacksboro, Texas, 76056, 800-825-4936
- Maurice Chambers, P.O. Box 479, Sabinal, Texas, 78881, 512-363-4252
- Little Creek Ranch, Alan Baier, P.O. Box 171, Colibran, Colorado, 81624, 303-858-9555
- Trophy Ranch, Kevin Anthony, 4076 Spencer Road, Ubly, Michigan, 48475, 517-658-8634
- Turtle Creek Farms, Chuck Strauss, P.O. Box 477, Bridgeport, New York, 13030, 315-633-2651
- Renegade Ranch, 2690 North Riggsville Road, Cheboygan, Michigan, 49721, 616-627-7232

102

EQUIPMENT: Nugent-Oneida WhackMaster at 65-pounds, Aluminum arrows, 2213, 125-grain WhackMaster Broadheads, two-blade
ANIMAL: Wild Boar at 360 pounds, Commie Hogs from HELL!!
HIT: Severed main artery, double-lung at twelve yards

Maurice Chambers is the ultimate American cowboy hero. Not only is he a world-champion rodeo star who walks, talks, acts and smells like a cowboy, but most importantly, he is an expert bow hunter! What a guy. As my Texas Lone Star Bowhunter Crazy Member buddies Greg Artz and Rod Rudino introduced me to Maurice, I shook his hand, knowing I'd made a new friend. He almost seemed like Fred Bear with a cowboy hat! It was hot Texas summer weather, but with a day off on the road, nothing beats a little bowhunting to keep a guy alive. Maurice and his lovely wife, Jamie, manage Marcia Smyth's big ranch for quality whitetails and genuine, wild Russian hogs. Maurice, Jamie and Marcia uphold the honorable tradition of wonderful Texas hospitality, and with the nice ranch headquarters, have one of the finest deer/hog bowhunting-only operations I have ever had the pleasure to visit. This was going to be fun.

Game preserve, exotic-game hunting can be fun, challenging, and is always interesting. First we have to admit just what the conditions really are, and always investigate to be sure it is to be a real hunt. Some are, some aren't. The great thing about Maurice's operation is that it is a bona-fide fair-chase bowhunt. The Smyth Ranch ain't no game preserve. These near-pure Russian hogs have been free ranging this Texas brush country for many, many years. These are wild animals. And there is nothing more wild than a big, old, nasty wild boar, that is used to having his way. Boss hog indeed.

In the heat of midday, we opted to explore the territory and get a feel for the land and the set-up. Some elevated stands were strategically located near the watering holes and some feeders. The thick, broken scrub was ideal for still-hunting. I decided to do a little stalking in the afternoon, and set off into the tangled mesquite and cedar, slowly sneaking into the crossing west breeze. I could see where the animals had rooted in the shade of the vegetation around the small stream course-distinct hog sign. Game trails cut in and out of the nastier thickets, and I sensed the pungent odor so unique to swine. Not twenty feet to my left, a huge black form exploded from beneath an impenetrable thorn screen. With a loud grunt and a cloud of dust, it vanished as fast as it appeared. And it was huge! Even in the instant that it all happened, the sheer bulk was impressive. I would guess after seeing an untold number of wild hogs, and killing hundreds myself, that this animal was certainly over three hundred pounds. That's a good hog in anyone's book. Or grill! That is fun. All the old wives' tales and folklore about charging wild boars tends to keep a guy on his toes. Though a charge is extremely rare, one never knows. These critters are certainly more than capable of grave bodily harm. I have seen them rip a big, tuff, mean hound to shreds.

I spent a few hours cruising the tangles, then took refuge out of the 100+ degree sun for a little iced tea and to prepare for the evening stand set. Rod, Greg and I spent the last three hours of daylight on stand, to no avail. Nobody liked this heat today. I had this feeling that sunrise would be a different story altogether. Love those sunrises.

With only a half a day to hunt before heading into San Antonio for the night's concert, the four of us loaded up Maurice's pack of fine hog hounds for a chase. The ground was saturated with a heavy dew, and the cool night had conditions perfect for a dog's nose and a hunter's heart. Gulping down the last of our steaming coffee, we headed out as the sun threatened to peak over the eastern horizon. At only a mile from the ranch house, we turned the strike dog loose and immediately got action. The second hound joined in with a boisterous howling, and the third and fourth blazed off in hot pursuit. Then I watched as Maurice, too, blazed off in hot pursuit. I knew I liked this guy.

Rod and Greg were doing their damnedest to operate their video cameras as we hauled ass thru the thorny underbrush, where hogs and dogs had no problem, but we were battling. At times I could not hear the dogs, but luckily the others' ears were less destroyed than mine. It all happened fast and furious, and finally we got a look at the beasts. Beautiful, big, black, commie hogs from hell!

Somehow the hounds actually singled out the biggest one of the three, and it was wild. I could only see the occasional flash of black-and-brown hide as the dogs and the boar lunged in and out at each other. My arrow was nocked as I attempted to push closer into the thorns, but I was still free enough to shoot. The hog could break away at any second, but I had to time and position my shot to hit the hog clear, without a dog in line. It was hairy.

In an instant I could clearly see the hog as he spun and faced me at about twelve yards. I had but a ten-inch window to lace my arrow thru to him, and came to full draw. Two dogs in front and two in back as the big boar spun to expose his shoulder in my window, and the arrow was gone; disappearing squarely behind the shoulder plate, passing thru the huge beast. Blood spurted freely, and within a second or two, the boar backed up and sat down, fell over and died. The hounds worried him awhile, and Maurice and I dragged him out into the open to admire the majestic old warrior. He was a prime specimen. You can't really say beautiful, but perfect. Weighing over 350 pounds, this old boy was in perfect shape. At least he was only a few moments ago! The shoulder plate was a solid two inches thick, and his razor-sharp tusks protruded almost three inches beyond his lips. The damage to two of the dogs was apparent. The one was gashed along his chest, but the other had a six-inch slice along his shoulder that was clear to the bone. Maurice doctored them up on the spot, confident that they would be raring to go the next day. The WhackMaster Broadhead had sliced clean thru the ribs, severing a major artery and both lungs for a quick, humane kill.

Of all the different wild boar hunts I have taken part in, I'm confident when I say that this was the best ever. The combination of good friends, good food, comfortable accommodations, wild country, great hounds and plenty of game is all a guy could ever ask for. The worst day bowhunting is better than the best day of anything else. But add all these conditions, and I feel like I've died and gone to heaven. If you ever find yourself headed west Texas way, and you're up for some fantastic bowhunting, give Maurice or Jamie a call, or drop them a line. This place is A-1. I will be returning to the Smyth Ranch off and on for both hogs and deer. If you are interested in a NUGENT-guided bowhunt, let them know, and we can try to coordinate our hunts together. Call Maurice or my staff at Ted Nugent World Bowhunters, 517-750-9060. We smoked that old boar, and got some terrific sausage and steaks for some of the best eating pork we have ever had. The trophy shoulder mount will be on display at Marcia's ranch house to live forever, mounted by Tom Piewitz of Victoria, Texas.

➤103 & 104

EQUIPMENT: Nugent-Oneida WhackMaster at 65-pounds,
Aluminum arrows, 2213, 125-grain WhackMaster Broadheads, two-blade
ANIMAL: Two Whitetail Bucks at 125 pounds and 135 pounds
HIT **#1:** Major artery, double-lung, running at twenty-five yards,
 went thirty-eight yards
 #2: Double-lung, went twenty-five yards

Once again, the magic lure of the north woods had me in its spell. As a guest
of the Pollingtons of Marion, Michigan, I had the opportunity to bowhunt as dense
a deer herd as there is anywhere in North America. Claude and his family live to
bowhunt, and manage their 1,500 acres for the critters. And critters there are. On
the numerous occasions when I have been fortunate enough to be the guest of their
generous hospitality, it is typical to see in excess of one hundred deer a day. I love
that. I sat quiet and still, fifteen feet up in the old cedar tree, as the wild around me
slowly came to life. I really love that.

Scanning the four trails visible from my perch, I had that feeling in my gut that
I get when game is nearby. With an arrow nocked, I was ready when the black, wet
nose of the little buck emerged from the ferns to my left. Stepping into the small
clearing, perfectly broadside, he paused to test the air currents. But it was too late,
as I released the WhackMaster two-blade on a mission of mercy, straight into the
pocket, tight behind his shoulder. At twenty-five yards, the black-and-white True-Flight
five-inch feathers vanished in one side and out the other. The game-tracker string
reeled out behind the fleeing buck, and I knew I had made a quick, humane kill.
They don't come any quicker. I watched him pile up in less than forty yards. He
was dead on his feet.

Even though the string tracker made for a simple trail to the animal, the blood
was solid from point of impact, thru the underbrush for thirty-eight yards, to the
four-point, one-and-a-half-year-old buck. The arrow had entered the right rib cage,
shot straight thru to exit low on the opposite side, severing a major artery and puncturing
both lungs. I tagged the beautiful animal and dragged him to the Bronco, with a
smile on my face that lit up the overcast fall woods. ☆☆☆☆

After rejoicing with the Pollingtons and other bowhunting companions,
following my good fortune of having made a perfect kill on my morning buck, we
had a little lunch and spent the day shooting the 3-D animal course, just to keep our
eyes sharp. I spent a few hours running Popeye, my Irish setter, and we killed five
woodcock and a grouse. Is this heaven or what? At about 4:30 in the afternoon, the
troops began preparations for the evening hunt.

Matt Pollington had generously let me use his favorite treestand that morning, and once again recommended that I return to it. Gladly. A slight misty rain had begun to fall, and the temperatures were dropping to the low 40s as I took up my repeat vigil. The sawgrass marsh to the east rose to maples and cedars, with a thick understory of ferns. Perfect bedding grounds. The rolling, broken tree line meandered above me to my right, leading to hay and corn fields in the distance. Perfect feeding grounds. I hadn't been in my tree for more than thirty minutes when the small six-point walked down the same trail as the morning four-point. Did I mention that I love that? This buck turned six feet closer to me on a secondary feeder trail as I completed my draw and released. KATHWACK!!! Dead center, low behind the shoulder again. Simply a thing of beauty. Again the game-tracker string spooled out frantically as the buck raced away, hitting the ground only twenty-five yards from the morning gut pile. The double-lung pass-thru was textbook perfect. The deer, weighing 135 pounds, about ten pounds more than the first deer. Both were prime, healthy specimens, and I was proud to have made the deadly hits. Conclusive proof, once again, as to the sure-kill deadliness of a razor-sharp, broadhead-tipped hunting arrow. Thank you very much. ✰✰✰✰

105

EQUIPMENT: Nugent-Oneida WhackMaster at 65-pound, Aluminum arrows, 2213, 125-grain WhackMaster Broadheads, two-blade
ANIMAL: Whitetail Doe at 165 pounds
HIT: Jugular vein at thirty yards, went a quarter mile

Geese had been flying over me all afternoon, just above the treetops. Should have had my ten-gauge. Pheasants cackled and flushed at regular intervals out in the expansive swamp below me. Should have had the 12-gauge. Fox squirrels seemed to delight in running straight towards me on the branches of my oak tree set. Should have had the .22 pistol. Heck, who needs a gun? I've got my trusty WhackMaster! The next big, fat bushytail that ventured into range came along an apple tree limb, swinging up and down just fifteen yards in front of me. I focused on his head as I released and the arrow sliced clean thru his forehead and blew him to the ground. He didn't twitch. That was the fifth squirrel of the season with the bow and arrow. That is great. Makes a guy feel pretty confident about his shooting ability. Not to mention the delicious fricassee forthcoming.

Now I concentrated on the opening in front of me, as the sun descended slowly over the hill to my right. It was the bewitching hour, that magic last hour of fading daylight, when the big game get active. Footsteps approaching from behind warned me as three young button bucks boldly wandered into my little valley. Without as much as a look around, they began to munch on the sweet white oak acorns that all game love so dearly. A great sign. This year's button bucks are next year's eight- and ten-points, more often than not. I have a hard rule on my hunting grounds, to never shoot any button bucks. Doe fawns are the best thing to harvest, as they play no role in the herd condition. In fact, in the southern Michigan zone that I do most of my hunting, the doe population is so high that the DNR issues thousands of bonus antlerless deer tags under their block permit system. This will hopefully reduce the overall herd size to alleviate the large-scale losses to the farmers, and the 50,000-plus deer killed on the highways. I requested and got twenty such tags this particular year and was looking forward to using them to further manage my herd for quality, optimum conditions and animals.

After twenty-five entertaining minutes of fawn-watching, a big, mature doe cautiously stepped into the opening, head up, ever alert. At thirty yards she turned to walk away, and I came back to full draw, holding for a center-neck shot. Her head went down for an acorn as the two-blade WhackMaster hit the middle of her neck, in the base, out the throat, into the jaw and out the top of the head.

She exploded straight away, yanking the tracker string fast and furiously behind her. I waited a few minutes, slowly lowered my bow to the ground, and climbed down to examine the site of the hit. Blood was sprayed wide on the ground and leaves. I followed the string for ninety yards to where it broke, with ample blood.

It was getting too dark to follow without a flashlight, so I returned home to get one. She had traveled about a quarter mile already, when I came upon her in a corn row. The two-blade had slit the jugular vein. The BLOOD TRAIL was primo, and would have been very easy to follow with the naked eye during daylight. It was also very easy to follow with a flashlight under the existing conditions. Even though the game-tracker string had broken after ninety yards, if in fact there would have been insufficient blood, the first ninety yards of string would have certainly been a major assist in determining the line of flight of the animal. This is always a big asset, and can be the difference between lost and found game. Get one and practice with it, and use it.

Remember, a string tracker CAN affect the flight of the arrow. It is essential to practice with it ahead of time. When I prepare to take a shot past twenty yards or so, I will sometimes slice the string off the end of the arrow. This shot was made at thirty yards, and had no effect on the arrow flight. ☆☆☆☆

106

EQUIPMENT: Nugent-Oneida WhackMaster at 65-pounds, Aluminum arrows, 2213, 125 grain WhackMaster Broadheads, two-blade
ANIMAL: Whitetail Doe at ninety pounds
HIT: Liver at five paces, went fifty-five yards

I had one day off from the road, and I knew exactly how I would spend it-in a tree! It was late October, with a strong north wind, as I sat quietly twenty feet up in my homemade ladder stand, leaning up against a giant old white oak tree bordering a large muck swamp. Waterfowl traded back and forth from lake to marsh all afternoon, and I could hear the carpenters pounding away on the staircase of my new home, which was near completion. Red squirrels darted up and down the big oaks in this grove, and doves landed within reach of my set-up. I had placed a large pile of fresh-cut corn as bait twenty yards upwind of this stand, to assist in luring deer into range. In possession of twenty antlerless tags for my property, it was my goal to kill a number of extra deer from the area. The farmer who works the property and I lose thousands of dollars each year to crop depredation, and I was going to do something about it.

The first deer in was a young, ninety-pound doe. She fidgeted around behind me for awhile, then walked directly in front of me at five paces. I picked a spot tight behind her shoulder, and sent a 125-grain two-blade WhackMaster broadhead a little too far back. The white 2213 passed thru her and she bolted, pulling the string tracker behind her. She made a complete circle around to my right, and as she humped up and walked by at twenty-five yards, I sent a second arrow thru her midsection. She continued ahead about thirty more yards, and laid down. I could see thru my binoculars that her head was still up. I waited twenty minutes 'til dark, and carefully climbed down and went home. Though I knew she was down for good, I felt it prudent to leave the area, just in case it was a gut shot.

At daybreak the following morning, I found her dead where I had seen her fall the night before. The arrow had sliced thru the liver and had opened up her belly a good five inches, with blood all along path she had traveled. The second arrow had entered just forward of the first, and had, in fact, enlarged the hole under belly for a perfect drain of liver blood. Once again, the game-tracker string had stayed with her the entire route, making a BLOOD TRAIL unnecessary. Even so, it was a beauty. ☆☆☆☆

107

EQUIPMENT: Nugent-Oneida WhackMaster at 65-pounds,
Aluminum arrows, 2213, 125 grain WhackMaster Broadheads, two-blade
ANIMAL: Whitetail Buck
HIT: Heart at eighteen yards, went forty yards

This small, one-acre knob of high ground in the middle of the big marsh was a natural. Years ago, my good buddy Bryan Schupbach had whacked the Banzai buck from hell right here with his shotgun. It's beautiful. The four-and-a-half-year-old deer field-dressed over two hundred pounds and had a twenty-eight-inch outside spread of eleven points, scoring 167 B&C. We have to cross a little feeder creek and a lot of black muck and briars to get to it, but there is always the chance the big boy's descendent might show up! That's exciting. I had taken a number of animals from this place over the years, but never a trophy. So be it. Even after hundreds of big game bow kills, any animal in range is a trophy to me.

The wind was whipping up a storm and I sat still, buckled into my Bucksy treestand, twenty-two feet up in the big oak. As always, the wildlife activity around me kept me mesmerized and entertained. And just as usual, like smoke, where a moment ago there was nothing, now stood a small whitetail buck. Where do they come from? I love that. As he nuzzled the ground for his dinner of acorns, walking from left to right, I waited for him to pass me slightly, barely moving my body into position with each of his movements. This time it worked. Maybe the wind helped, but as he was eighteen yards quartering away, I touched my anchor and watched my 2213 arrow vanish right thru his shoulder, making a loud WHACK as it shattered bone. This time the string from the tracker broke upon release, wadding up in a pile under my tree. The buck dashed off at a dead run, unable to use his right foreleg. These were the signs of a certain heart shot. Skirting the edge of the knoll, he died after covering only forty yards, with the top of his heart cut right off. Surprisingly, there was very little blood on the ground, and though I walked straight to him, it could have been difficult to follow. No matter what, even if I witness the animal fall and die, I ALWAYS backtrack and examine the BLOOD TRAIL for the sake of practice and experience. ☆☆

108

EQUIPMENT: Nugent-Oneida WhackMaster at 65-pounds,
Aluminum arrows, 2213, 125-grain WhackMaster Broadheads, two-blade
ANIMAL: Whitetail Buck, approximately 160 pounds
HIT: Double-lung, went forty yards

George Nicholls has a touch for the wild that most of us can only envy. Whenever I hear the term "good life," I think of George. Not because of the material things that most people attribute to the good life, but because George has a valuable sense of relation with wildlife. Like Fred Bear, he just knows. He can look at a piece of ground, no matter how unfamiliar he may be with it, and figure it out right away, nine times out of ten. Someday I would like to be able to do that. Someday.

Meanwhile, when I get a chance to hunt with George, I jump at it. He and Bryan Schupbach were hunting a big farmland swamp area along the I-94 highway. These were ideal conditions, I had learned, as the continual highway noise seemed to lull these animals into a false sense of security. Something like that, I'm not sure. At any rate, I am sure the traffic noise lets you get away with a little more.

Bryan had set up a number of hot stands along the watery island area, where the sawgrass marsh separated the high ground. George was hanging tight along the house fence rows where the big Pope and Young buck had been seen. Bryan chose the north stand, and I headed thru the swamp water for the island treestand, overlooking an old hay field. In the dark of pre-morning, I climbed fifteen feet up and settled in.

It was 7:20 before I could really see more than a few feet. A cold mist and fog accompanied the frosty sunrise. At 8:10 on the nose, as I pulled my glove back over my wristwatch, the first buck showed his head, thirty yards to my left. His body was large, I figured a good 160 pounds on the hoof, but his tiny two-inch spikes bespoke of his inferior genetics. Instantly, a second, larger, four-point buck emerged from the same sapling tangle. Behind them was a maple tree whipping back and forth, being thrashed by a third, even larger buck. I eased ever so slowly into shooting position, just as number three showed himself. He passed behind a small oak while I pulled back to full draw, and I picked a spot below his shoulder. He paused, I released, and everybody scattered. I saw the feathers enter his shoulder for a certain double-lunger. On these kinds of hits, I do not wait, but rather get right after the animals after the normal time it takes me to slowly descend my tree, and slowly gather my stuff. I literally stalk the Blood Trail, checking blood and tracks, and glance ahead for the animal.

The tracker string broke after thirty yards, but that didn't matter, as the big deer was dead ten yards further. The two-blade had entered at the point of the shoulder, but had turned and followed the path of least resistance, and after slicing both lungs, had exited the rear right hip. COOL! All the good stuff had been sliced for an immediate, humane kill. ☆☆☆

# 109

EQUIPMENT: Nugent-Oneida WhackMaster at 65-pound, Aluminum arrows, 2213, 125-grain WhackMaster broadheads, two-blade
ANIMAL: Nilgai Indian Antelope (Blue Bull), five hundred pounds
HIT: Liver at seventy-five yards

Shemane and I needed a getaway. The kids were off on spring break, and I needed to kill something, big time. We had first met Mike Mireles at the Oneida Idaho Pronghorn Hunt the previous August, and knew of the majestic "blue bull," famous for its wariness and tenacity, found in great numbers on the world-renowned Kennedy ranch. It had a well-earned reputation for being an extremely challenging animal, and I was itching to fly into Corpus Christi, Texas, for a week of hunting.

The Nilgai was imported into this part of the country back in the '30s, and has proliferated over the years. Some animals have certain characteristics that make them a super challenge for the bowhunter, and this big antelope could very well be at the top of the list. Like the wonderful whitetail, Nilgai have a sense of awareness that most often makes them unkillable. Their senses are like a whitetail's, but they are even more fidgety and spooky. The landscape in this part of Texas is jagged, broken and brush-choked, ideal for critters to vanish and escape in. These are free-ranging, wild animals, not contained by any fences. With an out-of-the-ordinary abundant rainfall, the vegetation was at an all-time high, lush and green. Waterholes were at record-high levels, making for chancy water-blind sets. For five days, I stalked and sneaked thru every nook and cranny, looking for a bow shot at a big bull. The clear, calm conditions were no good for stalking much past nine or ten each morning, and the trail sets were used heavily by the abundant deer, hogs, and turkey. As usual, the conditions for bowhunting were less than desirable.

Mike is the ranch manager, and more importantly, an experienced, knowledgeable bowhunter himself. He knows every inch of this vast hunting ranch intimately and, in fact, holds the number-one Texas non-typical whitetail himself. Having bowhunted for most of his life, Mike knows the specific requirements we need to manipulate as best as we can for a chance at a bow kill.

My chance came on the second day, with windy, cold, overcast skies that improved stalking conditions. I snuck along the edges of the thickest brush tangles, taking peeks as they came, into every nook and cranny. About an hour of stalking after sunrise, I rounded a slight depression and found myself forty-five yards from a feeding bull Nilgai with his head stuck in a bush, totally unaware of my presence. I was caught completely off guard, and reacted almost desperately, quickly yanking an arrow out of my bow quiver and preparing for the shot.

Normally a forty-five-yarder ain't that big a deal, but if I had calmed down a little, I am confident that I could have closed the distance to less than thirty yards, because his head was completely consumed by heavy vegetation, nearly to his front leg. But as it was, I touched off a shot and watched the damn shaft zing right over his back! Now, here is the interesting part, just to remind myself of the possible within! The bull did not react at all to the arrow shot, but rather continued to nonchalantly feed on the bush! It was windy, but still, with his uncanny hearing, I expected the bull to blast out of there.

Arrow number two was ridiculous! Right under his armpit! Good shootin', Ted ol' boy!! YOU DOLT!!! Simple case of buck fever. Pisses me off big time. The presence of a new species of game tends to knock me off center for awhile.

Anticipation ran high throughout each hour of each day. Plenty of game was seen, and the big blue bulls appeared regularly. On a cool, dark morning, with drizzle off and on, we spotted a herd of seven bulls not far from the Gulf of Mexico. They were a long way off as they filtered into the mesquite line.

The wind was with me as I skirted the brush and saw the bulls nosing out of the distant screen of trees 150 yards ahead. They were totally unaware of my presence. I squatted down to figure my next move, and watched them slowly feed on a line that looked good for my position. Another small bush materialized ahead, so I crawled to cut the range down to eighty yards.

The largest of the bulls was slightly in front of the rest, and I was considering a shot. The second largest bull nipped at a subordinate, moving another ten yards closer, and my mind was made up. With his gaze still on his target, the good-sized Nilgai was perfectly broadside at what I figured to be seventy to seventy-five yards.

From the kneeling position, I drew back for the long shot, just long enough for everything to look good, and touched 'er off. The zebra-striped shaft arched up and over, looking prettier all the time, and disappeared center into the big antelope's side. SHAZAM!!!! Off they went, in a cloud of dust and a hearty HI-HO SILVER! I was excited, but at the same time, nervous. Always am. Was it too far back? Too high?

Boy was I relieved when I saw all that beautiful blood sprayed all over the grass, limbs, brush and ground. I marked the spot and ran like hell to where Mike said he would be waiting. I got to the road and saw him down a few hundred yards. I thrust by bow into the sky, legs and arms akimbo. Mike came racing up in the truck and jumped out to take a picture. He said I looked just like the photo on the first World Bowhunter Night flyer! Cool!

We picked up the BLOOD TRAIL easily, and I called the hit as a liver, middle-artery shot. I knew I was a little far back, but still felt confident I was in the good stuff. Now the rain was starting to fall pretty good, endangering our trail. To make it even more thrilling and somewhat scary, we saw a herd of eight bulls a mile ahead that, for all practical purposes, was probably my group. Not fun.

We had gone a couple hundred yards and Mike decided to return to the truck, since we were approaching a pipeline road. I watched the eight bulls fade into the trees, and kept on the blood. It was still easy to follow, but the rain was threatening the whole deal. Mike rejoined me and we took blood another fifty to sixty yards to the tree line.

A glance to the left startled us. We saw the bull lying down as if asleep, twenty yards to the side. I don't trust critters that look dead, so immediately I nocked another arrow. I took a bead on his neck where it met the body, as Mike tossed a stick at the old boy. Even though he didn't budge, and we knew he was dead, I still put the arrow into him.

It's real interesting here to note that though this animal is famous for his tuff, difficult-to-penetrate hide, my WhackMaster two-blade, without the insert bleeder, went clean thru. Cool! Our estimate of the original hit was right on. The first WhackMaster had sliced slightly back, severing the top lobe of the liver and the main artery running up the middle. Glory Hallelujah! Three-star BLOOD TRAIL!

The big bonus to this great animal and hunt is the spectacularly delicious meat it yielded. All my buddies that have had the pleasure of tasting Nilgai meat agree that it is the best of all venison. Great! Cuz I got the appetite and recipes.

Hunts at this fantastic ranch can be booked year round for Nilgai and other exotics, such as wild hogs, javelina, axis, sika and fallow deer, ibex, blackbuck antelope and eland (from Africa). Seasonally, you can also hunt unbelievable whitetail deer, turkey, quail, pheasant, duck and geese. The ranch has terrific accommodations and food, with a professional crew of friendly, hard-working guides and assistants. I couldn't recommend a hunt more eagerly. ☆☆☆

➤110

EQUIPMENT: Nugent-Oneida WhackMaster at 65-pound, Aluminum arrows, 2213, 125-grain WhackMaster Broadheads, two-blade
ANIMAL: Wild, free-ranging Spanish Goat, one hundred-pound nanny
HIT: High left ham at thirty-five yards, artery, traveled ten yards

The ringing in my ears had not yet subsided, but Wayne Endicott and his Bow Rack buddies were determined to be the world's greatest fox-hunting hosts in Eugene, Oregon, and they were doing a fine job of it. Seems the homesteaders outside the area had let their Spanish and mohair goats go wild and unrestrained over the years, to the point of overpopulation. There were too many. Enter the WhackMaster Squadron, a division of Orkin, specializing in smelly goat problems.

After a wonderfully scenic drive thru the beautiful mountainous countryside outside the environs of Eugene, Oregon, we pulled into a valley of rolling timber and pasture land. Elk were seen wintering in meadows, and the elusive blacktail deer were spotted here and there. Wayne, Roy and I climbed straight up to the top of the butte above the grazing cattle and silently slipped thru the Douglas fir forest line, glassing each and every pocket and thicket. After huffing and puffing to the top of each rise, Roy spotted a large group of fifteen to eighteen goats ahead, hillsiding below us. We scrambled as quietly as possible to intersect them, hopefully, in one of the deep ravines. Keeping the intervening ridges and second growth between us and the strong wind in our faces, we lucked out by slipping into a cut that the goats decided to climb slowly towards.

Wayne readied his video camera, Roy hunkered behind a deadfall, and I slid to a huge stump to position myself for a clear shot, just as they appeared below us. Like second nature, I nocked an arrow, adjusted my cap, and angled my body for the shot. Four or five decent billies were in the bunch, but I wasn't going to be picky, since the goal here was simple: kill the pests.

A good-sized billy fed slowly across the steep incline, and my arrow went high because I was not used to the hard downward angle. Nonetheless, the WhackMaster head buried deep into a mature nanny's hip, and she was down in seconds with a severed femoral artery. One down, and the others scattered for cover. ☆☆☆☆☆

111

EQUIPMENT: Nugent-Martin Gonzo Safari bow, 65-pound, WhackMaster head and arrow
ANIMAL: Wild Spanish Goat, 125 pounds
HIT: Center right rib cage, exit left shoulder, double-lung at thirty-five yards, steep downhill, went twenty yards

The herd of fifteen to eighteen wild goats vanished into the thick understory of vegetation, sidehilling to where they had come from. They did not appear to be spooked badly, so we climbed to the top in an effort to get above and in front of them. A light rain was falling with a good wind in our faces. Within a half mile I saw the white forms hidden in the brush. I hit the dirt and belly crawled thru the trees, slowly positioning myself behind a thick screen of limbs as I came to full draw. Leaning slightly to my right, I cleared the debris, exposing a clear lane to the steep downhill shots. I picked a spot low in the animal's armpit and released my arrow, hitting perfectly behind the shoulder. The 2213 sailed clean thru and into the valley below as the herd darted ahead. My billy ran twenty short yards and fell over dead in about three seconds.

 # 112

EQUIPMENT: Nugent-Martin Gonzo Safari bow, 65-pound, WhackMaster head and arrow
ANIMAL: Spanish Goat, seventy pounds
HIT: Walking away, hip artery hit at forty yards, went ten yards

Within two seconds, literally, my second arrow was nocked, cocked, and ready to rock, doc! Three goats stopped on the trail at forty yards for just a second, and I instinctively envisioned the arch of the arrow as I released. The WhackMaster, white-fletched shaft sailed gracefully down the hillside, connecting solidly into the hip of the near animal as it stood facing away, burying to the feathers.

Besides the femoral artery being severed completely, the single-blade WhackMaster head sliced thru the length of the body, terminally damaging, with its razor-sharp edges, liver, pancreas, and the off lung. The seventy-pound goat barely made it ten yards before expiring in a clump of brush. ☆☆☆☆

 # 113

EQUIPMENT: Nugent-Martin Gonzo Safari bow, 65-pound, WhackMaster head and 2213 arrow
ANIMAL: Feral Goat, thirty-five pounds
HIT: Running, hit high on the back at fifteen yards, severing the main artery, went ten yards

The rain was whipping pretty good now, and I appreciated my heavy wool clothing. Deer kept bounding out of the thickets, making for a real enjoyable day. An undetermined number of goats had been seen moving into the far hillside. The vegetation was thicker there than anywhere else we had seen yet. Three bowmen moved in from the top, two from the far ledge and I crawled straight up the middle, clinging to brush and vines on the steep incline. The going was slow and slippery, but the conditions were helpful in keeping down any noise we made. Obvious trails were easy to pick out in the screen of brush, but I realized the extreme difficulty in threading an arrow thru any of it.

Three quarters of the way up the hillside, a patch of white became visible ahead. It had to be goats, so now I hugged the muddy ground, and stalked the greasy terrain. After twenty minutes, to cover five yards, I thought I saw a small opening ahead of the now apparent two billies. I pushed a knee into the slop for a toe-hold, and touched off an arrow just as the first billy entered my window. No such luck! The arrow clamored thru the intervening branches like so much bumper-pool action, with the goats squirting over the top. At this same instant I heard the unmistakable THUMP-THWACK!! of arrows striking flesh, and knew the boys were there when the animals topped out.

I searched for my arrow and was surprised by a small goat running towards me on the trail. Caught flat-footed, the goat stopped, I twisted an arrow out of my bow quiver, got it on the string just as the little billy darted around a tree. I touched my anchor as he emerged on the other side, and watched the shaft disappear a bit high and a hair far back. But the immediate change of color on the goat's side from white to red made it obvious that once again the big artery had jumped in front of my WhackMaster broadhead. The barbecued goat crashed lifeless in a leap. A real whopper BLOOD TRAIL. ☆☆☆☆

114

EQUIPMENT: Nugent-Martin Gonzo Safari bow, 65-pounds, WhackMaster head and 2213 arrow
ANIMAL: Spanish Billy Goat, 130 pounds
HIT: Left hip, exit right shoulder, at forty yards, seven-eighths quartering away, went forty yards

For all intents and purposes, we were ready to call it a day. Some serious up-and-down country had been negotiated, and everybody was cold, wet, tired and hungry. Especially me! We had dragged eight goats already to a rendezvous point. Now we were prepared to haul them downhill for pictures and then load them up in the trucks. Nonchalantly, we started to walk along, bullshitting and carrying on about what a great day we had, with me and Wayne out front for a few yards. I really wanted some chow! We were on the peak of the ridge when I saw a white back ahead, just below the crest. I hit the dirt and I nocked my last straight arrow with Wayne Endicott right behind me. Wayne's 90-pound, twenty-seven inch over-draw got there first, but went a bit high. My arrow arced smack dab in the left hip and buried in as far as the feathers. AGAIN! I love that. And again, the single-blade designed WhackMaster slid oh so efficiently thru all the vitals. A real nice billy goat, my best for the day. He had a tall, thick set of horns as an exciting and fitting end to a glorious day in the wilds of Oregon, and with a bunch of great bowhunters and friends. This is the life. ☆☆☆☆

**115**

EQUIPMENT: Nugent-Martin Gonzo Safari bow, 65-pounds,
WhackMaster head and 2213 arrow
ANIMAL: Russian Boar, 325 pounds
HIT: Left shoulder, double-lung, severed main ventricles at top of heart,
went twenty yards

Seems wherever there is wet slop, you got the best hunting. Critters prefer the boondocks just like I do. My over-the-shin LaCrosse boots are a mainstay on ninety percent of my adventures, and today they would be essential.

We had pussy-footed thru the nastiest stuff we could find for the last three hours and had encountered many signs of hogs. Large patches of moist ground were rooted up by an apparent roto-tiller from hell, and tracks and rubs were everywhere. I like that. Maybe my left ear doesn't work very well, but I think I have more than made up for that loss with increased capability of sight, instinct and even my sense of smell. I could smell a hog. Like elk, your first awareness of a hog is its odor. Stinky to the poor city slicker, eau-de-cologne of porkfest to us hunters!

My friend Jim Young had made a great moving shot, clean thru the boiler room, on a beautiful 250-pounder earlier that morning, and after no sightings for a few hours, my nose told me to be ready.

The standing water in all directions, interspersed with short vegetation clumps scattered here and there, focused our attention on a living room-sized thicket ahead. Standing forty yards downwind made it clear thru my nostrils that pork was either in that clump, or had recently been there. With a 2213 nocked and ready to rock, I side-stepped, angling crosswind, ever so slowly, trying my damnedest to x-ray the overgrown puckerbrush. As is the rule for bowhunters, I knew it would be impossible to thread an arrow into the tangle of willow and vines. I would have to hope for a shot at moving animals as they emerged from the tangle. If they were actually in there. Being the eternal optimist, I was geared for action.

Jim painstakingly slipped into the wind, circumventing the cover, carefully, slowly, letting his scent find its way into the cover from fifty to sixty yards out. The hogs could virtually explode from their hiding place at a high velocity, making for a very difficult running shot. I like 'em standing still, broadside, at thirty yards. But I practice all the time on moving targets at home and small-game hunting, so I have a pretty good feel on the shotgun-type swing necessary to execute these tricky shots. The speed and trajectory of an arrow can be printed on your mind after thousands and thousands of arrows are shot, under all types of shooting conditions. If you plan on taking moving shots, PRACTICE, PRACTICE, PRACTICE, PRACTICE, AND THEN MORE PRACTICE!!!! Please!

As the initial movement caught my eye, the hunter's mind started clicking. Black-and-grey bulk was busting brush from the center of the brush. This wasn't the best set-up, but it sure as hell wasn't the worst. They were moving, but luckily at a code-two pace instead of out-and-out full-boar panic. Maybe they hadn't heard who was in town! My angle was excellent as the three boar parted the screen of limbs, and I could see number three was the boss hog. With my guide standing right over my right shoulder, I drew the 65-pound Gonzo Safari bow back, touched my release to the corner of my mouth, swung easy with the animal's pace, and sent a WhackMaster two-blade payload on an instinctive path of intersection. And intersect it did!

Having witnessed hundreds of wild boar kills with magnum rifles, shotguns and hand cannons, as well as archery tackle, my hosts were dumbfounded when they watched the shaft whack hard, perfectly behind the left shoulder, impacting the far shoulder bone, penetrating both lungs, severing the main ventricles from the top of the heart, and witnessing the hog DOWN AND OUT, after two seconds and twenty yards! The WhackMaster strikes again!! You want humane, you got it. They exclaimed that they had never seen a big three hundred-plus-pound boar die so quickly. Like he had a choice! Farmer Pete should be so kind.

Like all of my kills and, in fact, even all of my misses (man, have there been a bunch of those!!), the absolutely mesmerizing beauty of that arrow's flight will be burned in my guide's and eyes and mine forever. It is something to behold. There is something mystical and poetic about the flight of an arrow, especially when it leaves your own hands. I love it. And I love a quick, humane, instant kill. Yes, I do. Remember, like my mamma said, "Do unto others as you would have them to unto you, carry a clean hanky, and never, I say never, eat dinner 'til it's DEAD!" Yes mother dear, anything you say. Such words of wisdom. Pork chops-R-us.

116

EQUIPMENT: Nugent-Martin Gonzo Safari bow, 65-pound, WhackMaster head and 2213 arrow
ANIMAL: Nigerian Dwarf Ibex, fifty pounds
HIT: Lengthwise thru the heart

I think I had one of these working on my crew at one time! Seems like it. Anyhow, this little booger was one quick, tricky little goat. And I mean little. At a pinch over twenty inches at the shoulder, and a mere forty pounds, I wouldn't have much mass to shoot at when the opportunity did arise. Actually, animal size doesn't really enter into it, because you only aim for the vitals, and that is always demanding and challenging. The mountainous terrain always compounds the difficulty, not only in shooting angles, trajectory and point of arrow impact, but just in the logistics of getting in on the animal, and physical strain. But who loves it? You and me, that's who.

I had jumped a small band of goats and sheep together from a dense tangle. My guard was somewhat down after hours in the sweltering summer heat of Colorado, and they vanished in a flash. The vegetation was thick throughout the mountainside, so I slowly eased my way towards the sloped and higher ground. Glassing carefully every inch of the way, pausing, I had plenty of time to enjoy the grandeur of the Rockies. I could relive my memorable adventures of the past of mule deer and elk, and smile knowing I would return in the crisp fall mountain air to live it again soon.

Out of nowhere, the small black Ibex darted onto a rock ledge, twenty-five yards above. Like second nature, my arrow found the string as my release grasp closed, anchor and release all in about four seconds. By the time our eyes met, the 2213 WhackMaster entered the forward chest at the shoulder, penetrated half length, separated the ball joint and sliced thru the heart. He somersaulted and fell dead ten feet away. ✩✩✩✩

117

EQUIPMENT: Nugent-Martin Gonzo Safari bow 65-pound, WhackMaster head and 2213 arrow
ANIMAL: Asian Four-Horn Ram
HIT: Double-lung

Kevin Towsley, Grover and I had seen the beautiful ram at a far distance. He was the largest four-horn I had ever seen or even heard of, so I decided to give it a whack. (My M.O.) With the boys perched atop a high meadow, I began my mile-long stalk into the wind. With daylight fading, I covered ground quickly when topography allowed. As I closed the gap to fifty yards, I found myself on my hands and knees crawling thru water and muck. The ram stood and occasionally grazed on the opposite end of a two-acre pond, unaware of my presence, as the wind began to whip up a bit more.

Four unseen mallards abruptly flushed, startling both me and the ram to attention. He watched the ducks fly off, but was now on red alert. I figured it was all over. He took two steps closer to the pond, giving me a new advantage as he separated us with a screen of brush. Nearly face down in the muck, I nocked my arrow and slowly attempted to rise to a knee. The wind was now gusting as he actually took steps towards me, glancing to the side from where the ducks took flight. I made a small move for every move he made, and was now thirty-five yards from him, face to face.

The frontal shot is not preferred, but if exact shot placement is possible, under

Red hartebeest, South Africa

9-point whitetail, Texas, 2002

9-point whitetail, Texas, 2003

American Rock 'n' Roll fueled by pure venison and spirit!

8-point whitetail, Michigan, 1998

5x5 bull elk, Texas, 2002

African Scimitar horned oryx, Young Ranch, Texas, 2002

The Beastmaster Live!

Double bag! Pollington's Buckpole Ranch, Michigan, 1999

9-point whitetail, Camp Verde, Texas, 1996

6x6 bull elk, Young Ranch, Texas, 2002

6x6 Rocky Mountain bull elk, Young Ranch, Texas, 2001

ideal circumstances, it is a direct path to the vitals. He cocked his head as I slowly drew back, and buried the shaft to the feathers, dead center. He scrambled and fell backwards, two seconds later my second arrow penetrated both lungs. He was dead.

The guys had a ringside seat, with their binoculars, for a two-hour stalk theater. The ram was spectacular, and will be a very special trophy on the TED NUGENT WORLD BOWHUNTER Headquarters wall. ☆☆☆☆

➤118

EQUIPMENT: Gonzo Safari bow 65-pound, WhackMaster head and 2213 arrow
ANIMAL: Russian Boar, three hundred-plus pounds
HIT: Broadside, upper lungs at thirty-seven yards, complete penetration, went twenty-five yards

A day off on the road is rare, but appreciated. Usually it provides a seriously needed break to relax, hang out at the pool, order a little room service, and sleep. But for those of us hopelessly addicted to the wild, fat chance.

There is a big swamp surrounded by dense woods and puckerbrush in upstate New York. My good bowhunting buddy, Jim Young, had his order in for a load of pork for an upcoming barbecue. Why not? I never leave home without my trusty GONZO SAFARI and a wad of WhackMaster arrows and heads, so let's rock!

Chuck Strauss runs Turtle Creek for the discerning pork-chop connoisseur, and we merrily tromped into the tangles with a troop of six fellow WhackMasters for a couple days of boar hunting.

After setting up four guys at various trail crossings, Chuck, Jim and I set out to dog the hell holes to see if we could rustle some hogs out of their daytime hot beds. I enjoy this. John Neiman managed to whack a fine two hundred-pounder right off. It was one we apparently scooted from a thicket. He made a perfect two-yard double-lung hit, and the black boar died within seconds, at twenty-five yards away. The slaughterhouse porkers wish they had it so good!

Big Jim Froio's luck wasn't good, so we kept stalking the ridgelines. As Chuck and I rounded a dry wash, I could make out a massive dark form ahead, rooting in the old, soft riverbed. I backed away, circumvented the wall of downed trees and thickets, faced the slight breeze, and crawled slowly forward. At forty yards, the feeding boar looked huge, with a black, silver and grey coat of coarse hair, the distinct characteristics of true European lineage.

He plowed along, nose near the earth while he ate, and all the while I inched closer. The vegetation was very thick, with few holes of shooting opportunities visible. At thirty-seven-ish yards, he lifted his head as I peered from behind a small maple tree, arrow nocked and ready. He sensed something and turned to move on, when I came to a full draw and picked a spot, centered on his broadside chest. The white fletch of my arrow hit the spot, he burped then exploded thru the vegetation. In under two seconds and within twenty-five yards, he was down and thrashed a moment while he tried to lift himself up.

From twenty-five yards away I released my follow-up shot, connecting dead-center between the eyes, penetrating the skull for a brain finisher (ask Chuck). You want humane, you got it. The WhackMaster two-blade sliced thru both shoulder plates on the first shot, while the second shot penetrated the thick heavy skull bone. Can't ask for better performance from a broadhead. Both heads are in perfect shape and ready for more. This design rules. Just ask Porky. ☆☆☆☆

119

EQUIPMENT: Nugent-Martin Gonzo Safari bow 65-pound, WhackMaster head and 2213 arrow
ANIMAL: Wild Boar, 150 pounds
HIT: Right hip at twenty-five yards, finished with a double-lung

I bring this recent kill up because I want to stress the importance of quick preparation for follow-up shots.

This hog jumped from his bed at twenty-five yards and presented what appeared to be a clear shot. The flight of the arrow looked fine 'til the last second, when a tiny, invisible, intervening twig deflected it. Instead of a nice quartering away chest hit, the shaft swung left and into the hip of the pig. The pig bolted away, but I saw the BLOOD TRAIL immediately. I charged ahead to a small clearing in the path of the animal. A mere five-six seconds later, I nocked my follow-up arrow and made a difficult, hunched-over, kneeling shot thru the shoulders, knocking the pig off his feet. This breakdown shot has occurred many times on hogs, javelina and warthogs, apparently breaking central nervous system skeletal formation, resulting in complete immobilization of the animal. Though the first arrow was mortal, being prepared for a quick second shot can sometimes make the difference in a long trail versus and expeditious anchoring of the animal. As documentation clearly shows, in this source and others, a single arrow is all that is needed ninety-nine percent of the time. But whether shot-gunning for upland game, rifle-hunting for moose or slashing at the local slaughterhouse, one must be ready for the unexpected. Our mental frame of mind reaction for a follow-up move is prudent. ☆☆

 **120**

EQUIPMENT: Nugent-Martin Gonzo Safari bow 65-pound, WhackMaster head and 2213 arrow
ANIMAL: Whitetail Deer at thirty yards
HIT: Three-quarters angle away hit last right rib, exit throat, penetrated liver, lung, heart, neck

The sumac was shiny, beet red, and the sky and maples were vying for fire-of-the-year award. Hickory glowed hard yellow, with rust oaks deepening the autumn backdrop. Wood ducks whistled and swhooshed overhead in harmony with the big Canadas dropping into my lake. Man-oh-man!! Do I deserve this heaven on earth or what? Yes, I say. YES!! Just the right, light breeze was stirring from the southwest, and my twenty-foot perch in the old tri-trunked choke cherry, gave me a special swamp-man's view of my wild. And as long as I am here, it is my wild. I take care of it, I love it, and I truly appreciate it beyond anyone's wildest dreams. Except my wildest dreams. Those are wild. This is the wild, and it is right where I belong. Two solid hours is usually plenty of time for the evening vigil, but tonight I came early, just because. Sixteen months and 281 concerts calls for some drastic rehab. Thank you very much. Batteries, get to recharging!

My two-by-four platform was solid, and the Seat-a-Tree comfortable. I was totally relaxed with my safety belt snug. A guy could fade right away up here in this fall air. A set aside sudan grass and weed field was off to my left, forty yards beyond the tangle of dogwood and alders. A beautiful marsh gurgled on my right, as I faced into the wind. The black muck below rose straight up in front of me to a forty-acre hell hole of impenetrable briars and willow thickets. A network of high-rope, well-defined game trails crisscrossed here and there, to red and white oaks, and I breathed easy. Red sky at night, bowhunters delight! And now it came! One second there was brush, an instant later, there stood a beautiful doe.

I had killed two this week on my block tags, but upon seeing her broken, gimped leg, I decided to mercy kill her. Hit by a car, probably, she would never out-run the local dog pack. For sure. As she walked directly away, she turned a hair at thirty yards. I picked a small yellow leaf at her last rib, and watched and heard the WhackMaster "Phunk" in and out. She lunged but fifty feet, penetrated full length, dead in three seconds. Everything was severed. Mercy killing indeed. Shemane and I carted her home for another glorious Michigan fall night. The kids love backstraps and onions. ✩✩✩✩✩

Highlight Hunts

A Miracle Triple
on Barbary Sheep of Texas

The adobe-brown buffalo grass and creamy broomweed swayed and glistened in the hot Texas sun before me, as far as the eyes could see. Like a sea of pulsating creme de la creme beige waves undulating in perfect harmony with the gentle southwest wind, my eyes hath seen the glory of the coming of the Spirit of the Wild. And it was good. Accented by reddish purple stalks of thistle and bluestem whipping here and there, the whole scene was the most beautiful, earth-tonal graphic I had ever witnessed. Off-white ribbons of sun-bleached gravel created a series of abstract halos amidst the broken fields. I blinked twice and swore I saw a clump of mobile vegetation shift from cedar tree to cedar tree. Replicating the exact color of their surroundings, the great horned head of an African Aoudad ram emerged from the field's center. Much to my astonishment, upon closer examination with my binoculars, an entire herd of more than thirty Aoudad appeared as if out of nowhere. Their camouflage was so complete, I actually lost sight of them as they paused with my eyes still on them. Miraculous defense mechanism for sure. At one hundred yards, the herd of mature rams, ewes and mixed young mingled about and browsed amongst the scattered islands of puckerbrush. They grazed and I gazed. My eyes followed the huge, grayish, darker male with the long, heavy sweeping horns that almost reached back and touched his hindquarters. Long,

Aoudad, Heartsill Ranch, Texas, 2000

shaggy chaps of coarse horse mane-like hair flowed down his neck, brisket and the front of his forelegs, nearly to the ground. He was magnificent. My eyes drooled lustfully for him. My predator instincts went on point. We were meant for each other. I named him BBQ Boy. I have a dream.

I was sixteen feet up in my North Starr ladderstand, concealed perfectly, deep in the body-hiding, thick, green boughs of a giant Texas cedar tree, bow and arrows in hand, ready for a perfect predator party. Much effort had been put forth to choose this ambush location at the foot of the rolling hills on the Heartsill Ranch near Walnut

Springs in central Texas. Walls of heavy cedar punctuated the islands of live oaks and brilliant red and Spanish oaks, with fiery splashes of golden sycamores and yellow cottonwoods. I was smack dab in the middle of the most beautiful nature art available to mankind. I sighed and smiled at the glory of it all.

The dense cedar I was hiding in eliminated any visible human silhouette. When I position my treestand in cedar, I never cut any limbs that I don't have to. Rather, I tie back any branches that could interfere with arrow flight so that I retain the cover they afford. Every time I hunt in or near cedar, I vigorously rub the aromatic green vegetation together in my hands and forcefully onto my clothing to permeate the zone with indigenous stink. It's delicious and fools the ultimate defensive olfactory radar in the prey's amazing nose. I use every trick I can when I bowhunt. With my ScentLok suit, Nature's Essence cover scent and the prevailing wind crossing to the east, I was in ideal position to waylay the beast. I was feeling pretty cocky. It's a good feeling.

And here they come. Slowly but surely, cautious step by ultra-cautious step, the wary herd of African beasts came on. The older females would pause every step, and rotate their noses into the air, sniffing for any danger. Each pair of radar eyes constantly scanned 360 degrees on vigilant alert for predators. The huge, older males brought up the rear, more cautious than any. As masters of evasion and escape, Aoudad have no equals. They represent the most difficult quarry in America for the bowhunter. It could make a guy real nervous if he didn't pray. Prey pray; it's good for the soul.

With a smattering of shellcorn spread on the ground where the cedars met the rimrock at the base of my hide-out, the first young ram halted and began gobbling up the bait. As a diversionary tactic, bait can help stop your target just long enough for the perfect shot. I happen to crave perfect shots. They're my favorite, and I felt one coming on. With the confidence exhibited by the now-feeding juveniles, an enormous old monarch marched into view between my dark-green cedar limbs. He dominantly rousted the other sheep, and turned broadside to display his alpha male supremacy. In an instant, a beautiful white-feathered arrow punched hard into the crease behind his right shoulder and zinged out the far ball joint. WHACK! And the stampede exploded into the mystical wildzone of Texas, and all was wonderful with the world. I fell back against the warm cedar trunk and gently laughed out loud. Aoudad sizzle on the BBQ tonight my friends. I could feel it. I knew it.

But wait, something else was going on here. With my arrowed trophy ram dead in a heap forty yards out in the field, the rest of the herd was standing and staring at the fallen beast. My fingers instinctively extracted another white arrow from my quiver and notched it. I watched as the nervous herd pranced back and forth around the dead ram, then slowly made their way back towards the mountain trail I guarded. Could it be that I would get another crack at another Aoudad like this? My Sims-equipped Renegade bow is so completely silent, it had produced no audible alarm to the herd. Sure as can be, they skulked back to the base of my cedar and began feeding yet again. Well I'm here to tell you, my nerves and heart began pounding double time with the prospect of a double unfolding before me.

After a nerve-rattling thirty minutes of uncertain come-and-go torture, another monster thirty-plus-inch boss ram presented his vitals broadside to me, and with my little archer's prayer for the Wild Things resonating deep in my heart, I sent another perfect 500-grain carbon arrow square into the crease behind his massive bullet-proof shoulder, the super-highway to his royal pump station. We had ram-jam number two in full force all over again. It was awesome.

Running past my first dead ram, this beast made it but another thirty yards and tipped over, stone dead in mere seconds. Again the confused herd stared in astonishment. My ace video cameraman and Texas Blood Brother, Bobby Bohannon, was once again zeroed in on the whole scene, capturing amazing footage on digital tape for our Spirit of the Wild TV show and video series. It's a good thing we had proof of this event, for it would be hard to describe to anyone familiar with Aoudad sheep that such a thing was possible. Giddy all around.

Did I mention; but wait!? What have we here? Is it my imagination or is the herd returning for round three? Good God almighty ladies and gentlemen! There was already another white arrow on my bowstring and Bobby was up and running with me as the herd mingled around the field edge gawking at the fallen monarch. It took the herd a while longer to turn around, having nervously moved away into the grove of oaks a few times. But then, led by a pair of juvenile rams, the herd slowly meandered our way by a circuitous route that brought them in on our left side this time. Unbelievable! With their heads thrust into the deeper grasses and prickly pear cactus clumps, the largest ram of the morning stood twenty yards away and turned perfectly broadside looking back into the woodline. My arrow was drawn smoothly back, nock snug into the corner of my mouth, and ZING! Another beautiful white arrow square into the kill zone. This giant ram exploded in a hell-bent for leather dead run due north as fast as his four legs could carry him, vanishing into the stunning colorful tree grove and beyond. WOW! Was this a dream, or did I just put the kabash to a third monstrous trophy Aoudad in a single setting? Good grief.

All was silent but for the pounding in my chest. Bobby and I looked at each other wide eyed and dazed, without a word. All our extensive scouting and planning had paid off enormously. We had accomplished the impossible. We were high as a kite.

On videotape, I tried my best to articulate what miracle had just transpired, and I hope I adequately conveyed the outrage of it all. We methodically tracked and recovered each of the three monster rams, showing true awe, satisfaction and reverence for each beast. More than two or three rolls of film were exposed to capture the spine-tingling memories we had just produced. Each creature was a wonder. The colors, shapes, features and majesty of each animal was marveled at and admired. Much work was in it for us to get these four hundred-plus pound giants back to the Heartsill Ranch camp, gutted, skinned and butchered. Stories and laughter resonated well into the not-so-quiet Texas night, and a very intense hunting revelry went on for hours.

We celebrated the fact that Texas has a thriving, in some regions exploding population of these amazing creatures. Amazingly, Texas has more Aoudad than all of Africa. Many years ago, Texas landowners and hunters imported this special animal, and now they roam Texas and New Mexico healthier and larger than in their historical homelands. When such critters are managed for balance and health, they thrive. It is the value placed on them by hunters as renewable resources that makes this possible. In this region, the landowner had determined an expanding population was approaching the carrying capacity of the habitat, so he contacted Sunrize Safaris to balance the herd. With regional homeless shelters and soup kitchens begging for quality meat, we were more than happy to oblige. A perfect win-win if ever there was one. Aoudad chili, steaks and lasagna for everyone!

A Trophy for Rocco

Ahhhh . . . What a great feeling. In fact, what a relief. My young son Rocco was at my side, back in the wild again, as a glorious rising, golden sun cut through the canopy of trees overhead with a shower of penetrating bursts of light. Thank God my children love the shooting sports as much as their critter-addicted old man does. I crave my sacred hunting season so much, it would be nothing short of a catastrophe

Ted, Shemane, and Rocco at home, Michigan, 1992

if I ever had to face it without my beloved family along for the fun. I get giddy enough when I simply sneak a peak at the months of October, November, December and January on my calendar, joyously anticipating my stimulating, natural predator time afield. But when I add to the dynamic of these precious experiences the increased joys of having my whole tribe along for the Spirit of the Wild campfire and adventure, well, I'm here to tell you, I about come unglued. God bless the ultimate American Dream we are so blessed with. Rocco and I were in the zone and going deeper by the minute.

And so it was, together again, on another bone-chilling cold December dawn, that young son Rocco Winchester joined dear old dad on a mesquite-choked Texas hillside, greeting another wonderful soul-awakening daybreak, side by side. Toting his trusty Remington Model Seven in the venerable .243 Winchester caliber, the all-time NugeClan favorite, we cautiously stepped our way up the steep incline toward a high outcropping of white rocks, overlooking a gorgeous green valley. At only eleven years of age, he had become a master of stalking, and at times so quiet, I had to glance back occasionally to confirm he was still with me. In hushed whispers, we strategized our game plan for Texas whitetails here outside Meridian, not far from Waco, in the heart of great southwest American deer country. How cool.

With a solid south wind, Rocco knew instinctively how to approach an ambush set-up from the north for this rugged, almost mountainous terrain. Whenever I hunt with my kids, I always let them do the most thinking, planning, and decision making, providing as little input as I dare. This way, they learn to not only think for themselves by applying the ongoing hunting lessons we have shared over the years together, but they prove that this structured independence will assist them at school, on the playground, in athletics and in peer gatherings, and even at parties too. It may very well be the most important lessons they will ever learn. After all, the American Dream is about being the best that you can be, as much on your own as possible, and a little push for self-sufficiency goes a long way in nurturing rugged individualism. Rocco was doing it and doing it well. As far as I was concerned, the hunt was already a resounding success.

Rocco was leading the way now, and he paused to look things over. He signaled to a thick edge of brush at the point of our ridge rim, and we silently made our way onto this natural vantage point. We settled in and began to glass the area slowly with our binoculars, a wonderful calm enveloping the silent father-son celebration. Even at this young age, his movements were those of a pro. He put forth that extra effort, so atypical of a modern youngster, to be unobtrusive and quiet. With exaggerated slowness, he scanned and watched. I was mighty proud of him.

As usual, he was the first to spot game, and alerted me to a pair of does working amongst the sheltered scrub on the next shelf to our east. The two deer remained in the shadows for the most part, but a creeping light was eating up darkness across the valley when I caught movement about four hundred yards due south. Immediately my hunter radar beeped a red alarm, for the headgear on this deer was more than apparently outsized compared to its body. Following my shaking finger, Rocco now looked at the walking deer through his crystal clear Leica riflescope as I studied it intensely through my 10x40 Nikons. We both let out a subtle gasp, doing all we could to minimize our inevitably exploding excitement. Without a word, we could both tell we were looking at a real trophy whitetail buck sauntering down the steep slope. Gentlemen, start your engines! We have liftoff!

It was this moment of intense and ultra-demanding scrambling that most impressed me about my little boy. With calm and focus, he carefully avoided moving rocks or scraping vegetation, and quietly positioned himself for a good shooting angle, taking advantage of cover and a solid rifle rest for precision sniping accuracy. I stayed back while Bobby Bohannon kept the video camera rolling, capturing a very special moment in time for our Spirit of the Wild TV show. I had trained Rocco to do just such maneuvering back home on our shooting range, confronting multiple-shooting scenarios and angles, training him to always consider minimizing movement and noise. He had learned his lessons well, for now, at the moment of truth, he silently squirmed into perfect prone position, and tracked the beautiful deer in his crosshairs. He was calm, but I was trembling.

When the buck paused, the rifle cracked and the deer went down. Smoothly chambering another round, Rocco stayed on the buck like he was supposed to. If I had killed a huge buck like this when I was eleven, I assure you I would have acted with far less control. That's probably why I never did kill a buck till I was twenty years old!

The killing lasted but a nanosecond compared to the elongated overall hunt, and our memory bank was now overflowing. We merrily but carefully made our way down and across the now sunny valley to the majestic beast. We marveled at the stunning whitetail buck with his royal crown of thirteen-point antlers and beautiful tawny winter coat. We hugged the deer and each other. Rocco relived and shared his thoughts and concerns as he had prepared for the shot, displaying the kind of intense passion for a job well done that every father hopes and prays for out of his children.

The buck was nowhere near as big as I had figured, as he was only a two-and-a-half-year-old youngster. Yet his head of bone was still most impressive. Scoring roughly in the 140-inch category, compared to his smallish body, it was apparent why his rack appeared so large from such a long distance. There was no question this deer had magical genealogy and would have eventually been a sure book animal in but a few short years.

Dragging our prize across the rugged valley floor towards the truck, Rocco and I talked for a long time about every detail of not only this morning's adventure, but of past exploits and future ones we looked forward to. That it happened to be my father's birthday made it all that much more emotional and impacting for both of us. This is one for the spiritual record books, that's for sure.

Annual Baptizmal Deer Hunt

Ouch! That's gotta leave a mark! Ninety days and ninety nights of sheer Rock 'n' Roll R&B hell/heaven outrage. Heavy on the rage. And it is out there. That's the American Dream I'm talkin' 'bout. What this ol' bowhunting guitardog needs following the intense bombast after every hi-energy concert tour year after unholy year is a massive dose of shut-up. Maximus backdown. Backoff. Peace. Quiet. Shutdown. The Great Escape. Vanishtime. Comfortably numb but without the drugs. Try to picture an angry, unkempt Quasimoto dragging two bad legs and a heaving, malformed torso across a backdrop of steaming rubble, drooling, squinting, staggering, and making little wounded puppy noises. That's me after a wonderful Full Bluntal Nugity summer-long tour of loud, over-the-top tribal guitar mating sounds. Think of the thousands of rock fans each night as curious, dancing prairie dogs, and that's me

8-point whitetail, Michigan, around 1992

onstage, my Gibson guitar a virtual varmint howitzer. "What's with all the red mist?" one might ask. Happiness is exhaustion and a puddle of sweat, grinning ear to wounded ear. As Mellancamp would say, "hurts so good, baby!" I am Crave Man, dammit.

So just how does an old rockin' guitarboy come back to earth after all this abuse? A naked swandive headfirst into the Spirit of the Wild, that's how. Fall. Autumn. Hunting season. Phase three in the four-part seasons of nature. The best time of year. Balance time all around. Let the healing begin! So there I was, the electric decibel orgy but a grand, painful recent memory, with nothing but silence and tranquility all around me only one day later. Twenty feet up in the gentle embrace of a strong, towering white pine tree, I sat

139

with the birds and the wind, grinning and calm, like a stoned Cheshire cat, but predator pumped to the hilt. And not just any old pine tree will do. The magnificent forest where I now rested was created with my own greasy American hands. God and I work together on timber productivity each spring by planting thousands of trees, and now the soul-cleansing powers of all that hard work was paying off in gargantuan dividends. My twitching subsided, nerves relaxing and breathing slowing down as if caressed by the hand of God His bad Self. Cool. I don't care what you do or who you are, any and all life-support careers and jobs will eventually drain us, and we all desperately need some regular recharging. There is nothing that does it better than the great outdoors and the mystical dynamo of Ma Nature's natural medicine. Add a bow and arrows to the experience, with the desire to match wits with the beast, and I'm here to tell ya, the physical and spiritual upgrade is guaranteed. It's how it works.

This first evening out brought with its delicious fresh air, a fivesome of does and fawns, nibbling and browsing along the autumn olive patch on the edge of my sacred pine forest. Simply being in their presence made me feel calm and vitally alive, mesmerized by their interaction and constant maneuvers. A single boisterous crow suddenly swooped through the pines with us, raising hell and carrying on as only a raucous crow can. The deer ignored him. I smiled.

It went like that all afternoon 'til just before dusk, when a dark, handsome six-point buck appeared from nowhere in the deep shadows of my sanctuary. Our Spirit of the Wild cameraman Jim captured great footage of the mature buck as he nosed around the other deer, then stopped broadside at a close ten yards to groom himself. Though he was a huge-bodied buck in the perfect position, and the temptation to take him was strong, I talked myself out of it, hoping he would grow browtines for a much better rack next year. He really asked for it for a good five minutes, and then casually meandered off into the darkness. The transition from Rock 'n' Roll season into hunting season was moving along nicely. I sighed and called it a night. The slow walk back to the truck with owls hooting under a clear, starry sky was quiet and splendid. What guitars?

Day two of the cleansing was also wonderfully metaphysical. More deer, more birds, more spirit. I felt like the Wizard of Ahhhhs. Another, bigger buck was nosing around with a small group of does out in the distance most of the afternoon, and their antics delivered me to the tranquil suburbs of Nowhere Land. From the moment I saw this buck, I knew that I would take the shot if everything came together. It didn't, but I did feel like I had harvested spiritual backstraps for the soul. And they were delicious and fortifying.

Evening three was the charm. Relocated to the big timber on the west side of our property, Jim and I settled into our North Starr treestands for another chapter of awe-inspiring video footage and wildlife joy. Situated in a stand of giant white oak trees, we couldn't have timed it any better. As soon as we tightened our safety harnesses and I notched an arrow, we became aware of the continual pitter-patter of falling acorns. Big, juicy, ultimate-bait white oak acorns, the kind that whitetail deer crave. In the still of the forest, I could hear them hit the ground quite a ways off, and plenty were falling all around us. Within minutes, my binoculars caught the telltale movement of a flicking white tail about one hundred yards into the woods, and the old heart starting its hunt-pumping routine. Within minutes, numerous deer could be seen feeding in nearly every direction and getting closer by the minute. At one point, five does were all nosing forest floor debris within twenty yards of us, and then it happened. Apparently, our Scent Lok clothing and Essence of Fall cover scent were working perfectly, because from directly behind us, walking nose-first into what should have been our scent-stream, a beautiful eight-point buck walked into view. Stopping nearly underneath us, he sucked up yummy acorns one after another. Jim had the camera on him as he nonchalantly stepped over a dead log, turning broadside with his head nearly covered by a cherry tree. That's all I needed as my fifty-five-pound Renegade bow drew back smoothly to my face, and without hesitation, my 500-grain all-white carbon arrow zinged instantly across the opening, disappearing tight behind his muscled shoulder, square into his deep, broad rib cage with a solid WHACK! How cool is that?

The Renegade bow was so silent, especially with all the Sims Vibration Lab accessories, that there was no disrupting audible sound other than the arrow striking the beast. He exploded headstrong into the forest. All the other deer jumped a bit, and then stood erect, watching as the big buck stopped after only forty yards, stepped back and to the side, then tipped over with a kick or two. Then all was silent again. Some of the does cautiously approached the dead buck, noses outstretched and peering. None of them really spooked, but rather, after a circling looksee, wandered off searching for more acorns.

Jim and I were ecstatic. We captured the tracking and recovery celebration on digital tape and relived all the incredible details of the encounter, pre-shot and reaction. We were full-on giddy. Photos were taken, guts removed, and with the aid of our trusty Glenn's Deer Handle, we dragged the sacred beast to the truck and headed home. That night over sizzled tenderloins and potatoes smothered in garlic and onions, we toasted the sacred hunt, the mighty beast and a job well done. By the time I hit the sack, I had to think hard what it was like just a few nights ago on stage, jamming like a man possessed, loud and energized as all git-out. As I closed my eyes, the bright lights and blaring Rock 'n' Roll gave way to silence and a majestic white horned monarch in the forest, walking in slow motion and glowing in the hunter's moon. The beast is dead, long live the beast.

Ted with campers at Ted Nugent Kamp for Kids

Bowhunting Boy Scouts

My binoculars began to shake more intensely by the second, as the handsome buck closed the distance to my hideout in the leafy, vine-choked fence row. A herd of twenty does and fawns were already before me, grazing leisurely in the big, green hay field. It wasn't a huge buck, probably only a year-and-a-half-old forky, but I shook nonetheless. In fact, the shakes were not a result of my typical pre-shot adrenalin dump, since it was still late summer and all I was doing was pre-scouting my favorite huntzone. But the point is, I shook anyway. Life should be a series of shakes, the way I see it. Critters do that to us, don't they. Knowing all too well that these critter-encounter thrills cause varying levels of jitters for so many hunters, we must prepare for this physical phenomenon by stroking our predator psyche in anticipation of such dynamics. I watched the ever-increasing herd feed and interact, and slowly relaxed and calmed down a bit myself. It is always a wonderful experience being in the presence of wildlife. I make it a point to get out there and be amongst the animals at every opportunity. I have found over the years, that the more I am around game animals, the more relaxed I can become for an optimally executed shot when I'm actually hunting. When I scout, I think like a hunter, always envisioning the time and place-ment of my shot, forcing myself to put my mind in that unique and stimulating killer frame. Oftentimes I will actually draw an imaginary bow to see if I can get away with the movement to confirm that my decision was correct. I usually have my bow with me, and I draw back a blunt tipped arrow and pick an exact aiming spot on the animal, then let down. Early season practice on small game or exotics during the off-season is terrific practice and loads of fun. This all represents a great learning tool.

It's not good enough for us bowhunters to just get prepared; we must stay prepared. Pre-season tune-ups and practice sessions are essential to develop responsible, even ethical proficiency, that's for sure. Unless we maintain that reasoning predator mindset and capability throughout the actual hunting season, things can come unraveled pretty quickly when we are in the presence of the beast after all that prolonged waiting typical to the hunt. I learned long ago that the heartbreak of failure at the moment of truth is lesson enough to force me to hone my skills every day, before, during and after each hunt as the season progresses. From day-in-and-day-out consistent practice comes a very important level of confidence that we desperately need when the ultimate pressure of the shot arises. In order to bring home the sacred venison, second-nature trained and memorized responsive instincts must guide our bowhunting ballet. The mystical flight of the arrow is no fun at all when it ends up in the dirt over the back or under or thru the belly of the beast. That can drive a guy nuts.

Like a good Boy Scout, we must always be prepared. I shoot a few well-executed arrows each day to keep my archery touch hot. There can be long spells between shots at game, so daily practice is important.

All the successful bowhunters I know, from Bob Foulkrod, Chuck Adams, Myles Keller, Bob Fromme, Bill Winke and so many others, finalize their pre-season archery practice sessions by shooting with everything that they will be using on the hunt; the exact arrow, broadhead, and wearing the exact same clothing from their specific treestand as well. They all make it a point to practice shots from every imaginable angle and position, sitting, kneeling, standing, squatting, leaning, twisting, contorting their bodies as if the deer of their dreams sneaks up where they least expect it. It is amazing how much difference there can be in arrow flight based on these dynamic variables. The moment of truth is no time to find out. I hear far too many painful horror stories from inadequately prepared bowhunters each year due to an error in judgment that could have been avoided by a little advance thinking and practice. Do your homework right and have the season of your lives.

Buckos Encontado
Father-Son Texas Dream Hunt

Jack Brittingham is my hero. He's such a die-hard hunter, he almost makes me look like an animal right's geek. Now that's intense. He travels the globe year round, celebrating every imaginable wildlife encounter a man could dream of. And he does it with the true heart of the hunter. Whether it's Argali sheep in the wildest hellzones of Afghanistan, elephant in Tanzania, huge mule deer in the Rockies, legendary

Brown Bear in Alaska, or his beloved whitetail deer in the mega-buckzones of his various Texas properties, Jack lives the Great Spirit of the Wild to the fullest. And he and his wonderful wife, Chris, are raising their great children to do the same. God bless them all. The American Dream lives.

Fallow buck, Texas, 2003

I first met Jack via the ever-warming TNUSA campfire, as he and his children are all dedicated life members of our spirited organization. During one of my many concert tours through America a few years back, Jack had contacted me to visit him at his then primo Stuttgart, Arkansas, deer camp on a day off before a Little Rock not-so-little rockout. "Shonuff," I said as I zoomed down to experience one of the best hunts I had ever had in but two short days. With Jack's expert guidance, I managed to arrow three deer in those brief two days of bowhunting, and needless to say, performed one helluva soulful venison-infested concert that next night. I had inspiration to spare!

Jack and I struck up a genuine Blood Brother connection that thrives to this day. He has since sold both his expansive Arkansas and Illinois deer ranches, but still has what could best be described as possibly the most intensely managed deerground to be found in North America on his two Texas properties. This guy leaves no stones unturned. With full-time professional biologists and property managers working throughout the year, his ranches are glowing examples of game-ground conservation at its finest. The fact that he arrows mature, 190+ class bucks nearly every year, including a mind boggling 249-inch B&C monster in 1999, is testimony to his skills and dedication to wildlife management. His young children take impressive trophies every season as well. A family that hunts together, thrives together, that's for sure.

My nine-year-old son Rocco and I had a memorable first deer hunt together in December at the famed YO Ranch in the Texas Hill Country, where Rocco took two beautiful whitetail bucks with his trusty .223 boltgun. Now we were again jetting back into San Antonio, but in the cool overcast winter afternoon of late January 2000, we would wheel south this time instead of north, heading towards Cotulla and the semi-desert wilds of Jack's Rancho Encontado. With the expanding opportunities implemented by the now-progressive Texas Parks and Wildlife, private landowners are finally able to better manage their properties and indigenous wildlife. Unlimited doe tags and management buck tags are now available to these taxpayers to better balance the buck-doe ratio and overall health of their herds and land. The Texas deer herd is at an all-time prime, and with increased access and control, the future looks even better. And we were about to swan dive headfirst into the awesome dynamic of the whole thang! We were very excited. What a wonderful trip for a father and son from Michigan, who by law are not allowed to enjoy this simple, proper pleasure at home because the minimum age for deer hunting is twelve for bow and fourteen for gun. We are working hard to fix that unfounded, counterproductive regulation right now! Meanwhile, we spend our time and money in Texas, gladly.

As we pulled into Jack's sprawling hunt camp headquarters, his guides were busy skinning, weighing and measuring three dandy bucks just taken by hunters the day before. All three bucks were huge for South Texas deer, each slamming the scales into the two hundred pound plus range. And their impressive antlers kicked Rocco's and my heartbeat up a notch or ten, as the bucks scored around 140, 160 and 170! We wiped up our drool and hurried to unpack our gear and get ready for the afternoon hunt.

The accommodations were great, each of us getting our own fully equipped, comfortable modern room and bath. A grand living-dining room was set up like a classic hunting lodge and the bucolic atmosphere was ideal. Out the large back sliding glass doors was a huge feed trough, and already in the early afternoon, two handsome bucks were helping themselves to high-protein treats in the sun. No hunting was allowed near the lodge, and deer and hogs, as well as African sable antelope were seen regularly meandering about the thick mesquite and cacti scrub. What a setting.

Rocco double-checked his .223 and headed to the range for sight-in affirmation. His able guide took great care to adjust his approach for a young hunter, and Rocco immediately felt comfortable and confident. I appreciated that very much. I headed off into the green Texas tangles with Mike Hehman, a dedicated bowman in his own right, and within a short couple of miles, we sat comfortably in a wooden coop blind at the edge of a clearing. With three hours of shooting light to go, we settled in and immediately began to glass the surrounding sloping terrain in hopes of seeing the beast.

Colorful songbirds flitted all about the abstract vegetation before us and cottontail rabbits could be seen in amongst the shadows. A roadrunner scooted under the brushy canopy and then a flicker of white flashed within the dense scrub of prickly pear cactus, mesquite and a variety of south-Texas thorny vegetation. Through my binoculars I picked up the giveaway glint of antler, big antler, and we felt the swell of adrenalin that all hunters crave. We instantaneously went from condition yellow to code red alert.

The first deer to approach our clearing was a handsome three-year-old bruiser sporting genuine eight-point trophy headgear in the 135-inch category. But at only three years, he was off limits on Rancho Encontado, for only genetically inferior bucks under the age of five could be harvested here. Jack knows that given the chance to grow, many of these young deer will develop into huge 190+ class beasts, and the annual waiting game is sport unto itself for Jack and his hunters. I sat there shaking and smiling broadly admiring the beautiful animal, his grey winter coat shimmering in the Texas winter sun. Ol' Ted was high again.

He fed cautiously in the area for a half an hour, when at once his head jerked up, looking intently into the heavy brush behind us. Knowing any movement could ruin our chances for a shot, we just froze and waited. The buck before us backtracked a few yards, when to our left approached a much bigger buck, ears laid back, stiff legging his way into the arena. Even during this extended management season at the end of January, there was still some intense rutting activity occurring, and the big boy was ready to rock the subordinate buck the hell outta here. As they squared off and their back hairs bristled, the bigger deer stepped broadside in the front of our blind and I slowly lifted my bow into position. But something wasn't quite right, and the big bruiser side-stepped away to the farside, as I let down, waiting for that perfect shot opportunity.

Abruptly, the target buck gave me a clear view of his right shoulder as he stared at the other deer and I was at full draw instantly. With his attention riveted on the other deer again, I took my time for a deep breath and cut my arrow loose on its mission of mercy. The all-white shaft looked perfect on its path, but a mere nanosecond before impact, the huge buck lurched hard, crouching low for a powerful lunge into the cover of the scrub, and the arrow caught him midship, vanishing through his rib cage, kicking up dry Texas dust beyond. On instant slomo-replay [slow-mo?] of the digital video, the arrow did in fact slice neatly directly behind the shoulder bone, but in his extreme crouch, his elbow was thrust disproportionately back, causing the arrow to hit what looked to be mid-liver. Our spirits and hopes were running high nonetheless, but sadly, after searching intensely all that afternoon, evening and half the next day, even with tracking dogs, not a sign of the big deer was found. We were bewildered. Spirits were crushed, big time!

Rocco did not fare any better. He had seen a trio of beautiful, killable trophy bucks, but had difficulty in getting a comfortable rest to execute his shot to his liking. He was a little bummed out too, but we had a good meal and talk about the whole day, and concluded that we had certainly had a fascinating day of great hunting, and would try harder for the afternoon hunt on day two.

And we did! I was surrounded by deer and huge Russian boar all afternoon, but didn't take a shot. Rocco, as well, saw more big, mature whitetails this afternoon than most hunters would witness in a lifetime in average deer country. Spirits were getting back on track. Another great meal and good night's sleep was had by all, and another glorious day afield was dreamed about by father and son.

Settling into our ground blind well before daylight, Mike and I shared those special dynamics that are a hunter's sunrise. A big hog moved in front of us just before shooting light, then faded back into the thickets that surrounded us. With the exotic, shimmering light of first dawn sparkling upon all the dew-covered vegetation, our eyes took in the sight we were looking for. Out of the pre-dawn fog cover, a big, bulky-bodied, tall, heavy-racked nine-pointer casually strolled into view, just thirty yards out in front of us, paused briefly, then vanished just as quickly. We were up and intense, then down and perplexed in an instant. But as any experienced hunter knows, you do not let your guard down, ever. And it's a good thing I knew this, because he reappeared walking in the opposite direction, this time only fifteen yards out, and he stopped to nibble the corn we had spread out. I was already up and drawing, so that when he paused, I touched my anchorpoint, and with a quick prayer, the arrow was loosed and on its way. With a THUMPH! the white shaft vanished into the crease behind his foreleg, in and out in a flash, and the big buck exploded in an abrupt about-face. This time we knew we had our deer and some controlled laughter and high-fives slapped the morning stillness. I lay back against the blind wall and smiled a big sigh of relief. God bless the hunt, it don't get no better than this.

We relaxed and waited for about fifteen minutes, then took up the ample blood trail for a short twenty-five yard walk to our fallen prize. He was a beautiful, mature, five-year-old south-Texas beast, with nine good, heavy, massive, even points and a big, grey Roman nose. We exposed a roll of film and video taped the recovery for our Spirit of the Wild TV show, and slowly dragged him to the nearby lane, where we loaded him into the pickup. Everyone celebrated back at camp as we weighed him in at 210 pounds and green-scored his rack at roughly 133 inches. More photos were taken and another grand meal was toasted and prayers said in thanks for another great day in the wilds of Rancho Encontado.

The next day, Mike and I joined young Rocco in a tall Texas tower blind for a fitting end to our adventure, as he tagged a real dandy nine-point trophy of his own. In the four days of hunting, we had seen more than a dozen genuine trophy whitetails, many javelina, wild boar, quail and a nonstop parade of fascinating indigenous wildlife. It was all the dream hunt anyone could hope for, and our plans are nailed for a return in January every year possible henceforth. If you are interested in this very unique and specialized deer hunt, give us a call at SUNRIZE SAFARIS, 800-343-4868, as we can book up to four other hunters while we are there. It is the kind of adventure most people believe is out of their reach, but it is in fact quite the amazingly affordable hunting value, reasonable dollar for dollar for the extraordinary experience. Once you witness RANCHO ENCONTADO, you will have lived the dream.

Ted and Toby–father and son day afield.

Family Hunt Celebration

It could not have been a more soul-inspiring day. Here I was, strolling down a long and winding hill-country trail, deep in the heart of Texas, my entire, wonderful family all around me as the glowing winter sun filled our hearts with the American Dream fire. Daughters Sasha and Starr joined their brothers Toby and Rocco in a full belly laugh riot that is worth its weight in gold to Shemane and me. The evening before, my Queen of the Forest wife had arrowed a beautiful eight-point buck of her own, and Toby had captured the whole thing on videotape for our *Spirit of the Wild* TV show. The nightly YO Ranch BBQ celebration had gone a little later than usual, but we were back in the wild again, right where we belong, for a perfect afternoon and another round of the sacred hunt all together. It was as good as it gets.

Eleven-year-old Rocco Winchester was toting his Remington Model Seven .243 sniper rifle, and we were going to share a hunting blind for a few hours where the live oak groves rolled into the broken canyon lands of this historical YO Ranch terrain. There was a slight nip in the air, but the clear skies let the sun shine down on us, bringing warmth and comfort to our wild-zone party. We made our way to an elevated deer blind, where its ample roominess allowed us to all relax comfortably for a long day together. There's only one hope for the Nugent family to realistically expect wildlife to come anywhere near us when we are together, for we are a crazy bunch, always getting out of hand with laughter and outrageously funny stories. The Blynd, an enclosed weatherproof coop, provided adequate concealment and a grand party ensued. Our laughter was augmented with the songs of many birds, and

Shemane—Queen of the Forest.

great video of distant deer and turkey kept us entertained for the next four hours.

As various critters were observed in and out of the distant scrub, I was able to educate my clan about the history of thriving exotic species here in the wilds of Texas. We saw beautiful blackbuck antelope and axis deer from India, fallow deer from Europe, sika deer from Asia, Barbary sheep, oryx, eland and zebra from Africa and more. All these magnificent creatures are more abundant in Texas than they are in their original homelands for the simple reason that they are valued as renewable resources here and they are not there. Go figure. We home-school Rocco, and I would wager there is no science or biology lesson in environmentalism available that is anywhere near as effective as this ultimate hands-on hunting experience. We took it all in together, deep into our proud hunting-family hearts and souls. We were having a wildlife binocular feeding frenzy. Now that's a perfect Nugent party if ever there was one.

With a small group of handsome whitetail deer poking for acorns under a nearby oak grove in the stretching shadows, the final fiery glow of the setting sun splashed a reflective shine on orange hide way out there. Toby zeroed in with the video camera while the rest of us examined the trio of stunning axis deer about three hundred yards away. Rocco immediately settled his rifle's bipod on a small window ledge and peered through his 14x scope. We all identified the big buck at the same time and I asked Rocco how he felt about the long shot. I knew it was at the limits of his shooting practice back home, but as a dedicated rifleman, I also knew his marksmanship skills were up to the task at hand. He confirmed his confidence in getting his crosshairs to lock onto the now-stationary buck, and I told him to take his shot when he felt certain of his steadiness. One more step, and the big deer would be below the far-off ridgeline. Rocco's chest heaved in and out, his right thumb clicked off the safety and the rifle bucked. Instantly, my binoculars told me that he had nailed the buck perfectly behind the shoulder. With one lunge and a leap, the buck piled up in twenty feet, stone dead.

Well, to say the blind erupted in joyous whoops and hollers is an understatement for sure. Tribe Nuge was jubilant and we all hi-stepped it 312 paces out across the Texas veldt to recover and admire Rocco's trophy in that beautiful shimmer of a hunter's dusk. The golden light caressing the landscape and all of us at once was the perfect frosting on a perfect cake. Rocco's 95-grain Winchester bullet had punched the near three hundred-pound deer exactly where he said it would, killing the majestic animal instantly. Even without the gorgeous sunset, I would have glowed perfectly anyway.

Great video footage and photographs captured the precious, happy family moments and powerful memories forever. The trophy antlered beast was then gently loaded into the truck to be processed into more delicious family-sized packages. Axis deer is some of the best-tasting venison there is, and we all congratulated and thanked Rocco for a job well done.

We went on to enjoy more hunts together that season, like we do every year. I cannot express the deep, soulful gratification we experience on these family adventures together. Something very special happens in this natural environment as a family. Instead of saying good-bye to your tribe as you head out on this hunt or that, consider upgrading this special time by making as many hunts as you can a family affair. Over the years since we have been organizing our Sunrize Safaris for entire families, many have expressed this same wonderful feeling. A tribal, primal calm brings out the very best in everybody, and some of the most meaningful conversations and experiences we've had as a family have taken place at various hunting camps around the country. In this day and age of intense scheduling and crazy pace, I prescribe peaceful time in the wild together to bring a family closer together and upgrade and increase the happy times together. Life is a BBQ. These grand family hunting adventures are the sauce for the soul.

Frozen Pork
of the Virgin Tundra

A trillion brilliant sparkles erupted before us, like a sea of fiery diamonds, the hoarfrost beaming exploding crystals of sunlight across the stunning snow-blind landscape. Ice-cold fireworks danced in a frenzy of pulsating shapes and textures everywhere. I blinked to keep my eyes from catching fire, but gleefully ate up the heavenly dynamo for all it was worth. Each cluster of puckerbrush shined aglow against the snowy white backdrop of fields, fence rows and forests. The prickled multi-flora rose bushes were Spirit Jewelry for the gods of thunder. Everything had a shimmer, especially my soul, for I was treading ever so lightly into the hinterland of Ma Nature's frozen icebox, exposing my inner and outer self to one of the wild world's most amazing extremes. I crave extreme. I live extreme. I am extreme. As extreme as I can be, but humbled by this mind-boggling display of danger-

Wild boar, Sunrize Acres, Michigan, 1997

ous beauty. And make no mistake, no matter how artfully attractive to the human eyes and sensual radar, a numbing sunrise at twenty below zero is a force to reckon with any old time you play with it. Add the outrage of big, mean, nasty Austrian and Russian wild boar somewhere out there to the snarling scenario, and the reality of tooth, fang and claw is no joking matter. I like my pork pissed off and pure, and hunting these majestic creatures with the bow and arrow never lets me down. My ponytail was at full mast, frozen solid in total predator Tedator alert. It felt good to be alive. Extremely.

Crunching forward, careful step after careful step, as slowly and quietly as we could, Renegade Archery's Bill Weisner and I stalked the edge of the sacred Nugent forest, giddy with anticipation for the encounter with the gnarly, toothy beasts of primal lore. A steady curtain of big snowflakes cascaded down upon us, making an already gorgeous setting come to life with a vibrancy that is unique to the eye candy

151

of a Michiganiac snowstorm. Our predator tracks broke virgin ground, plunging a foot deep into the untouched white of season four; winter. Michigan is known as the Winter, Water, Wonderland, and we sure as hell were not examining a promotional postcard here. Nosireebob! We were extremely hands-on with this masterpiece of winter, and celebrating every step we took.

We paused at the confluence of two high hogback ridges, and were surprised to see tracks in the fresh snow just the other side of a giant tangle of blow-down treetops. In a still-steaming, dugout depression beneath the heavy limbs, we examined a fresh, still-warm bed of scattered forest debris, hog piss and prehistoric coarse hair. A peppering of big, scattered tracks from apparently four or five good-sized pigs straightlined down the ridge due west, heading for the thickest habitat in the region. With heavy snow still falling, we knew they had just fled ahead of us, certainly not more than a moment before. With Bill's wife Sandy and Big Jim both operating digital vidcams, we decided to split up in pairs, and like good Marines, adapt and overcome. Semper Fidelis all the way.

Bill and Sandy slowly cut northwest into the whiteout, and Jim and I backtracked and circled southwest, keeping a solid crosswind in our favor. Before you could blink, Sandy and Bill were gobbled up by curtain of the falling snow. My SnakeSkin Illusions snow camo outfit made me virtually invisible as well. With the abstract snakeskin patterns of speckled black against the basic white background, even the camera lost me in the depths of the winter woods. Cool. This would be a great benefit for getting into arrow range of an ultra-spooky, uppity wild boar. My confidence soared.

Hour after frozen hour, we glassed the beautiful world around us. Though much time elapsed without a hog sighting, being in the belly of this amazing winter beast was wonderful unto itself. Jim captured some of the most amazing snowscape footage of what can only be described as God's own black-and-white artwork for the soul! We found ourselves stopping often, simply standing still, scanning all around, and absorbing this uniquely amazing feeling of aliveness. One with the wind, but a pawn in the perfection of creation, we were following God's work orders to the best of our ability. It was heavenly.

We encountered our first sounder of toothy bulldozers late in the morning. Their dark calico hides made them quite visible in the snowy woods. We watched them for a long while as they grunted and plowed along into the heavy timber ahead of us. There were about a dozen of the beasts, and every one of them was a massive beauty. We had to balance our desire to get into bow range with the reality of some noisy, crusted snow underfoot, and we never did get a shot. Cat-and-mouse tactics prevailed throughout the first half of the day, when we eventually made our way back to the warmth of the Sunrize Acres cabin, its woodburner heat a most welcome relief to Jim and I. Unbeknownst to the two of us, Bill and Sandy were in the thick of things in the distant forest as their own exciting porkmonster encounter unfolded in that not-so-quiet wilderness.

Bill and Sandy had also taken it slow and easy all morning, coming upon a large sounder of assorted pig life in the towering oak ridge about midday. They got lucky, and with a steady snarl of snowflakes assisting their careful stalk, they were able to keep a giant boulder between them, and close the distance to a comfortable twenty-five yards from the biggest boar in the bunch. Truly one of America's best instinctive archers, BearCrazy Bill yanked back the bowstring on his sixty-five-pound Renegade recurve and sent a razor-sharp Nugent Blade square through the beast's ribs. As if that were not exciting enough, as that huge boar erupted headlong into the thicket, another monster, totally unaware of Bill and Sandy's presence, got a whiff of fresh blood and tore after the mortally wounded boar and attacked it with a vengeance. Losing blood fast, the wounded boar fought valiantly, but Bill was able to get in another perfect arrow post haste, and bring an end to the rumble in the jungle. Sandy captured the entire outrage on digital tape, and it will make a fascinating Spirit of the Wild TV show that no one will ever forget.

When Jim and I rendezvoused with the Weisners at dusk, we celebrated this most fulfilling experience with a rousing photo session and the retelling of every blow by blow detail of this wonderful day afield. It took all of us with all we had to lift this four hundred-pound mammoth into the big F250 4X4, and never before did a troop of adventurers so appreciate a hot shower and hot meal before the fireplace like we did.

Naked Soul

Light, friendly rain and pitch-black pre-dawn sky forebode one nasty, snotty swamp run. The steady blowing mist kept the big steel mallard weathervane on rock-solid point due west, slightly aglow in a fogged barnlight. I had the Browning 12 and a box of three-inch steel 3s already tossed in the back of the truck with my patched LaCrosse waders and a heap of old, beat-up decoys, excitedly turning to get the Labrador pack from their kennels when it hit me. This would be a great morning to ambush a buck on the mystical hogback ridge! Plan B, take five.

Luckily, the dogs didn't know I was thinking waterfowl, and they snoozed soundly in their insulated boxes while I snuck back into the house to swap shotgun for bow and arrows. I had a hunch. It's that hunter's sixth sense, an instinctual gift that us modern Gonzo rockers have to get back in touch with to maximize our primal moves. Hand-to-hand combat with the prehistoric spirit, not in conflict, but as one. Tooth, fang and claw in all its glory. And that primal scream erupts in me often. Uprising. I have learned to appreciate it and always respond. A few precious minutes were lost in my change of plans, and now I would have to outrun the oncoming eastern glow to my favorite west-wind set. It is times like this that the smile spreads uncontrollably, the adrenalin surges and an inner charge drives the hunter. It takes everything I got to

11-point whitetail, Dr. Brocks, Texas, 2003

keep from running into myself, to remain reasonably calm and collected in anticipation of the arrival of the beast. It overwhelms. As it should.

The familiar, wet forest floor helped me maneuver the dark timber by Braille, silently, for a stealthy arrival at the huge old white oak tree my pre-season scouting had determined was the killer ambush hot spot for this wind. It was beautiful. High on a massive, glacier-cut ridgeline overlooking an expansive sawgrass marshfield, my eagle-eye perch was positioned to not only access any deer traveling the historical rutted trails on both sides of the razorback, but provide a panoramic view for nearly a half mile out into the impenetrable swamp to the river. Thank you God! You sure do grand work! It was still pitch dark, and I felt as if I belonged. Because I do.

Carefully, I tied my bow to the pull-rope and slowly climbed aboard the elevated stimuli zone of the wild. This is how I have always gotten high. Nature surely heals but her preventive medicine is just what the good Doctor Wild ordered. With my full-body safety harness securely fastened, I settled in the rock-solid API treestand for what seemed to be my zillionth vigil of the season. This is very exciting stuff, my friends. Us hunters are genuinely moved just to be out here. The mist in the face, the air you taste, the dark that envelopes, the smells that flare, the stirring sounds, the breeze that invigorates, and those runaway visions of things to come, all make for an elixir of sensual stimuli the likes of which ain't available outside of childbirth. Soul stirring Spirit of the Wild stuff for warriors in the game of life.

Only a wildlife addict would sit twenty feet up, strapped in and snuggled by the gnarly embrace of a one-hundred-year-old burr oak tree, gripping a bow and arrow with the cold rain streaming down his nose. But this is the hunter's life! After all, life is not a smooth pond upon which we gaze, but rather snorting whitewater rapids we oughtta be breaststroking wildly in, never missing an adventurous lick! Couches are for Michael Jackson fans. YOWZA! YOWZA! And pass the Tedstosterone in megawads. I was goin' down for the third time. Again. I of the storm.

Sunrize never came to be. The sky went from black to a barely legal shooting light, dark grey as the precipitation slowed down and the bird life kick-started the reluctant day. The mental ponytail was at ritualistic full mast on its own accord, and my predator radar breathed invisible fire all around. A hawk shared my airspace, a squirrel my supporting limb. Supersonic wood ducks whistled past my head, following the river course from a night of acorn orgy. Distant crowspeak soothed me. A doe with twin fawns cautiously picked their way deep into the bowels of protective tree-rimmed puckerbrush hell for the day. A sea of gold, bronze and yellow grasses weaved artfully through black timber. Deep green tamaracks and hemlocks protruded up from off-white dogwoods and willow, melting into the gunmetal sky overhead. The dark purple weaving ribbon of river smoked unreal fog, filtering into the whole picture. Walt Disney wishes. Ray Charles can see these graphics. Nature breathed life into our world. I counted my blessings again. Excuse me whilst I kiss the sky.

Then I felt it. Zero warning for mere mortal city-man senses. A mystical intuition, like a mother knowing a child's thoughts. And the manifestation for a reasoning predator with a soul emerged, fangs first. Could I perform like the pure predator, my brother, the cougar? Or would the "advanced" human brain get in my way? I dared not turn, but stretched my eyes as far left as they could possibly go in their sockets without moving my head. At first only a mini-flicker within the screen of thick vegetation was maybe observed! The silence grew deafening. A peace blanketed the wild. A tufted titmouse landed in my face to provide a little comic relief, but I concentrated on the moment at hand. Time zoomed on but stood still. Then he was in the dangerzone. Grooming himself at thirty yards on the wide-open trail gave me a dynamic view of his majesty. His seven-point antlers were brown, with white, ivory-like tips, crowning his handsome contrasting facial markings. He was bold. Muscled but dainty. Cocky yet alert. This trail had provided him secure travel for two years and he appeared relaxed and confident. The wind did not betray me. My Mossy Oak camo turned me into indigenous fauna. The Great Spirit accepted me and my thoughts, spurring me on. We deserved each other.

I was well zoned. All I looked at was the crease behind his foreleg. As if Fred Bear called his name, the stag turned to look away. Perfect! My bow arm mirrored his head swing into shoot position and my arrow nock nestled tight into the corner of my pursed lips like a million times before. For a nanosecond I blanked like a zombie, the buck distorted at the end of a distorted, dreamlike tunnel. I forced my focus back to my bow, the arrow and the deer's armpit, pulled my back muscles to the max, leaned slightly forward at the waist, and the arrow was off. He nearly turned inside-out trying to pivot, but the 600-grain zebra-striped projectile was in and out of his vitals before his awesome defense mechanism could outflash the 250-foot-per-second aluminum 2315 arrow, white turkey feathers vanishing into the twelve-ring of his heart, perfecto! A Motown snare drum punched a beat like a Neanderthal heart's first thump.

The birds, the wind, my heartbeat, pulse and breathing, everything, stopped. The forest scrub devoured two hundred pounds of venison on the hoof, pronto. I sighed. Breathing came back smoothly. A small bird returned. I could hear the river again. I rested my bow on my lap and leaned back against the damp bark in slow motion. A clockwork camo. 2001: a Nuge odyssey. My eyes stared at the point of his final departure and I pulled my facemask down around my neck, a long, deep sigh whooshing from my open, grinning mouth. I just sat there calm, yet anxious. Smiling, silent. My watch read 8:48. The hours had gone by quickly. I closed my eyes to say a prayer of thanx and replayed the shot. No doubt the mystical flight of the arrow was true. No need to wait. Slowly, very slowly and methodically, I reversed my morning procedure, lowering my bow and climbing down, taking it all in. My red-coated arrow was stuck deep in terra firma, feathers blood-soaked and bubbly. Confidence soared. The leafy forest blanket showed clear sign of his exploding scramble, the blood spoor accenting each deep, disruptive, cloven divot. His escape trail stayed right on the game path the whole way, but I had to creep on hands and knees, snaking through the lower multi-flora rose brambles for a dozen yards here and there, giving up my Browning cap twice to the unforgiving thorns. Inches from the ground, the pungent, wet, earthy autumn smell was wonderful. I came to truly appreciate the role and joy of the alpha wolf and his pack. Wolves and bloodhounds are truly my Blood Brothers. All senses were connected and on fire.

I nearly crawled on top of him, surprised by his presence in my face. He appeared as if sleeping on his side, peacefully. His death run of fifty yards must have lasted but a flash. No more than seconds. This made me happy. Fast food in its purest form. A flood of emotions, as always, poured over me. I just sat next to him, stroking his tawny winter coat, impervious to the strait-jacket briar tangle that embraced us as one, lifting his antlers in my bare hands, counting the tines twice. I marveled as always at this awesome, perfect package of natural, hi-protein fresh flesh sustenance from the Great Spirit for my family. More than forty-five years' worth of stirring memories of family hunts consumed me. Xtreme at its most intense. Ultra alive.

Many missed shots flashed back. A small, happy boy with a long bow. A smiling dad. A walk with Fred Bear. A hunt with a son. Red dogs. A caveman at a circle of fire. A haunch roasting over fire. Paintings on stone walls. A handshake. Buffalo. A footprint in the mud at river's edge. Red braves on horseback. Leather-strapped hands, bleeding, bonding two Blood Brothers forever. Black hunters dancing. Antler tips protruding from a snowbank. Wind. A circling eagle. Naked soul.

Nyala–The Most Beautiful Antelope in the World

You could feel the intense pride of sixty-six-year-old Afrikaner landowner Wally Nels as he gently wheeled the combi along the winding, grassy trail, thru rich, colorful South African scrub. Record rainfall had produced an explosion of vegetation along the Klasserie River here, creating a jungle-like setting of perfect, dense, wildlife habitat. To constant, vibrant singing of colorful bird life, a trio of beautiful nyala ewes nibbled at the base of a giant, light-grey barked tree at river's edge, and casually looked up at us from a short thirty yards. I studied their stunning beauty through my binoculars, amazed at the white lines flowing down each side of their orange, graceful bodies. The two mature gals weighed around two hundred pounds each, with the yearling about half that. They fed off towards the gurgling rapids and disappeared into the green thicket.

Giraffe, South Africa, 1999

Wally explained why he had such a high population of the locally rare nyala antelope on his more than ten thousand acres, because of the twisting, flowing riverine topography that borders the Klasserie. This secretive, special antelope needs wetlands and extra-thick jungle-like habitat to thrive, and they, along with the abundant impala, warthog, kudu, wildebeest, waterbuck, bushbuck, zebra, buffalo, eland, giraffe, duiker, steenbok and numerous other African critters were well cared for here. Though occasional animals were killed quietly with a silenced .22 to feed his family and staff over the years, there had never been any organized hunting allowed on his grounds, and the animals had come to accept Wally and his wife, Sissy, on their daily drives in the small van. We drove right up to within feet of many animals. The moment the vehicle slowed down, however, the game would move off, and if a person tried to step out of the vehicle, they would run. These were, after all, historical prey animals in wild Africa, with lion, leopard, cheetah, jackal, hyenas and man pursuing them for food and sport since the beginning of time. Wally figured he had trained them, to some degree, to avoid people on foot so they would escape the local poachers who trespassed and killed game illegally. Wally knows his stuff. This would make extremely difficult bowhunting.

And he cares deeply about the condition of the habitat that supports his wildlife, which is why he and I were studying his diverse, undulating terrain. The nyala had overpopulated in the last few years, and the over-impacted browse line of preferred vegetation was most apparent. The more aggressive nyala had eaten so much that kudu and other game were beginning to die off, and Wally knew it was essential to reduce the number of animals on his ground before catastrophe struck. Harvest the surplus to maintain balance to save the majority. It's so simple, it's stupid.

A giant old bull giraffe had to be killed just yesterday because of a terrible wound he caused himself by scratching his head too aggressively, opening a bloody sore. Flies immediately began to lay eggs in the wound, and the result was a sickening infestation of maggots in the old bull's head, literally eating the agonized beast to death. Slow, prolonged, horrible death. Tooth, fang and claw are the law of the land in the wild. Not a damn thing we can do about it. Almost nothing. Like the thinking beings we are, man will respond to flood warnings by filling sandbags and saving his family and home. So, too, must we intervene when Mother Nature threatens other life. A well-placed 200-grain .30-06 bullet humanely ended the old bull's life in a matter of seconds, in deference to the long, agony-riddled weeks it would have taken by the wicked hand of Nature. Though our intervention denied the scavengers a huge meal, the local natives were very appreciative for the large amount of meat they received from the giraffe's flesh. The natural world knows no peaceful end. The only death out there is violent and nasty. It works while we sleep, but man can and, when possible, must do better. We are proud to be involved. Peace through superior intellect and firepower is a reality I subscribe to.

Nyala, South Africa, 1999

All of a sudden, as we rounded a brushy bend in the trail, a large, chocolate nyala bull appeared, head down, grazing, about fifty yards ahead in the reeds at the edge of small grove of trees. Wally kept the rpms of the vehicle's motor constant, as I quietly bailed out into the deep grasses. The combi continued on, and the bull lifted his head to give it but a moment's glance. I slowly peeked above the brush as the nyala returned to feed. The wind was solid from the north, and if I could stay beneath the scrubline, crosswind, I may be able to get within bow range. I thought catlike predator moves.

I had tried and failed many stalks so far, and now I was given another chance. I pushed the bow ahead as I crawled through the tunnel of reeds and grasses. At one point, my foot sank two feet into the lily pad-like vegetation with a gurgling sound, and I was afraid it would alert the trophy bull. Ever so slowly, cautious foot by cautious foot, I closed the distance, 'til only twenty yards separated us. The three hundred-plus pound antelope was consumed with feeding on the extraordinary supply of greenery, with, as if placed by the hand of fate, a dead tree trunk covering his face. He would raise his head for a look-see every few minutes, but my ultra-slow moves had so far paid off, and now, at fifteen yards, I carefully removed a 440-grain Carbon Express 400 arrow with white feathers from my bow quiver, nocked it, and raised up for the moment of truth. Just yesterday, I had missed a large, trophy impalla ram at about thirty yards, so I reminded myself to focus on "the spot" as I completed my seventy-three-pound draw. My bow hand shook extremely, and I felt like a buck-fever idiot, as my arrow wobbled all around the majestic animal's torso, knowing I couldn't shoot like this. I envisioned John Voigt in the movie *Deliverance*. Not good! I closed my eyes tightly, took a deep breath, opened my eyes, and saw the arrow settle down just under the bull's front legpit. As my trigger finger relaxed into the release, I witnessed the prettiest arrow I have ever delivered, as if in slow motion, fly straight into that vital pocket. Good God, I love that.

With a loud KERTHWACKKK the white feathers appeared angling forward in the middle of his rib cage, and he lurched ahead and vanished into the African scrub. I knew what that meant, and I sighed aloud, standing on my toes to watch his scrambled departure.

As he blazed across a small gap in the tree line, I ran to the high spot on the hill. Through my binoculars I could see the distinctive white lines of his face seventy-five yards out, as he wobbled to and fro, then tipped over sideways, dead in a matter of but a few seconds. I am sure my smile could be seen in Zimbabwe!

I fell to my knees and dropped my head. The one hundred degree humid heat had taken its toll, and I felt at once exhilarated yet exhausted. I picked up movement far to my right to see Wally waving his clenched fist with a signal of jubilation. I waved back and slowly made my way over to the old man, where we relived the entire episode from each other's perspective. Wally had been suspicious of bowhunting as a legitimate harvesting tool, but now I could feel his excitement as he recounted his amazement at the quickness of the kill. The bow and arrow had a new supporter.

I walked back to my nyala and lifted his stunningly beautiful head in my hands, admiring the twenty-six-inch, ivory-tipped, spiraling horns and gorgeous facial markings of Africa's most beautiful antelope, prized for his succulent flesh for the dinner table. I marveled at the graphic and artistic markings on his face and body. His legs were a reddish brown, with darker stockings accenting the cloven hooves. A long mane of chocolate brown gave way to lighter, creamy guard hairs on his neck and back. White lines traversed his deep chest and back. His face had white spots where the native hunters claim God laid his fingers upon creation of this handsome animal. Wally and I found ourselves standing there mezmerized by the dynamic for the longest time. In our silence was a certain prayer for the wild things of Africa.

With the conclusive effectiveness of the bow and arrow proven once again, Wally was ready to open his land to visiting American bowhunters. He liked how non-intrusive this stealthy style of hunting was in harmony with his land. He saw that the wildlife did not become alerted by the quiet bowhunting technique, and how peaceful his property remained, while at the same time, reducing the herd and the pressure on the delicate, finite habitat.

With abundant populations of many indigenous big-game species, Wally offers some dream bowhunting opportunities. We spent considerable time setting up tree-stands and ground-blind locations on waterholes, game trails and river crossings to optimize closerange critter encounters for bowhunters, and the experience is one of the very best available anywhere today. I bow killed three zebra and the trophy nyala, and have big plans for our next adventure there. It will only get better.

If you are interested in nyala, kudu, zebra, wildebeest, eland, bushbuck, impalla, warthog, bush pig, Cape buffalo, giraffe, and a unique, powerful, wild African experience, Wally has the key to paradise. Though his property is bowhunting only, great gun hunting is available on adjoining lands nearby, where handgunners, rifle and blackpowder hunting can be had. We organize trips every year in comfortable, even luxurious bushcamps near Hoedspruit, South Africa, and it is a trip you will never forget. Call Sunrize Safaris and get the details for this adventure of a lifetime at 800-343-4868. Your wake-up call will be the roar of the lion, and a lullaby of hippo grunts will lull you to sleep each night. Africa is alive and well and offering what many believe to be the best-ever safari opportunities in history. My nyala kill could very well be the best, most exciting sixty minutes of my bowhunting life. Join us in Africa and discover yours.

Rock 'n' Roll
Wild Boar Hunting–Hogmando

With fire in my eyes and an ever present tasty wisp of prehistoric foam bubbling at the corners of my mouth, I have madly and gleefully chased packs of wildly belling hounds over hill and dale, up ridiculous vine-gripped mountainsides and through the nastiest, puckerbrushed, flesh-ripping, briar-infested hellhole muckzonia swamps a sane white man dare not tread. The harder the run, the quicker the foam takes on a handsome cherry swirl appearance I'm told.

I love the full-throttled adrenalin-pumping hot pursuit of bear, lion, coons, housecats, escaped chimps, small children, scared women and everything else that can be legally chased and/or hunted. But the ultimate Rock 'n' Roll hellraiser for me is when there is some stinking, godawful putrid, tantalizingly pissed-off, mud-encrusted, musk-saturated, urine-infested fuming swine snapping ivory and hauling non-kosher ass ahead of the hungry spirithounds to bring out the best natural-born killer God ever created in all of us. Where I come from, hot houndsbreath is a spice. And wild pigs are just plain cool as hell. I love to watch 'em, hunt 'em, fight 'em, kill 'em, nut 'em, stab 'em, shoot 'em, slap 'em, gut 'em, bite 'em, eat 'em, know 'em, give 'em the finger and dance naked with 'em, before, during and after the BBQ. When it's time to have some good, clean all-American legal fun and games, bring on the cross-country pork chop slammajamboree. It's like a country and western concert without the bad music. Gotta luv that. Though a rabble-rousing hot-leg run with a pack of God's best-designed fire-eyed, chain-bustin, snort-master trail-blazing howlers is my favorite method of snagging BBQ pork on the hoof, I get

Wild boar, Sunrize Acres, Michigan, 1998

an absolute kick out of every pig-killin' maneuver you can possibly think of. I luv 'em, I run 'em, stalk 'em, kick 'em, wrestle 'em, slap 'em, bait 'em, trap 'em, call 'em, yell at 'em, corner 'em, jump 'em, ambush 'em and surprize 'em backstage at the Grand Old Opry. I love hog hunting so much, I have created my own hunting operation at home so I can have my own wild porkfun any old time I wanna. God bless America and pass the hot sauce!

At my Sunrize Acres Hunt Ranch in Michigan, I have the most beautiful pure Austrian, long-haired, cranky, Rock 'n' Roll, bent-attitude wild boar you have ever laid eyes on, or a knife or a bullet or arrow into. With long, coarse hair in black, brown, red, gold, silver, calico, brindle and varying combinations and shades of all of the above, accented with spectacular razor-sharp ivory jutting out of their prehistoric lips, and a disposition that only me, their mothers and God could love, these huge, ornery beasts are just what the good BBQ doctor ordered for a weary old Rock 'n' Roll guitarboy to cleanse the soul and humble the heart. Besides feeding my family with the best damn, healthy, pure-organic other white flesh known to man, the hunt provides equal protein for the soul. If nature heals, pork exhilarates.

So there I was, back in the pork chop wild again, feeling wild and free, hungry and alive. Perfect as perfect can be. I had my trusty bow and arrows tuned-up, Nugent Blade broadheads as razor sharp as my hunter's mindset, and as physically and psychologically cocked, locked and ready to rock, doc, ultra-primed for some serious

162

hands-on beast harvesting. My mind was right and I was in full-kill mode. The sky was dark and the air was cool, and I had just scared over two million unsuspecting civilians on the not-so-mean streets of America as I wrapped up my 5000th rockout concert, including 133 in the last seven months with KISS, on the number-one rock tour in the free world for the year 2000. I was both beat to a pulp and powered up for the best hunting season of my greasy fifty-two years, as I settled into the towering white oak treestand on my favorite ridge in Nugent Forest. Ahhhhh! I stand up next to the mountain, chop it down with the edge of my hand, indeed!

I couldn't drag my wounded Rock 'n' Roll ass outta bed early this first day home from the long tour, but the wind called my name and I heard her loud and clear, as the ideal southwest wind set me up for an afternoon ambush. If the sounder of handsome hogs I had seen recently repeated their acorn-orgy schedule, I would be porkbound with the hammer down in a short while. With my Rutherford safety harness snuggly attached around my shoulders, butt and hips, I nocked a 500-grain carbon arrow and put on my Primos Mossy Oak camo facemask with almost cocky confidence. I had experienced many a day afield on my sacred Sunrize hunt grounds without getting a shot at anything, but I always seem to believe I will. This day I felt it powerfully. Maybe it was the ever-darkening hunter's sky overhead, accented by the always stimulating, beautiful bird life all about. Maybe it was the long-overdue, intensely anticipated first bowhunt of the fall, or maybe I'm just stupid, but my grinning face and laughing heart could not be denied. I'm hunting baby, and nothing else matters!! Rooted deeply within the always wonderfully positive metaphysical power of the hunt, you couldn't convince me that anything like Janet Reno even existed. Even the oldest, scarred boars looked good compared to Reno. Everything was much too nice. I say YOWZA YOWZA and pass the spirit! Fully erect if you please.

A squadron of flitting, chirping robins staged above me in the leafy treetops, squawking and dive bombing with Tora Tora excitement as the driving instinct to prepare for their annual migration took over. I felt it and joined in as best I could, smiling even more now knowing how connected my natural buoyant position way up high here with them is. They eat worms, I eat pork. Beautiful. My kosher friends notwithstanding, pig meat is grand, natural ultra-yummy chow, and my desire to feed it to my family kicked my hunter's heart into overdrive now as a branch snapped in the distance directly behind me. My ESP hearing amplifiers made up for the forty some-odd years (and I do mean odd) of outrageous sonic bombast Rock 'n' Roll decibel overload abuse, and I turned ultra slowly to have a look-see. Through my ever-handy Leupold binos, I could see dark, animated forms down the tangled ravine, due south about seventy-five yards away in and out of the thick stuff. Oh yeah! A pork parade comin' my way! A grunting, huffing undertow resonated in the depths of the big timber. How lovely.

The sturdy API ladder stand was quiet enuf for me to turn hard left, positioning me for a possible arrowshot if they continued on their current path. For a while, they did, but before they cut the distance in half, the big black lead beast led them away from me to the east and I had to squirm silently around the tree the other way. Much to my surprise, when I turned left, there was a huge grey, silvery old boar directly under my perch, rooting and gobbling up the sweet white acorns that were scattered across the September forest floor. His huge head jerked up on point and alert as I froze in midspin, hoping I didn't blow it. After a momentary pause, the swine couldn't resist the succulent mast all around him and returned to pigging out. Ever so cautiously I tried to get on him, but by the time I got straightened out, he was too far right and I could not get the bow thataway. Had he been the only hog there, I suppose I could have stood up and pivoted hard for a shot, but lo and behold, an even bigger, mud-encrusted black boar was bringing up the rear, about to enter my ideal shotzone to the left as he, too, fed on the ultimate acorn bait. God baits. Go figure.

The moment really made me appreciate the extra effort I invest each spring, fertilizing my white oak groves in these family woods. Typically, oaks only produce acorns every other year or so, but since I began with my simple triple-19 fertilizing efforts, we get a great crop every year, and the deer, turkey, squirrel, grouse, wood ducks, mallards and hogs go wild for them. So do I! And it looked like I was about to get me some acorn-fed pork if I played my hunter's cards right. Blackjack!

I held my breath as the big boy snorted and grunted amongst the colored leaves and forest debris, vacuuming protein from Ma Nature's pantry below. I gracefully swung my upright bow along with his movements, and as he stopped to root a spot, I came to full draw and began my ritualistic bowhunter's prayer. My eyes and my pointing arrow were one with his forward rib cage, a third of the way up from his bellyline behind his foreleg and shoulder, and as I kissed my release trigger and finished " . . . and of the Holy Spirit, Amen," my shoulder muscles pulled tight and my arrow zinged across the thirty yards square into the muddy hair I was looking at with a solid THUMPH, in and out of his tuff, rugged torso in an instant. With a Courtney Love-like squeal and a jump, he scrambled wildly around the wooded rise, as the previously all-white, now all-red arrow stuck into the ground beyond him. Other hogs erupted behind me with a clamor and a chorus of grunting swine speak, but my hairy pork chop express slammed head-on into a giant maple tree with a terminal bang, and he kicked his last all within thirty-five yards and three seconds, POA (pork on arrival). The other white meat has landed. Shopping with Ted. Always an adventure. Always good food.

I watched the other gorgeous Austrian hogs mill about in pig-like confusion, much like a throng of stoned, lost Grateful Dead fans, 'til they melted away into the dark forest beyond. I breathed a happy sigh of relief and looked to the now burning-red and orange sun-setting heavens in solemn thanx to the good Lord for this awesome system of sustained yield Tooth, Fang and Claw truth. How cool is this?

The three-hundred-pound truck of a pig was so damn ugly, he was beautiful.

Though he hadn't actually torched any children that I knew of, we called him Janet anyway. The resemblance was frightening. The only thing missing was the purple dress and he-man haircut. Long, gnarly calico boarhair graced his muddy grey warrior head, snout and torso. Nearly four inches of sharp-edged fighting ivory sabers protruded from his mean-looking porcine lips. Rips and gouges and scars adorned his entire bulk, and he was a joy to look at. I exposed a roll of film on the stunning beast, gutted him and dragged him into a clearing drenched in the last glow of the day. Magic time for Nature lovers everywhere.

From the expert butchering shop of Joe Nagle in Homer, Michigan, his organic flesh produced the finest breakfast sausage that Bob Evans or Jimmy Dean could ever dream of, and I relive the moving encounter any old time I close my eyes and remember. No wonder I don't watch TV Compared to this dynamic thrill, it all sucks.

No matter where one lives in this wonderful country, we are never far from potential pig adventure. California abounds with great pig hunting. Of course Texas is pig heaven, and the south offers world-class wild-hog hunting for everybody. New Hampshire has a huntable population, as does Illinois, Missouri and Indiana to some degree, since the floods of '89 and '90 set a feral population wild. And they are beauties too. Commercial hog-hunting operations are everywhere, and some are great and some suck. A little homework goes a long way to discover quality hunt camps. My family operates SUNRIZE SAFARIS in response to a gazillion requests for hunting advice from the old Rock 'n' Roll dog. In this book and at tednugent.com, I list my favorite quality operations and personally guided annual hunts. Here are a few of my guaranteed favorites: Sunrize Acres in MI, 800-343-4868; Ken Moody's Clark Range in TN at 800-585-4868; Maurice Chambers in TX at 512-363-4252 or 365-4817; Scott Young in CA 707-579-3078; George Britton in FL at 727-934-7042.

Snowhogs

Damn! It was cold. It was so cold that the fresh snow was so solidly frozen, it had the consistency of tiny, airy, Styrofoam beads. Fortunately, and surprisingly, nothing crunched, and it made for silent stalking as I slowly pussyfooted my way through the icy, breathtaking winter woods. SnoBoy with bow was in search of Beasto McPorksicle; old hairtooth WildBoar McSnort of the frozen wilds his bad self, as pretty as ugly can be.

My sacred deer season in Michigan had finally come to a thrilling, and always heart-wrenching close for yet another glorious fall and wintertime of dream hunting. But now the real fun begins, chasing amazing wild hogs through the deeper winter months. Extremely harsh, even dangerous conditions scare some guys out of the woods, but with an adequately bold predator attitude and the ever-changing and

American bison, 2003

developing clothing technology, there is no such thing as too cold for the modern hunter.

My Browning polar fleece snow camo was good and warm and made me blend invisibly with my winter, watery wonderland surroundings. I not only felt as one with nature, I even looked it. Omaha's Carol Davis long johns and LaCrosse Arctic footwear insulated me completely from the bone-freezing ten below zero windswept hell-frio. I was so snug in my quality hunting clothing, the only danger for me was getting sweaty if I moved too fast. Nanuck of the Great North wishes!

Proper stalking is ninety-five percent looking and five percent cautious moving. All movement must be accomplished with ultra-predator-like stealth, for all prey animals, even the lowly ugly/handsome swine, is geared for full-flight survival escape capabilities. I have learned over the many years of trial and error that a foot hunter cannot possibly move too slowly when still-hunting or stalking. It is imperative that the hunter identifies his prey before the quarry senses a predator presence. The nearly impenetrable radar of ears, eyes and nose of all game species are augmented with an unidentifiable yet mystical network of sensory perceptions that truly boggles the human mind. If I hear one more city kid call wildlife "defenseless," I think I'm gonna puke! All the defenseless critters are dead and gone and found on your grocer's shelves. The rest of 'em are still getting away ninety percent of the time. That's why we call it hunting. So be it.

With judicious binocular work, my eyes gobbled up every inch of terrain all around me. I had a slight advantage in that the snowy white topography should provide a dramatic background, causing your average dark-colored wild boar to stand out. But I dared not rely on that presumption, for I had seen huge black beasts appear seemingly out of nowhere more times than not, without a hint of adequate hiding cover to be found. Game is like that. Even a pitch-black hog has enough various shades, textures and hues to help him disappear in average habitat. What the snow really provided was an advantage for me, the predator. Completely dressed head to toe in broken-white camo, I had a wild hair of advantage in pursuit of wild pigs, with their somewhat less-than-perfect eyesight. Though hogs can see the slightest movement, their overall vision is not as inescapable as that of their brother the deer or elk. Slow and easy was my best trick.

Slow and easy is not just the best approach for getting in arrow range of game, but ultimately the best lick for optimizing the overall outdoor experience. As one pauses between careful steps, an amazing array of observations become apparent and fill the mind, heart and soul with powerful, spirit-cleansing beauty and joy. The slower and fewer my steps, the more I see, hear, feel and ultimately celebrate. So every conscientious step of the hunt provides a smorgasbord of sensual stimuli and lessons of the wild that increase our level of respect and sense of duty to the Spirit of the Wild. My spirit cup runneth over every time I leave the pavement.

This day, like every moving day afield, brought dynamic encounters of the wild

Wild boar, Sunrize Acres, Michigan, 1999

kind at every turn. As I paused in a deep ravine surrounded by the most beautiful snow-covered world you could ever dream of, a trio of crows came overhead out of nowhere, screaming and cawing up a storm as they dive-bombed their arch-enemy, Mr. Predator, the Redtail hawk. Mr. TuffGuy Hawk seemed to take great joy in aggravating the black-winged rats, as he sat poised in the branches above, calm and cocky as can be while the crows carried on furiously. I wondered if the crows ever really attacked or hurt a hawk. I have watched them for years and all the crows ever do is fly about madly, raising hell, but never actually getting too close. It's wild and fascinating.

While all this was going on, a fat bushy-tailed fox squirrel, oblivious to my invisible presence, hopped and scurried within a few feet of my position, digging intently into the deep snow looking for last fall's acorn stash. He probed about all around me for a long time before ambling off into the towering white oak grove up the ridge and out of sight. On most occasions when I am bowhunting big game, I will take advantage of these close encounters with other legal game to arrow one for the pot, but this time, for unknown reasons, I just watched the little booger make his way thru the snow.

And a good call it was, for the little limb rat had barely disappeared up the trunk of a distant oak when I picked up a slight grunt to my south. Slowly elevating my Leupold binoculars to my eyes, I focused into the tangle of multi-flora rose thickets fifty yards behind me and there he was, Sir Tuskerdo McPork!

My bone-numbing, patient standing still for so long in silence, appreciating the wild around me with my well-tuned predator radar, had paid off again. From a slight depression in the series of timbered ridges I was hunting this beautiful day came the unmistakable prehistoric hoary shape of one hell of a gorgeous Austrian boar. With the wind crossing away from him and my Mossy Oak snocamo doing its job of concealment, the old toothy Lord of the Swamp ambled slowly in my direction, rooting noisily as he aggressively power-tilled the frozen ground, desperate for winter-locked remnant feed. The crows abruptly ceased their caterwauling and silently winged off into the hinterland beyond the giant trees as I slowly extracted an arrow from my bow quiver. Without taking my eyes off the approaching beast, my arrow found its nock onto my bowstring as if with a mind of its own and my predator mind's eye scanned the world for porcine vitals. I breathed heavily now. We appeared on a perfect collision course but I had seen this before without getting a shot. I readied myself intensely.

He came on slowly, a beastly grunt per step to further antagonize my psyche. I always say a short Prayer for the Wild Things as I prepare to draw my bow, but I could feel the pressure building as he entered the dangerzone, so I took a deep breath and said an advance prayer now. He came. Ultra-slowly I lifted my bow and stared a hole into his chest. The Great Spirit's hand came from above, guiding the beautiful boar's head behind a single stump at twenty-five yards, covering his radar eyeballs, and my bow made the final elevation inline with the Mack Truck shoulder. I was one with the wind. There was no world outside my tractor-beam vision to his heart. The planets aligned and time stood still as the full drawn arrow snugged tightly into the corner of my mouth like a primal scream within, and I finished my hunter's prayer. In this totally snow-covered place, the heavy-white insulation helped my Sims-equipped bow discharge with nary a sound, the slice-punch of the razor-sharp Nugent Blade against muscled flesh the only sound in the wild, punctuated with the most wonderful deep, guttural beastly squeal you could ever imagine. In a dreamlike slow-motion explosion, the giant hog spun violently, the white feathers of the 500-grain projectile now against his massive shoulder, blood showing instantly as he slammed into the old oak stump, regained his footing and snorted madly off into the winter wonderland from whence he came. Whew!! I can breathe now.

I knew the shot was real good, and I felt a powerful tingling sensation all over. I have killed many magnificent big game animals in my lifetime, but each and every encounter and occurrence is truly moving. It takes a while to regain one's composure. This killing game for the dinner table is serious stuff, and I for one will never let its impact be diminished. I stood there for a few moments, smiling and shaking, and actually chuckling little laugh. I had done it. Luck had put me in this ravine, the Great Spirit had brought us together, and my lifetime of hunting and archery discipline had brought the good luck to its proper and ultimately gratifying conclusion. I wiped my nose with the back of my sleeve and let out a whoosh of visible breath, clenched my fist and audibly exalted a proud predator "YOWZA!" from my guts. My body began to relax.

I strolled over to the tattered stump, now covered on the south side with blood and hair. I knelt down and examined the evidence all around. A single set of parallel tracks meandered to this place, where his explosive departure tore up the ground like a bomb had gone off. The virgin snowfield now had a beautiful abstract artwork of splashed red sprayed along the bulldozed trail to the southeast, almost like but much more impressive than some post-modern artwork in a New York City gallery. And I could smell this sensually stimulating dynamo nature art. The pungent aroma of musky pig stench accented with blood on the snow and fresh-rotted oak stump torn asunder was an orgy for the senses. I slumped to the ground and actually sniffed the shrapnel of brown, yellow, grey and black around me. God, it was grand. I sat there taking it all in. Life itself soared on the wings of a bird of prey.

The blood trail was a graphic Five Star crimson-on-white beauty, taking me farther yet into the wonderment of a natural winter predator's postcard dream. I took my good old time, pausing to snack on a Three Musketeers candy bar and a sip of hi-protein juice from my water bottle. It was like a damn Spiritual picnic. The crows called again in the distance. There seemed to be a nuthatch or a downy woodpecker on every tree, hammering away and making their cute little squawking songs. I crossed a scramble of turkey tracks at the bottom of the gully, and deer prints were here and there where a small herd of maybe a dozen or so had moved through the oaks earlier this morning. I could see where the telltale spoor of a lone coyote had followed its hopeful meal a ways, then where he cut off for easier and smaller pickings. My smile grew exponentially with each sensually invigorating step and dynamic soul-expanding moment.

I nearly stepped on my giant hog as I moved around a clump of snow enveloped multi-flora snowcone rose, for he had died in midstep after a one hundred-yard flight. The arrow was still in him, sticking out both sides of his barrel like chest, having taken out both lungs and the main ventricles to his pumpstation. I had provided the beast the most efficient death to be had in the wild. He wasn't badgered and haggled to death, eaten alive by a canine predator. He wasn't torn to shreds by another wild boar in a fight for dominance, territory or breeding rights. He didn't contract a deadly disease and suffer a prolonged death. He didn't grow old and get chewed on by a pack of feral dogs. The gorgeous animal had not been tamed, controlled and caged all his life to be zapped for the canned-ham industry in order to provide for someone's Easter dinner. He had simply been killed cleanly, naturally, in the wild where he lived like a wild animal as God had designed him, brought to bag, full cycle, by my well-placed, razor-sharp arrow. He suffered none whatsoever, and bled to death painlessly in seconds. I was proud to be an active, reasoning predator.

I knelt at his side, stroked his prehistoric, gnarled coarse hair, examined his saber-like tusks and held his magnificent, heavy, handsome beasto head in my hands. With all I had within me, I absorbed the wonderment, anticipation, anxiety, hope, tension, excitement, fear, joy, respect, sights, sounds, smells, thrills, challenge, beauty, stimuli, participation and food that his very being had provided me.

Throughout my sacred ritual of forever imagining, preparing, dreaming, hunting, stalking, tracking, shooting, sensing, killing, trailing, looking, touching, remembering, photographing, gutting, dragging, loading, hanging, skinning, butchering, wrapping, barbecuing, seasoning, eating, and the ongoing, never-ending reminiscing of all these magical, mystical predator experiences, my soul soared higher and higher on the confident wings of a bird of prey. The spiciness of the delicious, nutritional pork dinner enjoyed by Tribe Nuge as a result of this hunting is outdone only by the spiritual twang of the powerful memories taken deep into my consciousness from every outing. These sensations raged and flowed on, like a whitewater torrent of emotions in my mind as I pulled the steaming carcass behind me on a grizzled hair sled through the moonlit, sparkling, mesmerizing white snowfield to my waiting truck. I caught myself short as I paused to breathe it all in, and there in the pure whiteness, my shadow walked beside me, as if an ancient, skulking ancestor accompanied me on this eternal quest for fire. He does. It's me.

The Beast from Nowhere

Ahhh! . . . Another day, another grand hunt. This glorious late-October sunrise brought with it an accumulation of moving sensations as could only be provided from sixty-six days of nonstop hunting so far this season. It seems to me, as experienced from the eagle-eye view atop a giant oak tree, that all is perfect with the world around me. The swamp was coming to life with a peaceful yet moving growth of throbbing life that touched my soul. Mallards and geese were carrying on as wood ducks whistled into the cattails to join them. I could hear their splashes. Sandhill cranes were squawking up a storm behind me in the flooded willows and crows began their ritualistic violent morning attack on a local screech owl off in the distant timber. Wave after wave of chickadees, juncos, nuthatches, titmice, finches, woodpeckers, song sparrows and a virtual squadron of dive-bombing robins traded all around me, singing and chirping like mad. The wilderness Mardi Gras has once again begun anew. It was beautiful. I of the storm indeed.

After touring the nonstop Rock 'n' Roll American Dream like a man possessed through the summer months each year for the last thirty-five years, the powerful forces of fall's seasonal changes provide me with a much-needed battery recharging jolt for both my body and soul. I take each outing beyond the pavement to heart and consider each hunt a sacred event in my life. Because of all the insane traveling I do, my home hunting grounds represent an important source of great spiritual peace and tranquility to me. The closer to home I stay, the better I feel. Because of the vast wildlife acreage we own, I must harvest quite a few deer each year in order to properly manage the precious ecosystem that is habitat for so much diverse flora and fauna. Biologists from various scientific groups and universities study our little piece of wetlands heaven because it is a unique fen that provides important habitat for endangered butterflies and their essential breeding and nesting vegetation. It is proven that the proper balance as provided by my killing surplus game and varmints, especially numerous deer, is the best thing possible for the ecosystem. Dr. Nuge reporting for duty!

With numerous does already in the walk-in cooler, even more processed in our freezer, and with the pre-rut still a week or so away, I was quite unpressured and relaxed in my treestand on swamp's edge, merely hoping for a possible shot at another doe or to simply take in all the awesome wild around me. That would be enough for me. Even with extensive advance scouting, I had not as of yet seen any mature bucks in this quadrant of our little paradise. Since I know all the scouting in the world is never conclusive, I am always cocked, locked and ready to rock for anything, anytime. I fully believe that the big boy could show up at any moment, and I'm committed to being ready.

By the time the opening rays of eastern gold warmed my backside, the first group of deer pussyfooted into my little grove of hardwoods. A huge old doe with two yearling does and four button bucks meandered amongst the red and black oak trees, probing for acorns amongst the bracken ferns. I watched their every move, fascinated as always by the interaction that animals display. As they approached my ambush position, I had decided that if the right shot were to present itself, I would try to arrow the big doe to donate her sacred flesh to our regional Hunters for the Hungry charity program. So many homeless shelters truly appreciate the donations of prime game meat from the hunters. Once that decision was made, I began to shake and breathe heavy, as usual. Giddy is fun.

The threesome balked in a thicket that disallowed any decent shot, so I just enjoyed their presence. It was then that my peripheral vision picked up a flash of white behind a screen of heavy brush. I slowly swung my head thataway, and gasped with eyes wide open and jaw dropped. Twisting in and out of the briars and impenetrable scrub came a set of antlers that I could not believe. Tall, wide, long, heavy white antlers rose up and down as a huge buck weaseled his way from the black slop of the marsh toward my personal predator dangerzone. I trembled and sucked air hard. I forced myself to close my eyes and settle down. I reminded myself of all the basics of my shooting discipline and talked myself into ignoring the amazing crown of bone on this monster's head. I was about to implode and burst into flames. I prayed for calm.

The beast from nowhere did everything in his power to destroy my nerves, as he paused and nibbled and sniffed and licked and rubbed every limb and twig around him. He walked left, then he went right. The gorgeous buck did a 180 and retraced his steps back into the shadows of the black swamp. I was high, then I was low. I was excited, then I was let down. Do ya love this hunting game or what? And here he comes again, only this time he's on a mission. It appears he decided to respond to that most moving of natural drives, that Wang Dang Sweet Doe Thang! Hot on the very trail that the she-deer had walked, he now came on with dogged determination. Just as he was about to enter my perfect shotzone, he spun hard left like a cutting horse at a rodeo and was about to disappear. I swung hard left with him, and with my own dogged predator determination, I yanked the Renegade bowstring back into the corner of my mouth, raced thru my hunter's prayer, picked a spot on his shoulder, all in a nanosecond, and let 'er rip. DAMN! My lower bow limb hit the base of my treestand on the final inch of travel and my white arrow punched clean through him midship. Guts! Paunch! Hell on earth! Dang!

He bounced thirty-five yards into the reed grass and stopped. Head swiveling, he scanned the area for the source of disruption, but found nothing. Slowly he hunched up and stiff legged into the puckerbrush and out of sight. I deflated. I intentionally whacked my head back hard against the tree bark, gritting my teeth and cursing myself. Huge buck. Maybe my biggest buck ever. What in the hell was I thinking. OK, relax. Review. Think, boy, think! I'm on a peninsula. I know the area intimately. I know where he was heading. I know where all those trails lead. Go home. Don't push him. We'll get that buck.

And sure enough, by heeding the advice of masters before me, my patience paid off huge time, for when I returned many hours later, I simply rounded the corner in the thicket to find my trophy whitetail buck, deader than a tuna only fifty yards from the hit. I thought I was gonna die. He was beautiful. My arrow had clipped the liver. I got him! His magnificent crown of antlers was spectacular. Twenty-two inches from tip to tip, with eleven heavy, thick, long tines, this beast would score well in the archery record books. But that was all secondary, for the encounter was everything. I sat there in the muck with him awhile, lifting his majestic head every which way, recounting the points, estimating each tine length, adding up and guestimating score, age and where in the hell he came from! Even the near-impossible chore of dragging him and loading him onto my Honda was painful yet exhilarating. The celebration back home was joyous. Video and photographs went on forever. At three-and-a-half years of age, we all wondered how deer can go undetected on our regularly traveled, monitored and scouted grounds. Needless to say, all hunting is good, but a huge surprise makes each adventure a special thrill, knowing the beast from nowhere just may show up.

Why I Hunt

L es Paul and Chuck Berry had just invented this electric Rock 'n' Roll thang, seemed to me. World War II and the Korean War had barely stopped smokin', the TV was finding its way into the first American homes. The "I" was born. Mom and Dad were into this industrial revolution thing. A disposable society sure sounded like a great idea. Life as simple as possible. On the surface. The American Dream. Father knows best. Wally and the Beaver along with the Nelsons were our models of family structure. A place for everything and everything in its place. The difference between right and wrong was so obvious. Sway from that path, and "Wait till your father gets home!" Right in the kisser. Whacked a good one. "Turn that damn guitar down!!"

Service. That's what we wanted. Milk delivered. Dry cleaning picked up. TV dinners. Trash collected on Saturdays. Turn on the TV for news and entertainment. Gas 19.9 cents. Give me a buck's worth. Service stations. Change the oil and filter, and a lube. Stop by the butcher and pick up a roast and some drumsticks, all cut up, wrapped and ready to go. This was the life. Sunday drives thru the country. Cool. Summer vacations to Uncle Morris's farm. Shootin' woodchucks because the draft horses could break a leg in their holes. Shoot a squirrel, and learn to clean it and cook it

Fallow deer, Heartsill Ranch, Texas, 2002

yourself. It all made perfect sense. My Dad would walk down the old farm lane with the single-shot, bolt-action Western .22, and I would follow right behind. He could put a .22 short between the eyes at one hundred yards. Swear. I remember cowboys and Indians, playin' wild absolutely fascinated me to no end. Something deep inside stirred me to the point of near hysteria. I would drag that woodchuck

8-point whitetail, Michigan, 2003

back to the farmhouse, watch Dad and Uncle Morris gut it and cut it up, then one of my aunts would prepare it for a feast. One plus one equals two. No foolin'.

The Rouge River flowed right across Hazelton Parkway from home. Woods, swamp, tangles. Ducks, geese, squirrels, coon, possum, skunk, ground-hogs, pheasant, quail, rabbits, rats, owls, hawks, crows and songbirds by the score. And silence. Sometimes it was scary. Mystery. I studied tracks and sounds. Learned how to move, and how not to move, in order to get close. I carried my bow and arrows everywhere. I was a shootin' fool. Cool.

Feelings. It all boils down to our gut feelings in life. There is no question as to which road to choose as our senses and intellect develop. Right is right, and wrong is wrong. Mistakes are made and one progresses. Most, hopefully, anyhow. I saw all the kid stuff going on as I grew up around the Motor City. The good, bad, and the ugly. My Dad made sure I avoided the bad and the ugly. I admit, I was lucky. My mother was the Rock of Gibraltar, a virtuous saint. And Dad took no shit. Not even a hint. We had very little worldly possessions. Values were the lesson of daily life. Do unto others as you would have them do unto you. Respect your elders. The Ten Commandments. It all made perfect sense. And of course if logic ever escaped us, Dad would remind us in an oh-so-certain manner! We were grateful for the food on our table every day. Thankful for the rare new piece of clothing. To share a bottle of coke was a treat. Dad worked very hard and there was a direct correlation between material goods and the effort expended. This respect for life was learned and appreciated as part of our daily existence. We knew where our chicken dinners came from. Hard-earned cash paid for that bird and America's Thanksgiving turkey. I watched Mom pull out the gizzards and liver. I knew the bird was recently killed for us. The dollar was earned and the price was paid. It was a bird. Cool. And delicious. We knew they were made to kill and eat. One plus one equals two. Still. I preferred grouse, quail

Fallow stag, YO Ranch, Texas, 1998

and pheasant, but turkey and chicken were easier at the time. My time in the wild reflected directly with the lifestyle of our modern ways. It is with the same callousness some people have receded into by disassociating themselves from certain of life's realities, such as the source of leather and chicken McNuggets, that has plummeted them into the abyss of sin, like killing for trendy sneakers. A pathetic disregard for moral values has stricken the weak. And there are too many of them. Man's worst crime against nature is not progress, but disassociation.

I remember the moments of decision as a young boy. Kids can be real troublemakers. Everybody had BB guns, slingshots, and bows and arrows. There was a time when it seemed as if all the kids in the neighborhood wanted to do was shoot street lights, windows and cars, just to be rotten. I did not dare! The fear of God and the fear of Dad. Good stuff. As soon as my buddies looked like they were going to pull that crap, I was outta there. Swamp, here I come. The wild ground was sanctuary. Every moment there was good. Something interesting was always going on. I crawled around on my belly, sneaking and a-stalkin' every life form I encountered. Here was a place where you couldn't get in trouble. Smart moves paid off in close, eye-to-eye encounters with wonderful, wild creatures. Mistakes in the wild were immediately reconciled with a lesson on how to more intelligently conduct oneself. Accountability in its purest form. One plus one still equalled two. The excitement I would feel and share in graphic detail each night with Mom, the family and my buddies was inspiring. I always had wild stories to tell. Like the owl that surprised me as he swooped down out of the big timber. The muskrat that ambled across the trail in front of me, only inches away. The Baltimore Oriole building its nest in the willow tree down in Skunk Hollow. The covey of quail that exploded underfoot, taking my breath away, as usual. Just as I do today, at the tender age of forty-two.

As time went on, these lessons of life continued, and became more profound

Scimitar horned oryx, Young Ranch, Texas, 1999

with the advance of age and experience. My choice between right and wrong became life-and-death decisions. No longer did I have to worry about some jerk shooting a street light out with his Wham-O slingshot. Now the "hip" thing to do was destroy your life with drugs and alcohol. Great. And once again, I was outta there. Fast. Back to the wild I went, and this sanctuary meant more to me than ever. I could not believe what was going on around me. Corpse after stupid corpse

8-point whitetail, Michigan, 2001

178

was stacked on TV news every night from drug-related deaths. And still EVERYBODY around me wanted to get high. I was livid with confusion. Not confusion as to what I would do. That was crystal clear. I was astounded that these other people could not see and respond to the same information that I embraced. Was I super-intelligent or were they complete morons? A little of each I would conclude. I was virtually shunned, and laughed at my by fellow musicians and age class. Not just for not indulging

6x6 bull elk, Texas, 2003

in this absurd death march, but also because I would venture off and kill "defenseless little animals." Perfect logic from people who would return from a drug addict's funeral, to mourn by GETTING HIGH!!! Absolutely unbelievable. Meanwhile, every time they would whip out their dope and chemical bullshit, I would throw my tent and longbow, with a quiver full of cedar shafts, into the trunk, and head up into the Manistee National Forest for some deer, squirrel and grouse hunting. These hippies continued to drool on themselves and die like so many mindless lemmings, and I would whack me some quality dinner, and cleanse my soul. The mental and spiritual therapy I received from my time in the forests, hunting, camping,

7-point whitetail, YO Ranch, Texas 2003

trapping and just reflecting, was the foundation by which my intellect and passion for life developed. I found myself focused on the human need for self worth and compassion, for not only myself and my fellow man, but all life around me. It was

7-point whitetail, Rancho Encontado, Texas, 2000

all too clear. From lessons on belonging in the wild, I would kill my dinner each night. Bow-and-arrow squirrel hunting is special. Grouse is a hard-earned delicacy! So meanwhile, while those "hip" fools were killing themselves, ol' Ted was improving his overall life with a retention of the earth's pulse. Cool. Cool as hell.

Man is young. America is an infant. Still, the sanctity of human life and existence is ingrained in our hearts and souls. I don't care where you are from, we all know what is right and wrong. It is just a matter of what we do with this knowledge that determines our caliber. Our species' sustenance comes from Mother Earth. Our intellect and unique sense of reasoning is unlike that of any other creature's. There is no living animal, besides ourselves, that can think out a response. Animals' instincts are powerful, and have facilitated their survival for time immemorial. But only man has a soul and the intellect to reason. It is this balance of existence that has determined man's use of animals for food, clothing, shelter, medicine and even religion. The same balance that determines the cougar eating the deer, the hawk killing the rabbit, and man killing the elk. It is good for the wolf to kill the caribou. It is good that Ted kills the moose. There exists a strange imbalance as well. Why does the mink go into a killing frenzy when he decimates an entire colony of muskrats? How is it that the heron kills hundreds of fish, but he only eats a few? The male lion eats his own offspring, as does the bear. Why is the heart-rending beauty of childbirth so prolonged, painful and bloody? Why do children die of myriad infections? I do not know.

There were seven hunters lying around one late summer day, somewhere in Alaska. One yawned and stretched, and stated that he felt like killing something. Even though there were no open seasons at that time of year, they all agreed it would be fun. No one even hinted an objection. After a short while, a cow moose was discovered at the edge of a willow and alder patch, and the whole bunch of them basically surrounded the beast. With no escape, the confused animal was pretty easy pickings for the group of hunters, and the leader caused a bad wound in the hindquarters of the moose. Instead of finishing her off, the seven hunters merely sat around for two hours and let the cow moose bleed to death. Were these the actions of the hunters represented and disrespected in the media of America? On the contrary, these hunters were revered and loved by ninety-nine percent of this country's citizens. Documented on video a few years ago, these seven hunters were Alaskan wolves, doing what they are supposed to do. Based on the claims of uninformed nature lovers, one would wonder where the so-called "balance of nature" was in this kill scenario. Predators DO NOT KILL THE OLD, SICK AND WEAK. Wild animal predators are pure OPPORTUNISTS. The cougar kills the first animal that walks by, or that it encounters. The eagle, coyote, fox and owl all do the same. Man, the hunter has proven with the implementation of hunting restrictions, game laws, license fees, self-imposed taxes, and heartfelt respect for the wild, can have REASONED, HOW to manage wildlife for the benefit of the future of wildlife and the wild ground needed to support it, FOREVER if we are smart enough to continue doing what is right.

With the implementation of hunting restrictions, game laws, license fees, self-imposed taxes, and heartfelt respect for the wild, the hunter has proven that man can manage wildlife for the benefit of the future of wildlife and the wild ground needed to support it, FOREVER. We just need to be reasonable enough, and smart enough, to continue doing what is right.

I know why I hunt. It is a drive deep inside of me, that pulls me into a wild piece of God's country, to experience, to smell, to touch, to vibrate a primal connection with my body, mind and spirit around me, on a level that is available nowhere else in our world. I have seen the good it has done for my life. I have seen the good hunting has done for the land and the animals I share it with. I have tasted the good it does for my family's sustenance at the dinner table, and the way we conduct ourselves with others. I will never go into a killing frenzy like the mink, the marten or the heron. I have reasoned that this is wasteful and wrong. I am better than the animal. I am a human being. Not only that, but my Dad would whack me!! God love him.

Hunting Techniques

Instinctive Bowhunting
The Hand-Eye Coordination Game

Some guys are just naturally better baseball pitchers than the rest of us. There is no doubt that certain individuals are gifted with special talents. There was this one guy back near Detroit when I was about eleven years old who could do anything. Baseball, football, basketball, pool, horseshoes, darts, seemed like anything. One day while I was shooting arrows in my backyard at a small matt target, Brian came over and was, as usual, interested in giving it a try. Sure enough, the first time he pulled back an arrow, he nailed the middle of the target, and did so with every arrow. No sweat! What's the big deal? There's the target, grab the bow, pull back and send the shaft straight to the center of the matt. How could you miss? That is what you call perfect hand-eye coordination, and an uncanny sense of perception. Lucky SOB!

Fallow stag, Young Ranch, Texas, 2001

I wasn't exactly a slouch with the bow and arrow, but I had to work at it. I, too, experienced the natural flow of youth, where nothing in my naive little mind got in the way of a simple function like directing an arrow into a specific spot on the target. Most of the time. My earliest years of shooting were some of my best. A thirtyish-pound longbow felt natural in my hands. Instinctively, I was able to matter-of-factly look at my intended target and nail it with confidence-building regularity. Maybe it was the takeover years of the guitar, or maybe I just thought about it too much, but after my teens, I developed many bad habits that really knocked my shooting ability down.

It is that mental aspect in archery, especially bowhunting, which gets in the way of perfect, consistent accuracy. When you consider our goal of arrow placement,

Black bear, Saskatchewan, Canada, 1995

it shouldn't be that tuff at all. At times, when I whacked that bulls-eye or boiler-room I could "feel" the arrow was true before I even released it. I looked right in perspective of hands, arrow, eye and target spot. It is a lot like throwing the baseball into the strike zone. Your eyes identify the target, and your brain tells you when to let go of the ball, at what moment to release its flight to the desired point of impact. Almost the same with archery, except for the fact that weird things start to happen when you tense and exert yourself drawing the bow, com-pounded with an acute mental desire to hit the bullseye, or worse yet, a big-game animal's vitals. All hell breaks loose, doesn't it? Of course, it is important that we NEVER let the functions and work overshadow the sheer excitement and joy of the challenge itself.

Keep in mind that our number-one goal should be the consistent accuracy with our equipment, and our touch with the wild and its critters. It will take sacrifice and loss of effort, but throughout the whole development process we should actually enjoy our fumbles and lessons learned. Think. Don't fight it and get frustrated and angry, but rather, have fun with the fact that it is going to be difficult, and may take many years to obtain our goal. Instant success would indicate a simple thing, and that wouldn't be any fun.

Now, your bow is tuned up right, your arrows are flying like a beam of light, and your close-shooting under fifteen yards is good. Proper stance and feel for the bow is basically ingrained, and you want to get to where you can nail the eight-inch vitals on our deer target every time from fifteen to thirty yards. Cool. Go for it. Practice smart. Make each shot count. Pay attention to your target SPOT, arrow, anchor, release, and then follow thru. There is only one way to rock! PRACTICE, PRACTICE, PRACTICE, PRACTICE, PRACTICE!!! Oh yeah, did I mention PRACTICE!!!???!!!

Stalking
The Bow-Hunter's Art

"Never step on anything that you can step over." Those are the words of possibly the greatest stalking bowhunter that ever crept into bow-range of world-class big-game animals across the globe, the one-and-only FRED BEAR. The thrust of hunting with the bow and arrow is such that it mandates the close-range encounter. Although probably seventy-five to eighty-five percent of all bowhunting today is done out of blinds, on the ground, and more so up in trees, more and more archers are rediscovering the challenge and thrill of "on-the-ground" hunting. We all know the excitement of having a critter by our treestand at close range. Or at least can envision it! Multiply that by two when you are on the same level as they are. Then, if you have intentionally made a successful sneak on one, multiply that by a hundred!! It is something else.

Productive stalking is the most difficult part of bowhunting. Depending on the species of the game you are after, it can seem to be almost impossible. In North America, mature deer, antelope and elk are the supreme challenge. The least wary, though always a demanding challenge, are the javelina and wild hog. No matter what the critter, you have to do everything right. EVERYTHING! You have to consider eyes, ears, nose, terrain, light, shadows, alarm-security animals, and how many of each there are. Though the actual stalk does not really begin until a target animal is identified, there is no real difference in your actions between still-hunting and stalking. I still-hunt until I see the animal. Once the move towards a specific animal is made, the stalk is on.

Wind

No stalk will ever accomplish a thing if you don't play the wind. I have discovered that the most effective approach is cross-wind at a ninety degree angle. Head-on straight into the wind is always good, as long as the wind is constant. Of course the more consistent the wind, the better. I carry a small plastic squeeze bottle of scent-free powder to occasionally puff into the air, plus a single down feather on a light thread tied to the end of my bow to drift freely in the wind, which indicates even the slightest breeze.

Light

If there is any significant sunlight, it is always ideal when the wind is in your face and the sun is at your back. Regardless of sunlight quality, you should always try to stay in the darkest part of the terrain. Shadows help diffuse shapes and motions. Returning to the immortal words of Fred Bear, in conjunction with avoiding sticks, stones and general debris underfoot, if you are faced with a clearing in the light of day, hustle right thru it and get it over with. If at all possible, skirt the edge of any clearing, staying well within the dark of the shadows.

Movement and Sound

A good stalk can never proceed too slowly. Scan thoroughly with your eyes prior to any step. Remember, the hunter MUST see the game before it sees him/her. One major lesson I have learned is that animals are never in a hurry. For the most part, they eat, sleep and hide. As they move thru the territory, even while eating, they keep their guards up at all times. Only during the rut is there the chance to catch them making a mistake, but I always pace myself under the assumption that they are looking for me. I spend a good deal of time remaining stationary, observing every detail I can within my vision before proceeding. Watch the ground in front of you prior to each step, being sure to avoid any item that could shift under your weight, causing a sound. When the weather permits, I prefer to wear lightweight footwear, to help me feel any debris underfoot. Oftentimes, on a final stalk, closing in on my quarry, I will remove my boots and cover the last yards in my stocking feet. It has made the difference on more than one occasion.

Ted and Rocco, Black buck, YO Ranch, Texas, 2000

Camoflauge

With all the different styles and patterns of camo clothing available today, it should be rather easy to match them to the terrain you are hunting in. Even the best camo set-up will not make up for mistaken movements. I believe the need for specific camo patterns. Any good, olive-drab or dull-green GI-type outfit will do under most conditions. You really can't beat the old standby GI woodland for nearly every terrain. Probably more important is the material of clothes to help muffle sound. Wool and soft cotton are best. I have mixed feelings about face-cover make-up, only because it is such a pain in the butt to get cleaned off. There is no question that it helps eliminate the telltale glare from our pinky little faces. Black bow hunters have got it made! If it does not interfere with shooting function, a face mask of some type is good. The tight-fitting Spando-flage offset the least interference. Practice and shoot with your actual hunting equipment to be sure a face cover does not

hamper your anchor or vision. Give equal attention to your equipment as well, making certain that there are no reflective surfaces that could shine or glow at an inappropriate time.

As a general rule, I do not keep an arrow nocked while I am still-hunting. However, in high-density game concentrations, I will keep an arrow ready to go at all times. Past experience has shown me that this can make the difference between being ready or not.

Maximum alertness and caution must be practiced in this code-three condition. NEVER EVER walk along with a

Axis deer, YO Ranch, Texas, 2002

187

4x4 bull elk, Young Ranch, 2002

9-point whitetail, Claude Pollington's Buck
Pole Deer Camp, Marion, Michigan, 1999

nocked arrow. Use cautious, step-by-step, pacing only. Pay attention to more than the animals as you make your moves. Look carefully for other hidden animals. If you don't see them before they see you, the gig is up. Also, always scour the entire area for an alternative approach route, considering a cut-off ambush possibility. It can usually improve your chances if you are able to position yourself ahead of an approaching animal, remaining still, quiet, and ready for the shot. Making a move straight towards an animal is the most difficult. Be prepared to rivet your eyes on your target, and be ready to "freeze" in place for long periods of time if the critter looks your way. It is a game of nerves and concentration. Only experience will prepare you for the perfect timing to make the right move in preparation for the shot. Under most conditions, it is realistic to be satisfied with a thirty-five to forty yard shot than anything closer. Accurate shot placement is essential at these ranges. I personally prefer to take my shot at fifty or so yards after a long stalk, because it allows me a little more freedom and forgiveness to get the bow up and the arrow back undetected for a relaxed, less-pressured shot.

The memory of a hard-earned stalk kill

will stay with you forever. The details will be clear in your mind because each step is an adventure in itself. How many can you get away with? Try it this season, particularly during the rut, when the game is active throughout the daylight hours. Remember, wind, pace, shadows, and eyes. It may seem an impossibility the first few times, but if a thrill is what you want, a thrill is what you'll get. Guaranteed.

Good luck, good stalking, and I'll see ya' in the wild again, back where we belong.

LOCATION OF HITS PERCENTAGES

Neck	12.0%
Lungs	44.4%
Artery	5.1%
Heart	8.5%
Chest	15.4%
Spine	3.4%
Rectal	2.6%
Hip	6.0%
Paunch	2.6%

Recipes

Ultimate Chow
Pure Game Meat for the Culinary Aware

Gamey is good. But what most people consider gamey is just mistreated meat. I hate when my meat is mistreated! The palatability of game is determined when it hits the ground. And its flavor. Real flavor is the main attraction here. No bullshit, Gonzo-additive injections to grow 'em fast. Just Mama Nature caressing the critters with organic sustenance, and of course us cool-as-hell hunters bringing out the best in them with our organic shopping spree! Our passion for the hunt and all of its diverse and intense experiences culminates when game is brought to the bag. It is our ultimate legal and ethical responsibility to maximize the utilization of this animal at the dinner table and beyond. As important as all the procedures of the hunt are, a thorough knowledge of game handling, butchering and rendering the different body parts now becomes number one.

#1 HIT 'EM RIGHT. A behind-the-shoulder hit is always preferable to avoid hydrostatic shock to flesh via bone impact and fragmentation. A double-lunger is perfect. Any bloodshot tissue that does result should be immediately cut away and saved for pet food or bait it for bear or other such legal practices.

#2 COOL OUT! Time is of the essence for getting the carcass cooled down to thirty-five to forty degrees F. Rush, I say speed to the nearest cool spot. If you are in a remote area, shade will do, but it is essential to get and keep the body temperature of the animal down. On some occasions in the past, I have cut up meat into small enough portions to wrap and put into the refrigerator at home. This will certainly do. I've heard two theories: 1. Cut it up right away and freeze it, or 2. Hang the carcass in a cooler for a week of aging to break down the enzymes that make the meat tuff. Both ways work, but I prefer the aging process. Bug free at thirty-five degrees F.

#3 KEEP IT CLEAN. The hide of the animal serves the purpose of keeping the flesh free of debris, and should be left on until the exposure to dirt, bugs and debris is reduced or eliminated. When the dead animal has to be dragged or hauled on horseback, the skin can be left on for the minimum amount of time necessary. Of course, a sufficient size and number of cheesecloth game bags should be part of every smart hunter's day pack supply. If it is good and cold, say below forty degrees, the hide can be left on while the carcass hangs in camp, or is transported to the cooler or home. A new product called Liquid Game Bag is great for keeping off the bugs and flies. Of course, a good dose of black pepper sprinkled liberally on all exposed meat will work good, too. Flies are the worst thing. My basic procedure is to bone-out all the meat in the shade, cover with pepper or Liquid Game Bag, double-wrap in game bags, stuff into my backpack or vehicle, separate when possible for max air flow, and get to a cold source pronto, Tonto.

At this point I would like to note my opinion on transporting game on the top of vehicles. DO IT! Keep it cold and clean and bloodless, but DO IT. I agree with Dan Quillian and other proud hunters, that one of the big problems with our society today is the propensity of denial. We would all function as more honest, in-touch human beings if we would just stop and admit how our chicken sandwiches got that way. They were raised, transported, at night usually, and WHACKED DEADER 'N' HELL. I believe in proudly displaying my beautiful dead deer on top of my truck for all to see. I am convinced that MORE people enjoy the sight of a successful hunter's animal than disapprove. Of course, if it is freshly killed, with blood still flowing, all steps should be taken to keep it clean. Just as game and stock used to be displayed at the counter and in the windows of butcher shops, and still is in Europe, without the blood. I feel this is a better method. More honest and more real. Remember too, that if the trip will expose the carcass to dirt, sunlight, heat, wind, rain or unwanted debris, don't do it. Oftentimes I will wrap the body in a tarp, leaving the head and antlers showing, and tie it facing forward on the roof rack, for short trips. The friendly waves, smiles, and thumbs up I get are cool.

#4 BUTCHERING. A trusted, professional butcher is the best. He knows what he is doing. But be real careful of the mass-mentality guys who don't give a damn. Your prized meat will be shit. In fact, it more than likely it won't be your meat at all, but rather lumped together with the other thousands of carcasses of God-knows-what origin. I butcher most of my own animals. It is easy. Get yourself a simple butcher's beef-cutting chart, if nothing else, and follow the lines. Deer and elk charts are available as well. Do a little homework on the subject and you will be gratified at yet another dimension on the overall hunting experience.

#5 COOKING. I believe any good beef, pork, lamb or fowl recipe is equally applicable to its game counterparts. There are volumes of good recipes for all kinds of game, and again, a little homework goes a long way. General rule for big game is always to cook it on the rare side. The center of red game meat should always be pink. Wild boar and bear, like all pork, should be well done.

S O M E   F A V O R I T E S

BIG MEATCAKES

This is a good way to prepare the tougher cuts of deer, elk, antelope, moose and bear, which the freezing plant or processor usually grinds for hunters. To each pound of ground lean meat, add one teaspoon salt, one-half teaspoon pepper, one quarter cup catsup and one quarter cup chopped onion. Mix well, shape in small flat cakes and cook in a hot greased skillet, usually about four minutes on each side. One pound of lean meat will serve two.

VENISON STROGANOFF

- 2 lbs. venison steaks
- 1 envelope Lipton Onion Soup
- Fresh mushrooms
- 1 beef bouillon cube
- Cooking sherry
- 1 cup sour cream
- Curry powder
- Garlic salt
- Butter

Cut meat into thin strips (eliminating fat). Brown quickly in three tablespoons or more butter with mushrooms. Stir in two-thirds cup liquid (one-third water, one-third sherry). Add the onion soup mix, a dash of garlic salt, a dash of curry powder, and the bouillon cube, mix well, cover and simmer for one and one-half hours or until meat is tender. Stir every fifteen minutes, adding liquid when necessary. Just before serving, add sour cream and increase heat. Serve over rice or noodles for four, unless Ted's eating over; then it'll serve two.

HUNTER'S STEW

Here at the Nugent ranch we prepare mashed potatoes with the skins on. Try it! As the potatoes are nearly done, brown one pound ground venison and fresh mushrooms 'til brown and tender. Drain, reserving grease for your huntin' dogs. Add one can cream of mushroom soup and mix well. Prepare mashed potatoes as you like and serve meat mix over it. Best when coming in from the cold.

BUBBLE BEAN PIRANHA A LA COLORADO MOOSE

This is it folks! The chow the whole world has been waitin' for! Proven at the hands of the most voracious of camp hogs, the ribstickin' slop is the ultimate in hunt-camp fortification. As the primary mainstay at the Nugent WhackMaster headquarters, many a hearty hunter has maintained the killer instinct by gettin' a belly full of my primo-extremo brew. First experimented with as early as 1968, the recipe has changed a little over the years, but rather improved with the spirit of adventure.

■ 2 green peppers
■ 2 red peppers
■ 1 large sweet onion
■ 1 large white onion
■ 1 bunch scallions
■ 1 large bowl fresh mushrooms
■ 1 whole clove garlic
■ 1 large box pasta noodles (creamettes or sea shells)
■ 1 pound ground venison (any)
■ 1 side deer backstrap
■ cayenne pepper
■ Mrs. Dash seasoning
■ wine vinegar
■ 1/2 pound butter
■ 1/4 cup olive oil

In a skillet, brown the ground meat. Dice up all of the vegetables, add half to the browned meat. Boil the pasta and drain. Singe the backstrap in bite-size pieces in hot olive oil and wine vinegar. Squash and add the garlic to the browned meat and vegetables, stirring vigorously. Throw the whole load into a large pot on low heat, including the remaining raw vegetables, and still stirring, add small amounts of water per desired consistency. Keep on lowest heat all day, refrigerate overnight, and reheat for days to come. It's best tow to three days old. Slop a load onto bread, mashed potatoes, rice, or serve by itself. Throw a log on the fire, kick back, relax, and swap huntin' lies. (Serves about five average, or two major swine.)

WILD BOAR CHOPS

Only a few campers are fortunate enough to enjoy this delicious game meat; the rest must be content with domestic pork chops. But if you should bag a wild boar, serve it this way.

Salt and pepper four chops, sprinkle with flour and brown well on both sides in three tablespoons of hot fat. Core (but do not peel) two pounds of apples and cut in thick slices. Put a dash of paprika and six raisins on top of each browned chop. Then cover with the apple slices, two tablespoons of brown sugar and one-quarter cup of hot water. Cover skillet and simmer until well done, about forty minutes. Cook one large or two small chops per person.

VENISON ROAST WITH SOUR CREAM SAUCE

- 1/3 cup cider vinegar
- 1 cup dry white wine
- cut each in half and chop:
  - 1 carrot
  - 1 celery stalk
  - 1 onion
- 2 tablespoons whole black peppercorns
- 1 teaspoon whole allspice
- 1 teaspoon juniper berries
- 1 teaspoon fresh thyme
- 3 or 4 bay leaves
- 1 3-pound boneless venison shoulder roast, trimmed of fat
- 8 ounces bacon, diced
- 1 cup sour cream at room temperature
- 3 tablespoons flour
- the minced peel of one lemon
- 1 rounded tablespoon of salad mustard

Make a marinade by combining cider vinegar, white wine, vegetables, peppercorns, allspice, juniper berries, thyme and bay leaves. Add the venison roast and refrigerate for three to four days, turning each day.

When ready to begin cooking, remove meat from marinade, brushing off vegetables and patting dry. Season meat lightly with salt and pepper.

Sauté bacon in a heavy skillet until bacon begins to crisp. Remove bacon with a slotted spoon. Into the hot fat, put the roast to sear quickly on all sides. Meanwhile, strain marinade and reserve juices. Remove roast when brown; place in crock pot. Quickly sear vegetables in remaining fat, to brown lightly. Place them in crock pot with the roast.

Pour strained marinade into a small saucepan; reduce over high heat by half, to about two-thirds cups. Pour over roast vegetables.

Turn on crock pot and cook roast until done, about four hours; choose setting according to how long you wish to cook (the lower the setting, the longer the braising will require).

When meat is tender, remove it from juices and keep warm. Combine sour cream and flour; add to juices in crockpot, and cook for fifteen minutes.

Strain sauce through a fine sieve, pressing vegetables to extract their juices. The sauce could also be put into a blender, if you want to make it very smooth.

Garnish plates with slices of lemon and lingonberries or cranberries. Spoon sauce over sliced roast. Serve with dumplings, spaetzle or noodles. Serves four to six.

HONEY SPICED TURKEY WITH ORANGE SAUCE

- 1/2-cup all purpose flour
- 2 tablespoons vegetable oil
- 3 to 3 1/2 lbs. of turkey, cut up or in 4 breast halves
- 1 teaspoon salt
- 1 teaspoon paprika
- 1/8-teaspoon pepper
- 1 medium onion, sliced
- 2 tablespoons cold water
- 2 tablespoons cornstarch
- 1 cup orange juice
- 1/2-teaspoon ground ginger
- 1 small can (3 1/2 ounces) ripe olives

Dredge turkey in flour to cover all sides. In large skillet, heat oil; add turkey and cook over medium heat until brown on all sides, about fifteen minutes. Place turkey in ungreased rectangular baking dish, 13x9x2 inches; sprinkle with salt, paprika and pepper; top with onions. Make a paste with water and cornstarch. Add orange juice, honey, lemon juice and ginger. Stir; pour over turkey, add olives. Cover and bake at 350 degrees F for forty-five minutes. Garnish with parsley, Serves six to eight.

TURKEY WITH CURRY SAUCE

- 1 lb. (freshly whacked) turkey breast tenderloin slices, cut one-half-inch thick
- 1 tablespoon margarine or butter
- 2 tablespoons all-purpose flour
- 1/2 teaspoon curry powder
- 1 cup chicken broth
- 1/4 cup milk
- 1/2 of a small banana, diced to one-half-cup
- 1/4 cup snipped, pitted dates or raisins
- 1/4 cup chopped cashews
- 1/2 teaspoon finely shredded lemon peel
- 3 cups hot cooked rice or bulgur

Wrap turkey slices in foil; place in a shallow baking pan. Cook in a 350 degree F oven for twenty-five minutes or until turkey is no longer pink.

Meanwhile, for sauce, in a small saucepan, melt margarine or butter. Stir in flour and curry powder till blended. Add broth and milk. Cook and stir over medium heat till thickened and bubbly. Cook and stir one minute more. Stir in banana, dates or raisins, cashews and lemon peel.

Arrange turkey over rice or bulgur. Pour sauce over turkey.

Serves six.

PAN-ROASTED VENISON STEAK

- 7 tablespoons unsalted butter
- 2 boneless venison steaks, each weighing one to one and one-half pounds and cut two-inches thick
- Coarse salt and cracked black pepper to taste
- Sprigs of fresh watercress for garnish

In a small saucepan, melt the butter over low heat. Skim off and discard the milky foam on top. Carefully pour the clarified butter into a large iron skillet, avoiding any milky solids at the bottom of the pan. Dry the venison steaks thoroughly on paper towels and season both sides with the coarse salt and lots of cracked pepper. Then heat the clarified butter in a twelve-inch skillet over high heat. Add the steaks without crowding the skillet and saute on one side for three minutes, until well browned. Turn and saute on the second side for three minutes. Reduce the heat to moderately low and continue cooking for ten minutes. Turn the steaks and cook for another ten minutes for rare or fourteen minutes for medium. The steaks are done when there is slight resistance to the touch. Transfer the steaks to a carving board and let sit for two to three minutes before cutting. Cut the steaks crosswise into thin slices and place in a decorative pattern on each of six warm individual serving plates. Garnish with sprigs of fresh watercress and serve at once. Serves six.

Ted and Shemane, 9-point whitetail, SpiritWild Ranch, Texas, 2003

Teditorials

Perfect Circle

As the goose bumps rippled across my flesh like an undulating swarm of buffalo stampeding the prairies, and the short hairs on my neck-back stood erect and quivering at full attention, my mind raced with the exploding anticipation for the moment of truth in my face. This handsome whitetail buck, glowing in the magic time of peak dawn firelight, was giving me his best show, teasing and tempting my inner soul, pushing my predator radar to the breaking point and stimulating the ringing earth tones all around. I had been watching him, celebrating him, for more than twenty intense minutes already, and it took everything I had to remain cool, calm, and collected, knowing for certain, that if I came unglued, I would blow the shot for sure. The ever-escalating encounter was more than enough to satisfy my cravings for the hunt, but there was something else going on here. My watery-eyed gaze shifted from beast to shadows, from songbird to tree line, sucking in the beauty of everything around me as if my brain was cataloging every inch of landscape and air current, every breath and thought, color, shape, sound, feel, and smell, a virtual feeding frenzy of sensuality. The crisp fall air brought every slight rustle of vegetation to my otherwise strained ears. My peripheral vision seemed to pick up nearly imperceptible movement off to each side far better than usual. I could smell the pungent gris gris of disrupted peatmoss with every cautious footfall the majestic creature took, and my spirit pumped a soulfood concoction of bellyaching adrenaline and hunger pangs for more. I was stoned on his beastness and all the dynamo of connected earth, wind, fire, tooth, fang and claw, time immemorial. This is how I get high. And I was soaring.

This stunning daybreak brought the realization that my hunting days were getting even more intense than I had previously expected could be. And that is saying a lot; for I do indeed crave every sacred moment beyond the pale pavement, weapon in hand, a joyous lifetime seeking pure flesh for my family's belly. There is no question that our pure survival instinct demands the killing of food, but my beloved hunt time was delivering much more than venison and mind-boggling happiness from each encounter. Surely, the spiritual dimensions were growing more and more volatile with each outing, and my mind raced to keep up. My smile stretched to its fullest as I realized the beautiful deer was emerging from a puckerbrush thicket of dense autumn olive bushes, interspersed with scattered clumps of dwarf pinetrees and vetch that my greasy old Rock 'n' Roll hands had planted here in this special place for more than thirty years. This ideal habitat we shared this wonderful morning didn't just happen to be there, for my inner sense of connection increased in velocity as I nodded in approval, celebrating the ultimate hands-on relationship with creation, heart-to-heart with the beast within the cover of trees and wild shrubs that I had personally plunged fist first into nostril flaring terra firma, together with my family, over many,

many years. I knew this buck was here because he felt comfortable and safe, at home, in perfect edge habitat that I had provided specifically for my wildlife brothers. I felt total ga-ga, pleased, proud, fulfilled, cocky. So did the butterball eight-point before me.

Maybe I shouldn't have planted so many bushes and trees here at the confluence of swamp and forest, for as close range as the buck was, the tangled thicket we now shared protected him from any chance of an arrow shot. I peered into the scrub, desperate for an opening for the mystical flight of my arrow. But alas, not a prayer. I forced myself to breathe slower and easier, telling myself that I should just take this close-up and personal encounter as joy enough for one morning. Then, with the shiny glow of golden light shimmering off his tall, ivory-tipped, mahogany antlers, he swung his huge head down into the lower branches of an autumn olive bush and began stripping the branches of juicy, red berries, thus bringing his heavy shoulder into clear view. Code red.

My bow already lifted into position, I held my breath and lasered my predator eyes into the life giving pump station zone of the beast, ignoring everything else. Beginning my little bowhunter prayer, I willed my arrow on its path. And before I knew it, white feathers were vanishing into that magical crease in his chest, directly behind his foreleg, and I knew the circle was complete. It was awesome. I was truly in awe of the perfection of our little dance of life and death here together. As he disappeared into the primal goop of our sacred marsh, I slowly leaned back in my tree, lifted my eyes to the heavens, let out a long, audible sigh, and simply closed my eyes and relaxed.

I sat there for quite awhile this morning, eyes closed, head back against the old gnarly oak, sponging omnisciently. I heard a pair of cock pheasants cackle back and forth to the north, a bobwhite quail sang somewhere below me. Squawking sandhill cranes raised hell in the distance, and a mesmerizing chorus of many different song-birds lit up the day. I concentrated on my sense of smell and snorted the welcome aromas of muck, autumn olive, sassafras, and God knows what wonderful scents of the wild. I could actually taste the delicious natural world all around me. Come on baby light my fire.

The buck's trail was just as much fun as every other moment of the encounter. I took it slow and poked along methodically. I examined every track, splotch, and splash of his sacred blood, and envisioned the tracks of history that I retraced here in perfect harmony with them. I gobbled it up. But it was the filling of my hands with the beast itself that drove me through the clouds. I just go nuts when I come upon a kill. It is a moment of spirited jubilation, celebrating a most difficult job well done. Intensified by the stunning appearance of the animal, taken to untold dimensions because of what each animal actually represents, I always find myself gushing almost uncontrollably at the scene of the last resting place. I count and recount the points of the antlers, rubbing them hard for good luck. I lift the amazing beast every which way, examining the mystery of creation that I hold in my hands.

I sat there with him, my spirit feeding on his. As I lay in the wet sawgrass beside him, his body heat slowly diminished as mine increased, channeled directly into me, like an IV transfusion of new life itself.

As the season went on and these moving experiences grew in number and intensity, Tribe Nuge dined on the succulent flesh of this deer and many others, showing ultimate reverence for these gifts of renewable protein. Though we masticated with exuberance on the delicious meat, and the atmosphere is full-on party time at every meal, the ritualistic Mardi Gras BBQ celebration is nothing less than a heartfelt prayer of thanx for all that these precious gifts have provided. I tell and retell the thrilling details of each hunt, and remind all of the importance of our annual spring tree and various plantings. Each bite of venison is that much better knowing how we played a partnership role in the quality for life for the animals that give us back so much. The equation of life calls upon each of us to tune in better as to how we can improve all life, all around. There is only one reasoning predator on planet earth. We've got a job to do, and when we do it properly, the dividends are unlimited. Good God almighty, does that ever make for a full tummy, mind, heart, body, and soul, or what?

Thunderbirds in the Texas Oakflats

A hoot owl let loose somewhere to our south and immediately, his lord of the roost, Sir ThunderChicken, double-breasted, iridescent feathergod of GobbleTown, USA, lit up nearby with a spine-tingling, throaty double gobble in retaliation. Real close nearby. I gulped. My head turned a glowing red, and I had a most powerful urge to spread my wings, tilt my head back, puff myself all up, and strut up a storm. There was even a deep rumble in my belly. I had to gather myself and try to remain calm. It was hopeless. It was beautiful.

As I bid farewell to Derek Derringer, my Texas hunting guide and friend, we both smiled knowingly in the pre-dawn Texas murk that a very special springtime ThanxGiving was unfolding before us. Ahhh . . . spring turkey hunting season in the Texas Hill Country. Excuse me whilst I kiss the sky.

Spring turkey, Tennessee, 1998

Derek's tail lights drifted out of sight into the thick scrub of the YO Ranch, as I unzipped the door to my Invisiblind, a nifty ground tent that I would call hunting home again this fine morning. Cleverly designed by Mark Mueller, primarily with the archery turkey hunter in mind, the ingenious shoot-thru camo screen is just what the good Drumstick Doctor ordered for hiding from the amazing eagle-eyes of the wild turkey. I have used this great product to help me take game for many years and it has been a godsend for frustrated turkey hunters everywhere. Though I've lucked out on a number of bowkilled gobblers over many years of trying, mostly hunting from makeshift groundblinds, my percentage of wild longbeard dinners has gone way up since using this advantageous concealment system. I settled in, opened the window covers, and genuflected in the predawn ritual of springtime renewal. I quivered and grinned with excited anticipation. It is truly wonderful to be alive in the turkey woods.

At first shooting light, with a few soft strokes on my box call, I broke the morning stillness. Nothing. Putting a little more oomph into my calling, I was immediately overwhelmed with a thunderous eruption of gobbles directly behind me. I actually flinched. How cool is that? I called back and peeked out from the side window of my blind to see four big birds walking my way through the scattered mottes of live oaks to the east. Here they come! I scrambled to position my tripod vidcam to both capture the excitement yet remain out of my way for a bowshot. The peeking sunrise was now glowing onto the beautiful iridescent plumage of all four toms, their beards nearly dragging on the caliche gravel trail heading my way. Gulp!

They hung up at about forty yards, picking, and scratching, the largest of the longbeards all puff-daddy'd up, strutting for all his worth. I now called with my mouth in subtle purrs and clucks, trying to sound my sexiest hen yelp flirtbirdy. That did it. The four thunderbirds were now walking with purpose straight for my hideout. I brought my Renegade bow up into shoot mode, and tried to breathe easy. You calm down mister!

With the slowest motion possible, I steered the camera onto the birds that were now only fifteen yards before me, centered the big boy in the lens, slowly zoomed in on him, and began my draw. WHACK!

The 500-grain all-white carbon arrow took him square in the wingbutt with a wonderful audible THUNK! It blew him off his feet and he scrambled to take flight, but the main engine was out of commission. He staggered a ways down into the draw as his three comrades surrounded him, pecking, and strutting in absolute confusion. Then he lay still, I breathed and the survivors moved off. Upon releasing my arrow, I had watched the entire thrilling episode unfold through the eye of my camera lens, and though I was ecstatic over the hunt and shot, I was much more thrilled that I had captured the whole deal on tape. This would surely make a fantastic show for our Spirit of the Wild television show for the whole world to share in the amazing American turkey hunting experience.

I filmed my excitement, a good show intro and a "stay tuned." Then I set the tripod up outside my blind, welcomed everyone back, then got the whole tracking and recovery on tape as well. With the camera whirring, I celebrated the fact that there are more wild turkeys in Texas right now, than could be found across North America when Christopher Columbus first got here. Wild! Like the record populations of deer, geese, cougars, and bears, the success story of wild turkey conservation is irrefutable testimony to the unprecedented, astonishing job the hunting community of America has accomplished, particularly in the face of dramatic habitat abuse for so long. God bless the National Wild Turkey Federation and all the hunting organizations dedicated to wildlife habitat and management.

I even filmed myself merrily walking off into the beauty of the Texas Hill Country with the gorgeous old YO Ranch thunderbird hung over my shoulder. We really look good together. WOW! What a great job I have. This is one of my favorites! I think I'll give myself a bonus of barbequed garlic and mesquite drumsticks for dinner tonight. The beast is dead; long live the beast.

The American Dream Begins at Home

Regardless of your profession, personal goals or hobbies, your number one job and responsibility is to be the parent of your kids.

I'm no longer convinced some of us understand that simple truism.

Parenting is a one-shot opportunity. You'll get no second chance. You either hit the bull's eye or you miss. The clock cannot be turned back so that you can try it again and again. I find it amazing that some of us act as though we'll get a second shot at parenting. Or is it some just don't give a damn?

This may sound odd coming from a parent who has made his living as a touring musician, but my children have always come first. I've literally forfeited millions of dollars by canceling tours to be with my children. I have intelligently taken off each hunting season since becoming a parent. This is not just the sacred time

Ted offers educational nature tours of his Michigan property to youth groups and organzations. *Credit: Matt Sherlock*

afield for the Nugent tribe, but of equal

importance, this represents school start-up season as well. This is opening day for their education and I insist on being a driving force therein.

When my kids were young, even while I was touring, I spoke to them twice, three, four times a day, every day. Each day I had off was spent traveling back to Michigan so that I could be with my kids. I checked their homework, attended their sporting events, took them hunting and fishing, and spent precious quiet time just listening to them. I attended nearly all of their school and athletic events as well to show them the dynamics of family bonding. Powerful medicine for sure.

Indeed, like all parents, I've made mistakes along the way. While I regret them, I don't dwell on them. For every mistake I made I have always strived to not only keep from making that mistake again, but dedicate myself to diligently upgrading my parenting skills by trying to find new, spiritually productive and quality-enhancing family activities that would make me a better dad. Continual personal upgrade is the key to not only parenting, but life as well.

I was blessed to have been raised by parents who believed and practiced being my parents, not my friends. They understood their role, which included a healthy dose of abundant love, guidance, and take-no-crap discipline. Thank you mom & dad!

If consistently and honestly practiced by parents, love, guidance and discipline are the very foundations by which a child will grow to be accountable, confident, responsible, polite, physically healthy, productive, and a caring adult member of society. The goal of every parent should be to pass on these vital characteristics to their kids. You shouldn't need a psychologist, family counselor, or a greasy rhythm and blues guitar player to tell you that. Self evident truth needs to be put back into common sense as soon as America is ready.

Seemingly daily, however, I read a newspaper or Internet article, or see a television report about parents who are failing miserably. The examples they are setting for their kids are counterproductive, unhealthy, and dangerous. It is not only their child they are failing, but ultimately our society. The insanity of drug, alcohol, tobacco and fast food abuse in America today can only be described as brain-dead. What example are you providing for your kids? Honestly?

Parents have the greatest influence on their children. Kids learn behaviors, attitudes, morals, and values from us. For example, if you have turned into a human blob by having a poor diet and a lack of exercise, your kid is bound to be lazy and fat as well. In fact, the statistics regarding the number of American kids who are overweight are appalling.

If you place no value on education then neither will your child. He or she will be as dumb as you. It takes no effort to be uninformed, stupid, and easily manipulated. If this is you, do us all a favor and don't vote.

If you don't enforce proper behavior through discipline, your child will grow up to be an out-of-control adult who does not know what the boundaries of decency are in our society. He or she will think the world revolves around them. It doesn't. The lack of parental discipline is the primary reason our prisons are full.

A home without love is the most dangerous of all. This will ultimately produce a child with low self-esteem and a sense of worthlessness. If you place your career or other interests before your child, you are selfish and undeserving of the most precious gift God has given you. Hug your kids every day and tell them that you love them. Spend quality time with them now. Push them. Intensely probe into their lives, showing them that you deeply care about their daily activities and content. That is an investment that will pay huge dividends down the road of life.

I encourage everyone to take a few moments and evaluate if you have your priorities in line. You get one shot at being the best parent you can be. Make it count. Your kids are counting on you. So is America.

The Great Uncle Ted Pork Story

It was certainly a scary bunch of heathens gathered about, their intimidating, animal-like scowling faces made even more frightening by the eerie glow of the tribal campfire. The flickering, flaming light on their rugged and disheveled features in the dank dark of pre-dawn was primal. Was this a clan of killers and thieves preparing for some heinous criminal orgy of terror on an unsuspecting innocent public? Maybe the rebirth of some new Attila the Hun fan club, or just dirty, drunken bums looking for trouble?

In fact, no book should ever be judged by its cover, for this handsome tribe of rugged individuals was indeed the best members of the American Dream society the world has ever known. It was the annual gathering of my esteemed fellow pig whackin' BloodBrothers of the Great Spirit of the Wild BBQ Pork Party. A little unkempt for sure, but after a sleepless night of adrenalin pumping anticipation for the big hunt, our sleepy, struggling-to-wake-up train-wreck appearance could not be confused with the sheer perfection of our readiness and the beauty of our pork gathering dreams of bio-diversity celebration. To kill many pigs is to not only bring the ultimate succulent flesh to the family dinner table, but indeed, a natural, positive function of simple balance for the environment. What at first appears to be scary guys and imminent doom, turns out to be the ultimate hands-on conservationists in the free world today, preparing for good, clean, gut pile fun. We may as well call ourselves the Mothers of Theresa Pork Posse and get it over with. We grinned and loaded our weapons while adjusting our halos. It was time to Man-Up. The grunting noises alone were beautiful.

Armed with blackpowder rifles and handguns, bows and arrows, crossbows, magnum handguns and hi-powered rifles of every imaginable caliber and description, not to mention unlimited attitude from hell, these hollow-pointed warriors slugged down the last of the aromatic race fuel Nuge Java and began to load up into the waiting pickup trucks. Some wild boar commandos slowly melted into the darkness on foot, heading into the sacred hunting grounds of Sunrize Acres. I loaded up and hauled a long bed full of pork-hungry hunters straight for the deep woods, and slowly dropped individuals off at prime ambush zones for their rendezvous with the beasts. Hearts beat wildly.

With all hunters positioned, and the threat of pre-glow sunrise behind us to the east, Big Jim and I walked slowly and stealthily into the big oak timber to the southwest, settling into our NorthStarr ladder-stands as quietly as possible. Jim readied our Spirit of the Wild vidcam gear while I notched an arrow and adjusted my Mossy Oak facemask. Goosebumps migrated up and down our spines in this wonderful, wild place, and all was good with the world. Knowing all our hunters were positioned in optimal game zones, we were giddy with excitement as we envisioned what would be taking place at some of our favorite stand sites. An ever-increasing thrill occurs when we have so many spots manned, waiting enthusiastically to hear the stories that would certainly gush forth later at the lunchtime campfire. I had to do everything in my power to calm down and prepare for my own hopeful porcine encounter. The east turned a light pink and my soul had liftoff. Here we go.

Invisible small birds are the first sensual alarm of the morning as they flutter about overhead, followed closely by distant crowspeak. Songbirds join in for the SpiritWild alarm clock soundoff, and shadows in the woods begin to take on life forms as the light slowly increases. And what a stunning light it is. Each wave of morning mist carries sparkling shards of colored, shimmering light as they slowly roll across the forest landscape. Then the status-quo aesthetics take a hit as a huge dark blob appears cresting the small woodland rise and Beasto McPorko emerges like a hairy Sherman tank, grunting and slobbering, ready for battle. He has death in his eyes. I love him.

He takes a few steps, then stops, nose in the air, course, brindle hair bristling. Surely he got wind of somebody somewhere off in his dawn travels, and now he is ultra alert, looking for trouble. He pivots hard to the left and we see a small whitetail buck staring back at the huge boar. At the same time, a brilliant shaft of stunning sunlight cuts through the leafy forest canopy, glowing, and glistening between the two beasts. I sneak a peak at Jim and he is capturing the whole, magic moment on digital tape. Just then, a pair of crows swoop in over us and provide a perfect, raucous soundtrack to the wild images before us. It's all quite moving and only a hunter will be here to absorb such beauty and thrills. We sponge it all in and thank God.

Now the handsome boar begins to walk straight down the trail in front of us, and, fortunately, still mostly paying attention to the small buck. As his head disappears behind a huge choke cherry tree, I draw my Renegade NugeBow back and begin my Prayer for the WildThings. As his fanny clears the tree, I let out a slight grunt that makes him stop. Instantly, my gorgeous white arrow vanishes dead center into his heaving chest with a hard whack. With a squeal and a whoof, he pivots hard 180 degrees and scrambles for the ridge, but does not make it. He runs in a small circle and tips over with a few last kicks. Then all is silent. The small buck stands and watches, totally confused by the whole show. Jim slowly zooms in on the fallen beast, pans to the buck and then to my smiling face. The light is magic now and I do my best to calmly articulate what just took place, trying to explain to a viewing audience how magnificent and wonderful this bowhunting life truly is. I think I do well because I love it so much. Reality rocks.

Jim films me drawing my bow for some cutaway close-ups for editing purposes, and then he documents the tracking and recovery of the great hog. He's a dandy, weighing more than three hundred pounds on the hoof. The razor-sharp two-blade broadhead killed him fast and clean. His long snout, protruding ivory, enormous chest, and narrow hips, long, rangy tail and heavy coat of coarse, iron-wool confirm his Austrian lineage and we take many photos to remember this magic moment in time.

After a struggle gutting and dragging the boar from the forest and hauling it back to camp, we are joined shortly by three more successful pig killers with their beautiful trophies. Larry arrowed a handsome calico boar and Rod made a perfect heart shot on a black beauty. James was responsible for the late morning bang we had heard, as he sent a blackpowder slug into a huge, heavy wild boar of his own. Their stories were conveyed with much passion and the excitement was very contagious. We were all pumped.

The entire weekend went like that, with much celebration and jubilation around the campfire. Stories and laughter were shared nonstop and all the world's problems were nonexistent. Massive amounts of delicious pork steaks and sausage were barbequed and consumed, and intense revelry went on into the nights. These were all good men, productive in their American Dreams of being the best that they can be. Taking care of their families, being assets to their communities, and hunting wild boar because they are driven to do the right things. Everyone took home giant coolers of the precious prizes of pure pork protein and unlimited memories that are unique and powerful. Enthusiasm was rampant, and ideas and concerns were shared by all to return home and to the workplace to fight for a better America. A stimulating boar hunt will do that for a guy, and the world will be a better place for it. We will do it again soon.

Helplessness Is for Wimps & Deadguyz

With all the yapping and hand wringing about Homeland Defense, I'm somewhat perplexed there hasn't been more discussion about how average Americans can secure their country from terrorists, thugs, and other assorted human debris and scum.

You heard it here first: Homeland defense begins at home. It is each American's responsibility to protect himself and his family from those who want to perpetrate harm upon us. I could care less what the creep's religious, political, or ideological intentions are, or whether he simply wants to steal your Buick at gunpoint. A killer is a killer and they must be stopped.

I pray the feds have the resources, intelligence, and commitment to exterminate terrorists around the world. I also pray the local cops have the same resources to lock up local punks who have instigated their own criminal jihad against law-abiding citizens. Pray as I might, I also adamantly believe each of us should be prepared to neutralize evil in its tracks whenever and wherever it may arise. Waiting for the feds or the cops to show up

Ted and Arbor Day student mentor, Kim Sobanski, demonstrate proper tree planting techniques.

might be a death sentence—our death sentence. Crime reports, studies, and honest cops will tell you that it is up to you to defend yourself and your loved ones against evil people. Fortunately, the majority of states allow their citizens to carry concealed weapons to do just that. After all, to be unarmed is to be helpless, and that's just irresponsible. Though the media won't tell you this, law-abiding citizens use guns to thwart crime roughly two million times a year. The media's silence on these facts is condemnable. Instead of reporting the facts, the media whores engage in journalistic prostitution as it pertains to guns. They will "report" or spin the story to meet their left-wing ideology that guns are evil, unnecessary instruments designed solely to kill other people. I'm sure two million people a year would beg to differ with the media's overt dishonesty and unprofessional anti-gun agenda.

The average American is much more likely to be the victim of a recidivistic punk who has a rap sheet a yard long than of a Muslim extremist. Therefore, it only stands to reason that we must be more vigilant to protect our homes and lives against the street rats than the religious numbskulls who kill in the name of their evil gods.

I'm not arguing that everyone run out and get a permit to carry a concealed weapon. First off, everyone is not going to do everything that makes sense all the time. Secondly, only those people who feel comfortable carrying a concealed weapon and who routinely practice with it should do so.

There are literally millions of Americans who carry concealed weapons on a daily basis. The media has unabashedly tried to convince Americans that this practice is extremely dangerous, that ordinary Americans will shoot at each other in traffic, and that accidental shootings will far outweigh any benefit. Again, the media whores couldn't be more wrong. The number of concealed carry permits that have been rescinded is literally minuscule, virtually a non-issue. There haven't been shootouts between concealed carry holders as the media tried in vain to scare Americans into believing. Concealed carry permit holders haven't shot the wrong guy. Concealed carry permit holders haven't committed crimes. Instead, these conscientious Americans have made America a safer place to live, work, and play. Isn't that the goal of Homeland Defense? Americans need to be vigilant. We need to get to know our neighbors better. We need to become more involved in great programs such as Neighborhood Watch. We need to establish better relationships with our police departments. I support any effort that will truly assist in stopping the next terrorist or thug who wishes to bring harm to innocent, law-abiding Americans. I will never, however, support any effort that will make it easier for criminals to prey on innocent Americans because Sarah Brady doesn't believe in us to take care of ourselves.

Homeland defense begins at home. There are millions of Americans each year that can attest to that. The heroic actions of these brave Americans need to be recognized, even celebrated, not hidden from the public view by the media, or worse, scorned.

We have the legal right and a moral duty to protect our loved ones and ourselves. I don't depend on anyone else for my family's protection. That would be foolish, dangerous, and cowardly. When I call 911 it will only be tell them to bring a dustpan and a broom. I shoot back, and depending on the circumstances, I'll shoot first. You're weird if you've got a problem with that. Good should live, evil should die. Make a stand America. Neutralize evil or get out of their way.

The Beast from Beyond

The Dirty Dozen had once again assembled on the spiritual battlefield of the GreatHunt and attitudes were running high with chilling anticipation for the arrival of the beast. Opening day, November 15, a day of infamy here in the wilds of Michigan's vast deer grounds, and we were proud and excited to be a part of the world's largest armed forces ever. With nearly 800,000 high-powered rifle-toting sporters converging across the hinterland on this mitten-shaped landmass, North America's largest peninsula was about to erupt in gunfire, spirit, and intense predator celebration. Our inner spirits were ablaze to say the least. I never felt more at home.

Good men all, this opener was especially celebratory as hunter number twelve was my son Toby. An expert hunter and marksman in his own right, having him at camp with the old man made every aspect of this wonderful event that much more intensely gratifying. There is nothing like a wilderness hunting adventure together as father and son and we were taking it all for all it was worth. Quality time in such a setting does wonders for the soul through more open communication as a direct result of the spiritual environment of this time-honored tradition of reconnecting with the good mother earth and all her critters. We all need as much reconnecting as we can get nowadays, especially parents and children. I was on cloud nine.

Following the soul-stirring revelry of a pre-dawn wake-up like no other, filling our guts with ample fortification, gathering guns and gear, twelve smiles lit the dim cabin with optimism and joy as we prepared for the wilderness plunge back to the sacred primal screamzone of the wild. With a hard-cutting chill in the black woodland air, we all trudged as silently as possible to our pre-designated ambush hides, doing our best to make the transition from downtown Charlie Brown to primordial Natty Bumppo predator. Chief guide, Jim Lawson, and I had positioned our intrepid sporters in prime locations for optimal deer encounters, but with the onslaught of humanity now descending on the once peaceful forest, we all knew the deer would be on red alert and poised to play this timeless tooth, fang, and claw game of predator and prey, as God had designed them to do so well. The challenge is intense to say the least. As outfitter for this annual Sunrize Safaris deer hunting party, I had thought long and hard about each hunter's setup, and was confident that we had chosen the very best spots for each hunter. The one hundred foot pine tree Jim and I headed for on this ceremonious morning was just too scary for your average hunter, but it gave us the perfect overview of the eternal landscape that our hunters surrounded. Son Toby was within earshot, about a mile northeast of us, situated in the most beautiful cedar swamp you've ever seen. We sensed enormous flocks of goose bumps fluttering everywhere. It is truly spine tingling.

As the first hint of dawn cleared the horizon, isolated gunshots began to build in the distance. It's ballistic music to my ears and an amazing feeling to be a part of, knowing that at any moment a buck could appear from nowhere, and all your training and practice will be tested to the hilt. Flying Vs of Canada geese appeared overhead, with giant skeins of snow geese soaring in formation, high in the stratosphere, singing their migration theme songs. Songbirds shared our pinetree perch with us, and a per-snippety red squirrel noisily scolded us for taking over his apartment building. Then, Jim poked me with his elbow as he slowly spun the video camera hard right. "Buck," is all he whispered and I strained to find the shape of a deer in the cutover puckerbrush hell to our south. I saw nothing 'till the white flag bolted in amongst the impenetrable wall of saplings about eighty yards out, and hopelessly tried to find an opening through my scope for the 95 grain .243 bullet to connect. No way! The handsome buck was much too cagey for this old hunter, always managing to keep just enough projectile-interfering brush between us to eliminate the chance for a clear shot. As the beast melted into the far off, thicker cedar cover to our east, I saw his tawny shape veer left and head in the general direction of Toby's stand. Jim and I looked at each other with wide, knowing grins, both of us excited that he was on course for a very special rendezvous.

In short order, a shot rang out and we knew. We high-five'd and held back our laughter as best we could. Settling down to let it all sink in, we continued our vigil till I couldn't take it any longer, and turned on my two-way radio to call Toby. Sure enough, he reported that he was standing over the most beautiful buck in the world, a dandy eight point trophy whitetail with unique white markings all over his muscled body. With much spark to his speech, Toby related the dynamo of the moment of truth and said he would meet us where the little creek forked at the ridgeline. He was one happy, excited deer hunter—almost as happy as his dad.

With vidcam purring, Jim captured the thrilling moments on digital tape for our Spirit of the Wild TV show, when father and son converge on a hard won trophy buck in such stunning surroundings. It was indeed a gorgeous, partially piebald buck, shot perfectly through the heart with his Browning .243 semi-auto at about sixty yards. The deer had run but a short forty yards before settling back to earth for its final rest. Many memorable photos were taken celebrating this special occurrence and together we dragged the heavy buck out of the cedar swamp. Back at camp, hanging on the historical NugeCamp buck pole next to our bow-killed deer, it became the epicenter of conversation at our little hideaway. Though no other hunters tagged a buck on this particular hunt, Toby's buck was celebrated as if each of us owned a part of the spirit of the beast. Over fresh backstraps and onions around a blazing fire that night, the transference of protein was but a small acknowledgment of what sustenance the beast provides. The memories and charging desire to save wild ground and wildlife burned in each of us, hot like a fire of dreams, fueled by the flesh and spirit of our deer.

The Prayer

Craig and I met up where the worn trails converged on the central Texas prairie. I was smiling ear to ear, Craig not. He could read my face and I sure as hell could read his. I knew that look. Pain. Heartbreak. Agony. Defeat. Good Lord I knew it well. For many years, and I do mean many, I too felt the pain of blown shots and missed opportunities. And there is no more intensely painful mistake than making a bad arrow shot following the typical mind, body, and heart-slamming torture and sacrifice of the average bowhunting waiting game. We scout, and plan, and strategize, and wait, and wait and wait and wait and wait and wait, so that when the shot finally does present itself, it is borderline unbearable, when for no damn good reason, we simply choke. It really hurts and the defeated look on my friend's face said it all.

I tried to liven him up with the joyous tale of my perfect morning and dandy Texas beast I had already recovered. And he did celebrate enthusiastically with me. But as he retold his story of woe, I knew we had to figure out a way to get him over this agonizing bowhunting hump. Reverend Nuge to the rescue!

Many years ago, I had forced myself, out of sheer frustration, to demand an end to my mindless, panicky arrow flinging misses at the moment of truth. I began a hard core procedure to eliminate the exploding tension and, at the very least, the uppity manifestation of critter encounter excitability that caused my own horror of blown ops. I had to train myself to memorize an exacting mental and physical procedure that would ensure consistent arrow accuracy under the pressurizing moments in the face of the beast. That's all.

Axis deer, Texas, 2003

When I listened to the master bowhunters I have been blessed to share campfires with, the likes of Fred Bear, Dick Mauch, Bob Foulkrod, Bruce Cull, Claude Pollington and others, I picked up on their reminders of archery's spiritually historical Zen beginnings. They all stressed the "keep it simple, stupid" approach to arrow flinging. I am convinced that the so called progression of archery technology, though certainly amazing in its own right, has provided improved possibilities for the masses with runaway compound bow development, perfected mechanical releases, sights, arrows, broadheads and more. This same technology has in many ways further complicated a once ultra-simple, graceful, natural hand-eye coordination game of man and basic tool. I have watched my stress-free friends turn into flinching, nervous wrecks as they seek to master the compound bow beast. It was when I applied the direction of better bowmen than I, that I finally turned back into the bowhunting killer of my youth. I crave proficient archery and game hanging on the pole is still the ultimate indicator of a job well done. Craig was about to unleash the killer inside, and I was as excited as he was.

We started out making sure Craig could draw his bow gracefully, without any straining effort. We ended up backing down his poundage by nearly ten pounds to a comfortable, easy-going fifty-five pounds. His draw length was AOK as his anchor settled properly into the corner of his mouth. No kisser button needed to complicate things as he memorized a specific lip lock for his release on every shot. We were rockin'.

His next step was critical. He was to learn that bad habits at the target range will guarantee missed game in the field. No more casual arrows ever again. Joining our friend and dedicated new bowhunting BloodBrother, we practiced at Calvin Ross' LoneStar Archery & Music in Waco, Texas. Both of them developed their own three-step mantra for perfect archery. I have my three-part sign of the cross, but Craig and Calvin determined their own personal prayer for every arrow they will ever shoot ever again.

Step 1. Pick and address an exact spot to hit and zero in on it with all your heart and soul. Step 2. Settle an exact anchor and overall relaxed form while maintaining step one's spot. And step 3, focus all systems on a back tension release for total consistency and follow-through as all three steps become a single gesture. It was beautiful.

Whew! It may sound wild and intense, but that may be because it's so wild and intense. But I am here to tell you, the smiles on these two guys faces joined mine for the ultimate three stooges archery party of all times. Sheer joy and giddiness was in the air. Did I mention. "Whew?" We couldn't wait to hit the woods.

The celebration went through the roof that weekend, as all three of us dragged home some dandy backstrappers as a result of some doggone good arrows. We all admitted it was without a doubt a direct result of our intense, hardcore three-step practice routine that took over as each shot began to present itself. It was agreed that it was as if the beast no longer really existed there before us, as our hunter's mind was totally consumed by our little bowhunter prayer. Cool, huh?

I am equally convinced that the number one cause of attrition in our wonderful bowhunting sport is the loss of archers due to target panic or other such maladies that cause us to miss. Especially when the chips are down at the target range or in the face of the beast. This loss of BloodBrothers would be bad enough under any circumstances, but in this cultural war against hunting and our honorable outdoor way of life, we cannot afford to lose conservationists or their votes. Spread this good idea far and wide, and let us all work hard to guide and nurture our fellow shooters, and of equal importance, the baptism of new bowhunters and archers every chance we get. The three-step shooter's prayer is the way to go. It works.

The Sacred Hunt
Is Where You Find It

It was a beautiful, sunny fall afternoon, September 10, 1975, yet another spectacular day on the mystical, wild grounds of the famous Uncompadre National Forest on Colorado's mythical Western Slope. Following legendary guide Jerry Byrum's expert instructions, young Ted slithered up the glowing, golden-quackie mountainside as quietly and stealthy as could be. Before I could attain my designated position, an eruption on the hillside exploded before me and as the magnificent trophy mule deer raced past me, my old Bear Kodiak take-down bow came back as if a part of me, and my Bear RazorHead tipped aluminum arrow sliced into the galloping beast's chest in a heartbeat, blood splashing everywhere. I didn't have a nanosecond to think, I merely responded as an instinctual, reasoning predator and let my lifelong archery training take over. It was beautiful.

As I knelt at the side of the gorgeous 5x5 buck, I reflected on the thousands of hours I had bowhunted with no such luck, and most poignantly, how it had all happened so fast this day. On the surface, it appeared to be just way too easy. Of course, it wasn't easy at all. Year after year of difficult pre-dawn adventure, bazillions of hours of hard core archery practice and woodsmanship lessons and, of course, the blessings of moving campfires with my family and the great Fred Bear, had prepared me to be the best bowhunter I could be. Nothing less would be tolerated in our camps. And now it had all paid off. I howled with laughter and happiness for a hard-earned job well done. I nearly cried at the stirring emotion of it all.

That wonderful moment, like so many others just like it, is tattooed on my spirit, never to be discounted or compromised as to the inescapable reality of our predatorship and natural consumerism in God's grand creation. After all, there is no other function available to mankind as pure, perfect, and absolutely tooth, fang, and claw as hunting. Nothing. Stalking, outwitting, outmaneuvering, and overcoming the awesome defense capabilities of such miraculous big game animals that God has created to do just so, especially with the short range restrictions of the bow and arrow, remains a driving quality of life force in millions of American families' lives, and I, for one, am proud as can be to be a part of it.

Now jettison forward thirty-eight years to my hunt season 2003, on the hallowed deer grounds of Jack Brittingham's South Texas' Rancho Encantado: five thousand amazing acres of prime whitetail hunting, the likes of which most of us only dream of. Though I was bowhunting during the most prime time possible at an intersection of killer habitat where mature bucks had been seen regularly, I wrapped up my second year here without getting a shot.

I've heard the presumptuousness of ignorant critics against such hi-fence operations as they condemn them as shooting "fish in a barrel," and I chuckle at such foolishness. Most of the greatest people I have had the pleasure to know in my fifty-five years have been fellow hunters. Intelligent, down-to-earth BloodBrothers of goodwill, respect and reciprocal integrity. But sadly, some of the biggest goofballs out there have been hunters as well. What drives these knee-jerk critics to be so close-minded, particularly during this cultural war against hunting, is beyond me.

I hunt every day of the season, usually more than two hundred days a year and I intelligently seek as varied and diverse hunting adventure as I can find with all my heart and soul; the wildest of wild grounds in and out of fences. I demand genuine "fair chase" and scoff at the notion that proper high fence ranches or the use of bait, sex scents, rattling and calling, drives, ultra-high treestands, scent-proof clothing, good optics, space-age materials, loud Rock 'n' Roll on the truck stereo or a good flashlight are somehow unsportsmanlike. Balderdash. There are critics of everything out there. It is all good. And bottomline, it is up to the individual hunter to choose his preferred method of legal hunting.

Not every hunter in America has access to a family's or friend's big buck heaven in Kansas, Iowa, Texas, or Illinois. I have killed great bucks under such conditions and deeply appreciate the opportunity. However, to bemoan, much less condemn, a private landowner for upgrading the quality of his herd and subsequent hunting with a deer-proof fence is intellectually bankrupt. On the numerous hi-fence ops I have hunted, I have never had the fence come into play, in any way, to help me ambush a deer. The main role of the fence is to limit outside impact on the herd, not vice versa.

I am and believe in, salute, and support the wilderness hunter. It is a great challenge. So goes the ultimate deer lover who dedicates his private land and invests in superior management of his natural resources by keeping the killer of young deer out. I hunt it all and love it all. Ethics are intensely personal and I also support the person who simply wants to eat venison but isn't interested in sportsmanship, challenge, or another's view of ethics or fair chase, but just wants to kill a deer on the back forty, fenced or not fenced, so he or she can eat the best renewable protein God has ever made. To each his own. Go for it.

Autopilot Kills

The exploding flush of the rocket-like bobwhite quail caught some of us off guard. Again. Even though the well-trained pointers were synchronized perfectly in their identification of the covey's exact location, the buzzsaw, whirlygig of wings is nerve-wracking and always intensely exhilarating no matter how much warning we have. Unless you've done it a thousand times before, the claymore-like covey rise will git ya everytime. Abruptly, three birds fell from the sky as the other twenty-some feathered bombs flashed away into the thick prickly pear scrub of Texas. The three dead birds were killed by two veteran quail hunters while the empty smoking guns held by the two novice's merely poked holes in the birdless sky before them. In order to hit such shocking, little targets, a shooter must experience many shocking little targets in order to develop the demanding, ever challenging feel for these fast, erratic flying, and always shocking little targets. Lots of hands-on experience is the only way to prepare one's psyche for such instantaneous hand-eye challenge. It all happens so fast, you must react instinctively on auto pilot, for if a nanosecond is lost to thinking, it's too late. Then we gotta buy chicken and that's no fun.

I was raised in a hunting family, but my dear old dad approached our outdoor adventures strictly as relaxed, laid back recreational time. And that is wonderful unto itself, for sure. But a fire erupted in me after but a few excursions beyond the pavement, and I went from easy-going wildlife observer, into full-bore, hard core predator addict by the time I hit my seventh Fall. I had it bad, I had it so good. With my increased excitement and anticipation for my wild time at such an early age, I had no idea how to manage my physical or psychological self for such stimulating critter encounters. I had

African Watusi bull, 1998

not been disciplined in the demands of stealth, level of awareness, or predator skills to any degree, and I found myself stumbling along with a very frustrating outdoor experiment of trial and error. Heavy duty emphasis on the error factor.

Though I learned much over the years, I certainly missed way more opportunities than those I had capitalized on. It was very, very frustrating. Eventually, I picked up many wise lessons from my uncle John, Fred Bear, Claude Pollington, George Nicholls and many other masters, but the big revelation came about with a life of its own. I had missed more nice bucks with my bow and arrow than I cared to admit and with an average of forty to fifty hours of intense hunting time invested before I even got a shot, made the blown opportunity that much more painful. Then I got angry.

A good emotion for sure, for as we channel anger towards certain failed procedures, we can punish ourselves by demanding upgrade by intellectually refusing to take it anymore. Ya think? I simply refused to waste my time missing anymore since I knew I could. A–position myself for a decent shot and B–put an arrow where I wanted it under most conditions. I suppose you could call my problem "buck fever," but I didn't really get nuts when the shot arrived, I just didn't function as I knew I must. So I started training myself in an ultra-disciplined fashion during every archery session no matter how informal. It was like a switch had been turned on.

Diligently practicing my guitar throughout my life should have taught me how simple repetitious activities can bring about precision and effectiveness. Sometimes, archery is just so much relaxing fun, that the serious aspects of bowhunting can be lost on the celebration of enjoyable arrow flinging. Bowhunting is NOT arrow flinging. In fact it is just the opposite. Bowhunting is ultimately discipline. And in its fullest appreciation, archery, too, should be taken seriously in order to perform it to its highest level. To witness a champion target archer in action is truly impressive. Arrow after arrow into a tiny spot on a distant target is an art form that shows the heightened capabilities of the human species. That's where I want to be when I'm in my treestand. And I'm there, finally.

Developing my three-part archery prayer taught me to combine a series of mechanical events in my shooting that became tattooed on my mind. Step one is to pick an exact spot to hit. Step two is to settle in at full draw with an exact anchor, relaxing for proper form. Step three is to pull my back muscles for a smooth, consistent release, locking all three steps into a learned regimen that is applied to every arrow I ever shoot. And man is it ever gratifying to say the least. I literally go into auto pilot when I prepare for a shot. The beast before me or the target on stage in front of a million people does not exist. It's just me and my three steps.

I have translated that same approach for my rifle, handgun, and shotgun shooting as well. By paying acute attention to each and every shot I take at the range or while just having fun plinking with my buddies, my mind, body, and soul memorize a systematic program that disciplines my every shot. Well, almost every shot. There is no question that my hunting time has become much more fulfilling and gratifying for me over the years because of this. And, of course, the increased rewards in the form of scrumptious nutrition at the family dinner table is BBQ testimony to the success of my auto-pilot program. It really is mind over matter or, better yet, mind in concert with matter that brings it all together. Next time you grab that bow or gun, or guitar, take a deep breath and make every shot count. Develop your own three step mantra and let the backstraps flow.

First Bow

It doesn't matter if you're five or fifty. Archery will turn you on. It can be as thrilling as loud, dangerous Rock 'n' Roll, but without the crowds. I promise. Over the

years, I have had the distinct plea-
sure of baptizing hundreds and
hundreds of families into the ever-
mystifying world of the mystical
flight of the arrow, and at this exciting
stage of my American Dream,
I'm not sure if I get a bigger kick
out of shooting my own arrows or
celebrating the immense joys I
share with so many people shooting their own. Everyone, man,
woman, boy, or girl, falls in love
with the Zen-like charge of making
that next arrow better. I can say

Ted Nugent Kamp for Kids

217

with total confidence, that archery, as a physical, mental, and spiritual discipline, has brought an immense quality of life upgrade for everyone I have personally witnessed discover it. It is truly that thrilling.

During hundreds of talk-radio programs each year, plus a daily infusion of e-mail and U.S. mail correspondence, I have been inundated with inquiries about my apparent bow and arrow giddiness. Everybody wants big fun in their lives and they see me go wild every time I fling an arrow on our *Spirit of the Wild* TV show, on stage at my concerts, or simply when I talk about it on radio. Even after more than fifty years of archery, my passion for each arrow continues to increase every day. It's wild.

At our annual Ted Nugent Kamp for Kids charity camp, the children have the times of their lives enjoying a plethora of outdoor recreation activities. But no other activity among the lengthy roster of enjoyable events compares with the excitement gushing forth at the archery range. Though many of the kids are already die-hard archers when they arrive, every boy and girl shows a marked excitability when they grip a bow, especially those who do so for the very first time. Witnessing such contagious fun, the parents immediately show rabid interest themselves, and we always find ourselves in a full-blown bow and arrow fun fest for the whole family.

The best archery is all about feel. Not technology, not competition, not killing record book trophies, not taking home awards. But rather, simple, gutsy, instinctual, individual feel. In its ultimate analysis, the flight of the arrow should be an extension of one's inner self. All the gadgets and hi-tech gear in the world won't mean diddly-squat if it doesn't feel right.

I'm six foot two, about 190 pounds dripping wet, without a belt full of hardware, and I can draw a ninety pound bow if I try hard enough. But a heavy bow does not feel comfortable for me. My current lightweight Renegade bow is set up for a girly fifty-five pounds, and it is a joy to shoot in every way. In fact, since I reduced the draw weight of my bows over the years, my accuracy has increased dramatically, and so has my bowhunting successes. I can pull back this rig with nary a struggle or hump, and my arrows go right where I'm looking. I always encourage new shooters and veterans alike to shoot a bow that comes back smoothly and gracefully. Whether we choose an old fashioned longbow, a beautiful handmade recurve, or a state-of-the-art hi-tech compound bow with all the bells and whistles, the style or brand name of the bow matters not. Just for the record, I know of youngsters and women who cleanly kill big deer, elk, hogs, moose, and caribou, as well as some big, tough African game without a problem. They thoroughly enjoy doing so by shooting razor sharp, two-blade broadheads from comfortable, properly fitted and setup bows in the thirty-five to forty pound range. Regardless of bow weight, killing big game responsibly has always been and will always be about stealth and shot placement. Not about arrow speed or bow weight.

Equal in importance to comfortable draw weight, is proper draw length. Archery pivots on hand-eye coordination. Our individual, natural, optimum hand-eye effectiveness is dictated by the simple alignment of the bow with our face and body. This archery form will come naturally, though some initial, reasonably experienced direction will go a long way in expediting the process.

For example, a right-handed shooter should address the target not unlike a golfer faces the ball. The target should be slightly quartered off the left shoulder to create a direct line from both eyes with the arrow an extension of our natural gaze. A few arrows from a smooth-shooting bow at close range will teach the body to adjust for optimum form and function. I recommend new archers shoot at big targets like paper plates with a safe backstop no farther than fifteen feet away. The best first bow should be a mushy, easy-to-draw recurve or longbow with feathered arrows properly matched to the bow and archery draw length. This simple outfit will immediately teach a newcomer how his or her body works in conjunction with the tools at hand.

There is a wonderful new bow on the market manufactured by Mathews Archery called the Genesis bow. It is a simple, small, lightweight compound model with a unique zero let-off system that I believe is ideal for the whole family to take turns shooting. Since this bow will allow a wide spectrum of natural draw lengths for young shooters that pull back a mere twenty inches, to adults who draw thirty, it can be shot all together. This way, other members of the family can observe and critique each other's shooting form and technique.

Discipline is what every kid needs, today more than ever. When it comes in the form of projectile fun and challenge, it goes straight to the heart and takes on a life of its own. There is a quality archery shop and shooting range around every corner in America today, and therein lies a guaranteed quality of life upgrade for the whole family to enjoy and cultivate together. As goes the mystical flight of the arrow, I believe, can go the soul of man. Go for it!

Whitetails in Your Face

I didn't dare move. Not a budge. No fidget. I didn't dare breathe. No blinking. Frozen. StatueBoy. This is where I try to go into a state of suspended animation while at the same time maintaining maximum awareness. It ain't easy. The beast's eyes appeared to be locked square into mine, burning deep into my soul and beyond, maybe even reading my mind. It was eerie, yet wonderful. We've all been there. It's powerfully titillating, intensely stimulating, nerve-wracking, spell-bindingly glorious for sure. Inside is a mental blitzkrieg, but on the exterior, we must be like a rock. It's a test. The test rocks!

But now what? Is the spoiled, indulgent, impatient modern man, (especially uppity guitar players) capable of out-staring his majesty the whitetail deer, MasterBeast of patience of all times? Well, I'm here to tell ya booby, this BeastMaster is and there is no way I'm gonna blink, twitch, flinch, or give it up. No way. I'm The Bowhunting Marine. Semper Fidelis. "Improvise, Overcome, Adapt" is my credo. Let's get it on, you horny herbivore SOB. Give me your best shot, cuz I'm gonna give you mine.

And he did. Minutes feel like days when terminally eye-locked with a prey animal at spitting distance. But challenge and discipline and testing my personal best out here in the wild against the masters of escape is my drug of choice and my spirit was high as a kite and soaring on the wings of an American Eagle in perfect predator radar delirium overload for all it was worth, again.

Finally, the handsome buck bought my deceptive ruse and lowered his head to momentarily look away. I stood my ground. But I was cheating. At least I think I was cheating. For you see, it wasn't just my bulldog attitude or carefully chosen camouflage clothing, facemask, and creative cover that allowed me to stare down the beast so near. I was actually hiding behind a screen of camouflaged netting, hidden even further by the darkness of the interior of my black-walled Invisiblind ground blind. I don't think that is cheating anymore than ambushing a deer from high above in a perfectly designed treestand, deep in the leafy branches of a giant multi-trunked towering oak tree. I've done that so many times, most people can't believe it. But when trying to arrow big game within the constraints of typical archery close range demands, man, the oft bumbling predator needs all the help we can get.

Game animals for the most part are walking, breathing, living radars of nearly impenetrable defense capabilities. The higher our treestands, the better chance we have of drawing our bow without being detected. So, too, the more thorough our conceal-ment on the ground, the better our hopes of getting away with the necessary movements needed to shoot our bows. I have spent many a day constructing the ultimate ground hides all over the world out of brush and leafy branches. Sometimes they pay off, sometimes they don't. But with the introduction of these shoot-thru ground blinds invented by Mark Mueller in Missouri, my success on the ground now rivals my kill rate from high in the sky treestands. Along with Mark's original Invisiblind, there are many incredible quality shoot-thru units manufactured by Lucky, AmeriStep, GameTracker, and Double Bull, just to name a few. The older I get, the more I'm inclined to stay earthbound. And with my feet planted on solid terra firma, my comfort, safety, and confidence levels make me a better hunter overall. That's the American Dream the way I see it–being the best that we can be. You've got to try these babies if you haven't already. They kill.

Now the dandy buck swung slowly to his left and my graceful fifty-three-pound Renegade NugeBow flexed back to full draw like butter. As his foreleg stretched ahead, I finished my requisite Prayer for the WildThings and my razor-sharp broadhead silently sliced through the thin Invisiblind window like it wasn't even there. The white-feathered shaft swished across the twenty yard opening like a ghostly vapor trail and disappeared into the crease behind his outstretched leg with a melodious THWACK! How beautiful is that!

As the muscled beast pivoted in a flash, I saw the now all-red arrow fly out his right side and zing into a cluster of bushes beyond, just as the racing deer vanished into the very same bushes. Through the camo screen, now with a tiny slice in its center, I could clearly see the tracks of the deer and my bloody arrow in the settling dust, shimmering in that special morning light where everything shines and sparkles. I sat back in amazement at how clever this blind design is that allows us to see outward so clearly, yet remain concealed enough to fool the eyes of the beast.

In fact, not only do these new shoot-thru ground blinds help overcome the amazing eyeball radar of deer, but with the innovative Scent-Lok carbon technology lining the entire interior I can even fool the ultimate noses in the world. The construction is so good that it provides substantial forgiveness for noise as well. I'm telling you, these things are just what the good Dr. Backstrap ordered. Thank God for clever inventors.

We captured the whole exciting ordeal on videotape for our *Spirit of the Wild* TV show, including a most momentous tracking and recovery of my gorgeous ten-point Texas whitetail. I'm sure we will have to edit the scene at the beast, because I spent way too much time celebrating the always-mesmerizing giddiness of a bowkill, especially when the drama and tension we all so love is extended, like in today's encounter. I went on and on and on and on. My passion for the beast and love of the hunt gushed forth uncontrollably. How could I not? Bowhunting has always played a pivotal role in my overall American Dream as my favorite pursuit of happiness. My mind raced with exploding memories of failed encounters, bad shots, and, of course, many powerful memories of past hunts with family and friends. Holding onto the beast upon claiming the kill brings forth a torrent of positive emotions and sensations everytime. The beast is dead. Long live the beast.

Goodfire in the Heart

I'm sitting here in a cushy old beat-up, faded brown leather club-chair in front of a beautiful fireplace, with snapping, crackling, flickering flames touching the depths of my soul. The masterful craftsmanship of black and grey slabs of indigenous bluestone sheetrock, layered ever so artfully, frame the warming fire perfectly. Cedar walls, beams, and flooring complete the stirring beauty of the interior of this Frank Lloyd Wright creation. My older brother Jeff is at my side, reminiscing all things Tribe Nuge. The wilderness-like setting summons wonderful memories from a lifelong flow of family hunting and outdoor adventure that is spiritually energizing to the entire setting. Earthtones resonate.

Another glorious, beautiful fall is in the air as the pattering raindrops outside the open windows bring in light, gentle wave after wave of delicious fifty-nine degree clean air from the enchanted forest around his beautiful upstate New York home. We feel it. A towering forest of oaks, poplar, elm, beech, shagbark hickory, maple, giant

"Up North," Michigan, 1999

white pines, and both red and white cedar, add to the stimulating olfactory aroma that blankets our precious, deeply appreciated Spirit of the Wild atmosphere here. Bubbling water over rocks from a fast running creek join the gurgling Esopus River, winding and meandering throughout this sacred new Nugent homeground. The very presence of abundant wildlife is felt all around. Increasing raindrops have a cadence that is thoroughly calming. It is indeed heaven on earth.

Jeff's friend Kevin arrives with his new Browning A-Bolt .338 magnum, and a synthetic-stocked Sig Arms Blaser in .30-06. The addition of artillery puts the finishing touches on this American Dream. We swap stories about our guns and hunts from around the world and talk about the condition of the ever-changing world as we sit down to a steaming bowl of the only meal worthy of such wonderment—the ultimate rib-sticking BubbleBean Piranha ala Colorado Moose. It gets emotional amongst the slurping and laughing. Primal scream BloodBrothers are alive and well in 2003. We have spirit liftoff.

It is times, places, and people like this that drive our quality of life at Camp Nuge. Like so many millions of American families still connected to the good mother earth and her dynamic tooth, fang, and claw reality, we celebrate the last perfect hands-on conservation lifestyle remaining in the world today. As natural hunters, we intuitively and instinctively know the logic of nature and science as our management vision statement. Record populations of deer, elk, buffalo, bear, cougar, turkey, geese, and other game animals are irrefutable testimony to the honorable hunting, fishing, and trapping success stories in America. We salute the abundant wildlife, goodwill, attitude, and spirit all around. It is in the air and we fill our lungs and hearts with it.

After a fun shooting session with the rifles and handguns, equipment is cleaned and put away, and we bid farewell and good hunting to Kevin on his upcoming adventure to Alaska. As dusk settles within the canopy of our forest, fog drifts in with the darkness and a blanket of welcome silence envelopes the night. The creatures are beginning to stir and that is surely stirring to us. We return to the stone hearth and the fire is stoked while more tales and laughter end a grand day of true brotherhood. Jeff and I are past the mid-fifties mark now. Dad and Uncle John are long gone, but their presence and powerful memories around the traditional hunting fireplace remain palpable. Any time spent with family is good, but there is something more open, invigorating, and lasting about the quietness and spirituality of a hunting camp. Everyone just seems to be more relaxed, unencumbered, open, and communicative. All guards are let down and the spirit seems freer. This is good and much too rare in America today.

As the summer nights take on that cooler fall zing, the awesome forces of nature are alive in each of us. The trick in this modern world is to let them run and to heed their call. The entire planet changes with the seasons, but man has fought to defy these natural fluctuations and somehow function independent of nature herself. I am convinced this is wrong and at the root of all our environmental and social problems. From pollution to global warming, to resource and land abuse and tribal uprisings wherever they occur, it is this intentional disconnect with the very earth that provides us life that allows irresponsible behavior to continue. Cause and effect should be celebrated, not denied. I for one believe we need more communication at the fireplace. We need more hands-on, eye-witness cause and effect conservation honesty. That we hire men to dig enormous holes in the ground with giant earth-moving machines every time we flick on a light switch is a reality most people need to confront and, therefore, fess up to. If man were to manage energy resources with the passion and dedication that sporters have managed wildlife, we would not be in an energy scramble around the world.

More Americans need to think, talk, and act more as "we the people" in this glorious experiment in self-government, if upgrade is our goal. And upgrade must be our goal, period. Find the time. Make the time. Find a fireplace, literally or figuratively. Let the positive energy flow. Many brothers and many families, and many neighbors, opening up with each other around the country would be good for America. The system of sitting back and expecting bureaucrats to get the job done has created a mess. They vote themselves pay raises and benefits and pass politically correct "feel good" wasteful and counterproductive legislation without the minor inconvenience of consulting with their bosses. Their bosses, of course, are supposed to be "we the people." What have you told your employees lately?

The Nugent family Spirit of America fire burns hot. We are proud to celebrate that most of our friends and family are involved, active and responsible Americans. Truly, there are many of us out there. But a new prioritization must be demanded by each of us, and I for one am convinced it will begin within families, spread to the workplace and neighborhoods, churches and schools and eventually into the halls of state and federal government. Believe it or not, during that great day hanging out with my brother, I walked away knowing that as active as we are as a family, there is always room for upgrade and improvement. I'm splitting and stacking spiritual firewood today for more productive American family fires. I hope you are too.

Goofball Fever–The Agony of Blown Shots

I went limp and dropped my head in disgust, nearly sobbing. The magnificent ten-point trophy whitetail beast bounded off into the distant jungle with my white arrow sticking out of his backstraps like an embarrassing antennae of stupidity. Or, was that the middle finger of defeat waving good-bye to me? Ouch.

Twenty yards. When I miss a squirrel with my bow at twenty yards, I seldom miss by more than an inch or two. I usually don't miss at all. How in God's good name I could miss the entire football-sized vitals on another huge-chested buck by more than a foot at dumper range is one of my life's tragic not-so little mysteries. The actual missing isn't a mystery at all, really. It's the psychological hiccups that bring it about that mystifies me. Buck fever. Target panic. Nerves. Stress. Hyper tension. Lack of focus. Goofballitus. All the above. I was a wreck. I simply sat there torturing myself for blowing such a golden opportunity, a rare, much-dreamed-of, gimme dump shot gone with the wind yet again this season. Oh the humanity.

I want it too badly, that's what's goin' on here. I'm much too intense for a white guy. My cravings for bowhunting have gotten completely out of hand. I've always enjoyed, actually celebrated, my sacred time afield chasing critters with the bow and arrow, and for all the right reasons. The incredible demands of this ultra, close-range sport are a discipline unto itself that tests the mental, physical, and spiritual mettle in us all. The satisfaction of having overcome the land mine field of often overwhelming obstacles brings with it grand joys when it finally, painstakingly all comes together. The BBQ alone is, of course, worth the price of admission.

I've got a list of the usual suspects when it comes to excuse making. Another long, grueling tour of outland-o Rock 'n' Roll insanity and the intense transition from rock idiot to calm, reasoning predator is a journey you can't imagine. There's no question I take on too many things in my adventurous life. My namesake kids camp charity, hundreds of articles for dozens of magazines, nonstop daily media interviews, producing our *Spirit of the Wild* TV show, the VH1 specials, charity events all the time, meetings at schools, with politicians, NRA, and being on the board of directors for Gun Owners of America, etc., etc. Add to that a long list of unique complications in my life of late, and its no wonder I'm being eaten alive by the nerve-wracking in-your-face time with the oh-so-anticipated, bigger-than-average, dream bucks. We've had serious health problems exacerbated by the loss of our home and belongings due to toxic mold infestation, which makes it that much worse all around. With the resultant lack of oxygen in the blood as a result of a destroyed immune system and what we have here is a good old fashioned recipe for psyche hiccups. Intellectual blackouts. Brainfarts. That's my story and I'm sticking with it. Damn.

Kick that whole psycho cocktail up a notch with the added pressures of a video camera up my ass every time I go hunting and it's amazing I can even pull my bow back without shoot-ing myself in the foot. That "antennae buck" as we affectionately named him, was sadly only one of seven that had taken me to hell and back in the last two weeks. I couldn't handle it any more. I needed to escape. And the great escape was about to happen as I boarded a jet from our new home in Texas for the wonderful wilds of Michigan. God bless the Winter, Water, Wonderland of my youth. Maybe my traditional home hunting grounds would calm my nerves and soothe my soul to help me return to the friendly comfortzone of good arrows again. I prayed hard.

Let me tell you about it. All my fellow arrow flingin' BloodBrothers take note—there is hope. Never give up. Even as the big jumbo jet lowered its flaps for final descent into the Detroit airport, the blanket of fiery earth tones covering the Midwest autumn-colored land brought sighs of relief to the old guitarboy. It was beautiful and calming. The drive westward to the sacred huntswamp was increasingly revitalizing every mile of the way. By the time I slowly strolled down the ridge to my old familiar ravine treestand, I was a different man. The fact that none of my SpiritWild camera operators were available this evening removed any trace of pressure or stress. I was on my own and ready to rock with the wind. Slow and easy.

As I settled in and sat silently with bright, orange, and golden leaves falling all around, I could taste the flavor of wellness entering my system. A cock pheasant sounded off behind me as a trio of squawking sandhill cranes soared overhead. Geese honked from one direction to the next and squirrels scampered in celebration of the annual acorn orgy. I was joined by a foursome of fat raccoons when I first saw the dainty buttonbuck emerge from the cluster of autumn olive brush before me. Ahhhhh! Delicious.

Before I knew it, seven deer were browsing and doing the acorn boogie all around me. One huge old matriarch doe was bullying all the others. As she smacked a yearling doe hard with her cloven hoof, she gave me the perfect broadside look-away pose, and I came to full draw, lasering a path into her pumpstation at fifteen yards.

My Renegade NugeBow came back silently and upon release, with nary a sound, my aluminum arrow streaked down and into the old she-deer's chest for a perfect, pocket rocket shot. The curse was officially over. Now, mind you, I am more than aware of the psychological difference between a doe and a big old antlered buck beast, but the perfect arrow was what I was looking for, and I found it.

A short bloodtrail up and over the old orchard ridgeline brought me to the fallen deer and I was joyous. The transition was now complete and I went on that week to perfectly arrow two dandy bucks and numerous does. I had entered the wonderful land of Ahhhhhhhhhsssss! And it felt good.

Archery and, ultimately, bowhunting, is certainly a mental game. The mind must be clear and relaxed and basically empty of thought. Simply sending the arrow where it is supposed to go is what must take place for consistent accuracy, especially under pressur-ized hunting conditions. And, of course, the more antler, the more the pressure. The trick is to eliminate the sensation of any pressure. Shooting arrows where we want them to go is what it all boils down to and a genuine effort to get to that calm spirit is job Number One.

The sacred hunt season scorches on my friends and most of my arrows are just what the good Hunt Doctor ordered. Being the uppity goofball that I am demands a daily meditation on my part to keep the excitable demons at bay. So far, so good. But I will never have seven setups in a row like the ones I blew earlier this fall. Let that be a lesson to me and anyone who has felt the torture themselves. Say a prayer for the wildthings and you calm down mister!

Exotica–Year-Round Backstraps

My sacred Michigan deer season was still a month away, but I felt the urge to scent mark every tree I crossed paths with. I occasionally pulled off the side of the road and raked my head and eyes against sturdy saplings, pawing the ground beneath into a bare scrape of richly scented earth, upon which I would urinate and hump air. It just felt like the natural thing to do. I'm sure I scared many unsuspecting civilians whenever they may have caught sight of this most frightening of animalistic rituals by the pony-tailed madman. Ask me if I care. I am a predator, an Alpha male, a man, a natural born hunter, an independent, rugged individual American Dreamer, doing what comes perfectly natural. I don't shop. I kill. It's my job. I have powerful, positive instincts to be as alive as I can possibly be. Meat is my fuel, my drug of choice. Protein brings me energy and life itself. I hunt, therefore I am. The survival urge should be not only responded to, but intensely cultivated and celebrated as the mighty gift of life that it truly is. Let's rock.

A simple occurrence like a glowing sunset or seeing a flying V-formation of geese overhead only made it worse/better. The morning air was always a little cooler and each rare sunrise during my annual summer rock tour was a delightful luvsmack in the face, awakening my inner predator for the upcoming annual hunt season. A series of strange events had relocated Tribe Nuge into the wonderful huntzone of Texas and I rejoiced at the prospect of plucking those special, seemingly unlimited Texas meat apples from the abundant fruit-heavy branches of this most productive wild game orchard in the great Yellow Rose Lone Star state. An amazing hunting bonus for us Texans, in fact for all Americans who so desire to join us, are the year-round hunting opportunities that the flourishing exotic game species here provide. From Asian buffalo, sheep, antelope, and deer species, to European fallow deer and African big game, one never knows what strange critter we may come across in the wilds of this ultra hunting paradise. And even though everyone has probably heard of the famous Y.O. Ranch, 777 Ranch, The Diamond K and hundreds of others, exotic game of every imaginable description can show up anywhere at anytime on the endless acres of private property statewide. Even though Texas is limited on public land, many hunters have lucked into the occasional elk, redstag, fallow, sika, axis, Corsican, nilgai, blackbuck antelope, and, of course, wild hogs beyond your wildest imagination. Even the occasional kudu, buffalo, aoudad, ibex, eland, waterbuck, zebra, and God knows what else have been bagged on many a weekend outing by lucky Texas hunters over the years. Around the Hill Country of Leaky, Texas, for example, the axis deer population can only be described as out of control. And all these species can be hunted all year long. How cool is that?

Within a fifty mile radius of Waco, home of Calvin and Melissa Ross's LoneStar Archery & Music, there seem to be unlimited hunting opportunities. Calvin had scouted a wild piece of ground not far from Valley Mills with deep ravines and long, high rocky ridges, covered with thick groves of live oak trees and heavy cedar stands. Dotted with large and small patches of purple-fruited prickly pear cactus, this rocky terrain is alive with indigenous and exotic game. We had placed a pair of NorthStarr ladder stands in a long line of large oak trees where a steep ridgeline sloped into a valley and a meandering creek down below. Feeding shell corn and Purina protein pellets into the scattered openings throughout the timbered areas, we knew a herd of red stag, plus some fallow and sika deer were traveling this funnel to water each morning and afternoon. A few beautiful blackbuck antelope were seen on occasion as well, so we were well beyond psyched when we climbed into our stands this fine, cool, overcast summer morning. Calvin was operating the vidcam and I had my brand new prototype Renegade Archery NugeBow in my hands, with a quiver full of carbon arrows tipped with the new Magnus Stinger four-blade stainless steel broadheads. We had big plans to say the least. Strapped in securely, we basked in the warming rays of a gorgeous Texas sunrise and thanked God to be alive. The night before I had raised massive hell and fire on stage with the loudest, most intense rock-n-roll in the world. Now I was a million light years away, and this quiet morning was already doing me immense good. I was rockin', just a little differently.

In the deep grass of a distant hillside, a form moved in the brilliant sparkle of the glistening morning dew. Through my binoculars, I saw a stunning chocolate European fallow buck, grazing peacefully along the crest of the hill. As he slowly made his way towards us, another good buck brought up the rear, and a gaggle of does and fawns kept coming from every direction. There must have been twenty or more in the bunch and we had high hopes. Unfortunately, an hour later, they had teased us no end and wandered out of range and out of sight down the north edge of the tree line.

Crows cawed about, vultures soared overhead, and wave after wave of brilliant red cardinals and assorted songbirds came and went all morning. A pair of cottontails scampered into a giant brush pile to evade the talons of the red-tailed hawks nearby, and like the Spirit of the Wild, the temperature was also rising.

Then, I realized movement just below my sixteen-foot ladder as a brown body moved in amongst the thorny mesquite tangle. It was the chocolate fallow and right behind him was a white buck. They nervously picked and browsed, discovering the scattered grains of corn and pellets strewn about. They jostled a bit, clacking their palmated horns together in a half-assed sparring match. That was the perfect distraction for me to lift and draw my bow. For as they separated and began to nibble again, I picked a spot behind the white deer's shoulder, said my little bowhunting prayer and touched 'er off. The 500 grain projectile hit slightly

227

high on the shoulder with a resounding WHACK, severing the spinal column of the handsome buck, dropping him in his tracks. The brown buck exploded out of there along with a bunch of other deer behind us that we had not even seen. Within seconds, my follow-up arrow was on its way, this time the razor-sharp four-blade head slicing clean through the big, tough beast's chest, severing both lungs and the good heart plumbing. He kicked his last just seconds later and we descended to recover our pure, protein prize.

Fallow deer backstraps are a thing of beauty and we immediately gutted and cleaned up the carcass for expeditious processing. As the sun got higher along with the heat of the day, we took the deer into a local cooler to hang and age awhile for optimum palatability.

Later that week, we killed a pair of dandy red stags for more pre-season excitement and BBQ perfection, no doubt the power of the hunt going straight into my guitar strings for more outrageous, soulful Rock 'n' Roll to finish up the tour before deer season. If you want to celebrate opening day everyday, join me sometime in the beautiful wilds of Texas for the best deer hunting in all the world. The deer need killing, we all need BBQ, and everybody wins when we balance the herd.

Bowhunting Angles

Cade Green jabbed me in the ribs. I flinched and looked out the elevated blind window following his intense gaze. How in the world this handsome buck ever got past our ever vigilant, diligent predator radar, I'll never know, but sure as hell, there he was, ten stinking yards below us, big as life itself. I didn't know deer had middlefingers. Wild. Here come the shakes. Cool.

For sixty to seventy yards all around, there was nothing but shin-high scrub. Prickly pear cactus patches, dwarf mesquite, and silverbrush, with scattered clumps of various indigenous South Texas stabbers and jabbers here and there amongst the sandy, rocky, desert-like terrain as far as the eye could see. As so often occurs, the beast simply appeared out of that legendary nowhere, an apparition bursting forth from the good mother earth without warning or notice. God bless the beast. He turns me on.

Cade had the vidcam rolling, capturing magnificent footage of the stunning sunset glow on the beast's grey-black winter coat and all his shimmering world. The bowhunting moves were strictly up to me. A sandy sendero cut just below the blind's scaffolding, then, an ever-elevating wall of thick brush lay in the path of the dandy eight-pointer. I had to move quickly, but not too quickly as to give away my presence. Carefully lifting my Renegade bow into position, I monitored the slow step by step progress of the buck as he nibbled along and angled even closer to our box blind. I rose up into a semi-squat, poked my arrow through the blind window and silently snapped my Scott release onto the string loop, preparing for a straight downward shot. Eighteen feet below us, the buck sidestepped slightly right, which now put him on a beautiful quartering away angle and, fortunately, separating him a few yards from the base of the tower. Now I had an ideal fifteen yard, quartering-away shot instead of the extreme hard downward angle of just a moment before. My arrow's line to his pumpstation was changing with every second. Then he paused and my arrow was gone. WHACK!

Captured on digital tape for our *Spirit of the Wild* TV show, that gorgeous white arrow hit the

European red stag, Deep Creek Ranch, Texas, 2003

beast square behind the left shoulder, slightly above midway, and slipped out his right armpit, coated red. The mature buck exploded wildly for thirty yards, stopped abruptly, flashed a quick look left then right, backed up a step, then charged headfirst into a tangle of mesquite scrub twenty yards north and slammed to the ground in a heap. One dusty kick in the glowing magic light and it was over. Well, that's how ya do that. Can you say "Kowabunga?"

Much rejoicing took place in that elevated coop and upon exhausting an orgy of hi-fives and celebratory laughter, we carefully descended to recover our wonderful gift. The tracking job was performed as if we didn't know where the buck had gone, articulating on tape for our Outdoor Channel viewers why every tracking job is a valuable lesson in woodsmanship, reasoning predator responsibility, a higher level of earthly awareness and just plain exciting fun.

He was handsome all right, a seven-year-old grandpa of a whitetail. Long, grey Roman nose, heavy brisket and bellyline, somewhat gaunt in the withers, and a trophy head of handsome bone. The shot had been surgically exquisite, entering high-center through the top of the left lung and exiting out the bottom of the right lung, slicing a Nugent Blade smile clean through the middle of his pumper. It was textbook and I was proud of a disciplined shot and a job well done. That is the essence of bowhunting, all hunting for sure. Be the best that we can be or buy chicken.

The angle had been acute, but not as severe as it would have been if I had taken the shot only seconds earlier. It's always an instantaneous judgment call with the bow and arrow. When I hesitated on the straight downward shot, the buck could have easily escaped under our blind and straight away, but my hope for a quartering away shot materialized out of sheer luck. Believe me, I've misjudged often enough to know and I will take all the luck I can get.

An OK shot one second can become a no-way shot the next. What would represent a perfect twelve scoring hit on a 3-D target from ground level, would be a lost animal for sure with the shot angling below all vital organs from fifteen feet above. Though there is no better lesson than extended, varying, ongoing experience, a basic truism for arrow placement should always be to aim for the exit hole, concentrating on the path of the arrow through the central chest cavity between the shoulders. Learn this and practice it as often as possible to spare yourself the agony of bad hits. I've endured enough of them for all of us and it ain't no fun at all, believe me.

A mental 3-D image of the beast's internal organs and how to slice the center lungs must dictate the actual choice of the spot we choose to hit. A spot on a deer's chest for a perfect heart shot as seen from broadside ground level will certainly be too low from an elevated angle. Though a straight downward shot can bring home the bacon when executed perfectly, we are much better off when we can decrease the hard angle by putting some yardage between us and our target for optimal double-lung-ability. I've taken to groundblinds more and more these days for just such improved shot ops.

3-D target manufacturers are making some superb quality deer targets with accurate vital organ displays. I highly recommend using these educational devices during practice sessions from actual hunting positions. There is no better confidence-building mind-settler during the hunting season than daily shots under real world conditions, wearing the same clothing we will be hunting in that day and from anticipated ranges and angles. I place major importance on the fact that I take a few practice shots like this everyday before each morning and afternoon hunts as to why Tribe Nuge enjoys so many rewarding backstrap BBQs. It is truly worth the effort.

The National Field Archery Association and the National Bowhunter Education Foundation are two killer places to begin the anatomical lessons of our bow and arrow predatorship responsibilities. With the scientifically precise information available in their literature, publications, events, and classes, a huge frog jump to meaningful pragmatic conclusions will help us get past the guessing game of shot angles and arrow placement. Then as we go afield all giddied up for the moment of truth, we are much better prepared for the delivery of our deadly projectile. Like the American Dream, being the best that we can be is what archery and bowhunting is all about too. Take it to the limit and don't just dream of putting all our arrows into a single dead center hole; study the science of it all and put your heart and soul into the excellence that we are all capable of. The rewards are many, but just knowing you did your very best will bring the most joy of all.

Thanxgiving as Life

Another day, another change of dry clothes, then right back into the wild again, right where I belong. That's how it goes, day in and day out at the Sacred Nugent HuntGrounds. Nonstop from September straight on through into February, the hunting season drives me wild, literally and figuratively. My instinct to remain connected "hands on" with the Good Mother Earth is as powerful as any force in my life. Self-sufficiency, after all, is the ultimate American Dream of independence and individualism. How on God's good green earth we, the people, ever got to the dependent lifestyle so many have plummeted to I will never know. As more and more citizens take advantage of a plethora of available services in life, many Americans are spoiled rotten, no doubt about it. Not me. I like to plant and chop my own fuel, kill, butcher, and cook my own food and, most importantly, raise my own kids. But that's a whole different story. No doubt about it, hunting is the last and best way to remain in touch with a planet that miraculously sustains us all. As a hunter, I cannot escape this fact and apply myself accordingly.

Last night's beautiful Michigan butterball buck and this morning's fascinating bag of beautiful mallards and wood ducks are a perfect example of pure self-sufficiency at its finest. Each hunt for these amazing creatures was another series of dynamic occurrences that are just not available in any other experience available to man in this modern day and age. The spectacular forest from which the deer emerged and the breathtaking cattail wetlands in which I encountered the ducks, may have well taken place in the Year One. It was primordial in all its glory when the handsome buck browsed his way into my bow and arrow zone. And the incoming waterfowl that bombarded my son and I provided a high that nothing else in life can match. And as far as activities for a father and son go, there is nothing more wonderful, period.

The mystical forces of nature, so obviously at their peak during the natural season of harvest, continue day and night indoors as well. As we hunt together in the great outdoors each day, we also process our precious kills as a family unit and ultimately prepare the meals together too. It is a powerful lesson in reality when the kids take part in all these essential events that bring them life, particularly food. This eye-witness lesson in cause and effect comes to a climax as we join together in the kitchen to cook up our nightly meals from the daily harvest. Ya can't grill it till ya kill it, that's for sure.

Preparing wildgame for the table is so easy, even guitar players can do a great job of it. That's gotta tell ya something. Whether duck or deer, quail, squirrel, or mountain lion backstraps, it's simply a matter of quality control in the field and every step of the way. In our book, KILL IT & GRILL IT, Shemane and I celebrate the perfection that is properly handled flesh from renewable wildlife resources. Not only is it supremely delicious, but it surely represents the ultimate healthfood to be had. Making certain to keep the meat clean and cold, we butcher our kills into family-sized portions then head for the stove and the grill for the best meals on earth. The venison steaks and the duck breasts were prepared almost identically by heating up some olive oil in a cast iron skillet, then adding diced onions, celery, and garlic cloves. Our garlic is jarred with jabenero peppers to add some kick into our meals and we add this to the sauteed vegetables. Sometimes we add potatoes, sometimes sweet potatoes or even spinach, turnips, or sliced sugar beets. Seasoned with garlic pepper and garlic salt, a single pan is all we need for the entire cooking process most of the time. The vegetables saute a while, then are pushed to the side of the skillet while the meat singes quickly on both sides in the hot center of the pan. A splash of wine is added for the last minute or so, then we sit down to what can only be described as a dream feast fit for a king and queen. When you celebrate the Spirit of the Wild at every meal, you not only take in the sacred protein from the earth, but even more importantly, you better understand the real relationship we all have with the world around us.

231

Afterthoughts . . .

E very one of the animals killed in this book, like damn close to 100% of game harvested in this country with a bow and arrow, was killed in what I believe to be the most expeditious, humane manner possible, under any conditions. In most cases, a well-placed, sharp arrowhead causes imperceptible pain, zero hydrostatic shock, and literally puts the animal to sleep on its feet. Experience is a sure teacher. Literature is available, in volumes, on the management of wildlife. Recent, in-depth studies support 100% my findings regarding the humane death via the broadhead. Dr. Dave Samual, just this year (1991), completed an extensive study defining the hollowness of the lies about mass wounding of arrow-shot game. Pure lies. Even those animals that are hit and not recovered have survived the clean cut of modern broadhead with no ill effects. Deer have been recovered on some occasions with old arrow wounds, yet no ill effects. In the mid '60s, my good friend, George Nicholls, arrowed a small buck right between the eyes; it got away. A year later, Dave Gilpin killed the deer with a shotgun, and it was perfectly healthy. This has happened in Los Angeles and elsewhere. The wounding of game is a problem in as much as we wish to eliminate it. However, in the whole scheme of wildlife management, it has no impact compared to highway casualties, starvation, predation by domestic dogs or other natural causes of death. Once again, the cry of the animal rightists is one big ignorant lie.

Each animal was shot, trailed, gutted, skinned, butchered, and eaten. (No, I didn't eat the fox.) Every scrap of flesh, hides, horns, and even some body fluids and bone were respectfully utilized in the time-honored traditions of man and beast. There is an undeniable connection between hunters and animals that reflects the respected relationship of our Native American Indian brothers. (Peyote practices notwithstanding.) Remember, these kill stories are merely a sample, the tip of an iceberg, of the kills that I have personally made and/or witnessed. Death is a part of life for every living organism, and each living thing must take the place of some other living thing, therefore causing its death, one way or another, directly or indirectly. Period. If you don't understand that truism, go immediately to the library and kindly catch up on your homework. Your ignorance is in the way. Re-read again our TNWB By-Laws, and remember that these guidelines were not written just to look at, they are to be lived. To ultimately harmonize with nature is to eat some. The entire, wonderful procedure is a chorus.

When I first wrote the original *Blood Trails*, I thought I could whip it out in a few months. Had I locked myself up in the cabin, during the closed season, I believe I could have done just that. I did not know the Damn Yankees would EAT my calendar!! But that is OK. At two million tapes sold of our debut recording, I'm very pleased. But even more pleasing is the exciting growth of our Ted Nugent United Sporstmen of America magazine and organization. The reality of all-year-long hunting involvement is hitting home in a big way. Our members have come to grips with our duty to kick ass for nine months a year, so we can expect to hunt for three months a year. The heritage is being secured for the future hunters of America because we are standing up loud and

Black bear, Ontario, Canada, 1997

proud. As I smack this out on my wounded laptop computer, flying with the entire Nugent clan to continuing weeks of concerts and bowhunting connections in California and beyond, our growing membership approaches 6,000! That's in our second year folks! COOL!

I've received some flak. Cool. In order for a battery to get the job done, there must be a negative terminal to go with the positive terminal. TNWB is that positive terminal. Don't ignore those negative terminal clowns. Put them in their places. Send them home knowing the reality of our cause, our support, and our power. If you're not making waves, you're not paddling. We have done great things. In the two hundred cities I have visited and performed in the past year, I have met with bowhunters, Fish and Game personnel, conservation groups, kids looking for something, and the PRESS in every one of them. The positive message of our crusade was, and still is, being made clear. HUNTERS CARE!!! To put it bluntly (which I enjoy), I have spread this truth to more mainstream Americans via the general media, in a STRONG, POSITIVE manner, than has ever been attempted in the history of the shooting sports. Hundreds of prime-time radio shows, dozens of television appearances, and thousands of printed interviews that could not have been bought, like so many trophy hunts for shallow, greedy, pious hunters and writers. There are not many, but they are out there and obnoxious and unsophisticated. Small in-breds with cheap, phony, holier-than-thou, paid for smiles. You know who you are. I can handle the bullshit. In fact, I welcome it, because ultimately, it exposes the chumps for who they are, and that they are worse enemies than the animal-rights freaks. If you let a line of BS go unchallenged, you are part of the problem, not the solution. Do not stand for it.

Carefully re-read, over and over again, our fourteen By-Laws. Anyone who has a problem with Ted Nugent has a big-ass problem, and therefore must have a problem with our creed. That means they are scum. Pure and simple, bad people. Tell them to wake up, get smart, or get the hell out of our way because we have a job to do for wildlife conservation and hunters' rights. It's our duty. I did not write these By-Laws, I LIVE THEM. They flowed out of me onto paper as natural as breath itself. They represent a constitution shared by all of us who can reason intelligently-how to participate in harmony with nature.

Corsican ram, Heartsill Ranch, Texas, 2001

The hunting industry is learning what the music industry had to face years ago: You can't get rid of Ted Nugent. Period. Not until Ted Nugent is damn good and ready. And I am always damn good and ready to stand my ground, do what is right, and KICK ASS.

I foresee many great things for us. State chapters are on the way. Chumps are being put in their places and eliminated. Fence-sitters are figuring out the truth and joining in. America's non-hunters are identifying the immorality of the animal-rights freaks, and the ultimate winner is wildlife. Archery and bow-hunting are catching on to a whole new generation of bright-eyed, bushy-tailed enthusiasts. Again, the industry grows, equipment improves and becomes more of a value, and wildlife wins dollars, effort, and respect. We all now realize that we have to work all year, to some degree, if we are to save and earn opening day. By-Law number twelve says one great way to fight, DO IT. If we strive to perfect numbers two thru fourteen, then number one will be unstoppable, like me.

There are many different conditions surrounding the kills in this book. My goal is simple. Educate. Each of us has an obligation to conscientiously conduct ourselves in a responsible manner, in all the endeavors we pursue. Especially hunting. I do not recommend long-range shooting. I do not even recommend short-range shooting if you are not up to the task at hand. The National Bowhunter Education Foundation has excellent guidelines to assist us in making many serious decisions when bowhunting. Read their literature

Aoudad, Heartsill Ranch, Texas, 2001

6x6 bull elk, Young Ranch, Texas, 2002

carefully, understand these obligations, and act with care and safety. Shooting decisions should be guided by two basic premises: 1) Can you hit the vitals? 2) Does the position of the animal facilitate direct access to the vitals? Range and animal posture are most important, and also is its alertness. Be cautious, be sure. The jubilation of a successful kill, quick and clean, is nowhere near as intense as the heartbreak of a bad hit. You don't want it.

I've got some arrows to crest and fletch, some kids to teach, a few brush piles to stack, an editorial to write, some friends to enjoy, a family to love and protect, dogs to shoot birds for, broadheads to sharpen, treestands to secure, clover to plant, a bull to bugle, a buck to grunt, a goat to whack, shooting lanes to cut, ducks to feed, trees to plant, firewood to saw, diapers to change, deer to skin, pictures to take, a wife to squeeze, hair to brush, mucho Rock 'n' Roll to obliterate, a wad of guitars to destroy, a few odds and ends to button up, and some ass to kick. Other than that, keep your eyes open, because I have not yet begun to fight.

Now, all I ask is for all of you who truly care, and cherish this ultimate lifestyle and wildlife heritage, to please get out there and spread the word. Our TNWB organization will be the strongest conservation/hunter voice in America and beyond, if we all crusade to share our pride and dedication. Sign up the people in your lives. Anybody who embraces our By-Laws should be a member. It will be great. Do it for the kids, for the critters, for the planet. Is this fun or what??!!

Live It Up!
Bowhunting Forever!

Ted Nugent

TED NUGENT

- Born in Detroit, 12-13-48
- Began bowhunting in 1953, playing guitar in 1956
- Recorded 30 albums, 1967-2003
- Sold over 30 million albums worldwide
- Considered the #1 Guitar Showman in the world
- Performing professionally since 1958, nonstop yearly touring since 1967
- *Full Bluntal Nugity* DVD, on Spitfire, 2003
- *Craveman* recording, on Spitfire, 2002
- #1 Grossing Tour Act in the world 1977, 1978 and 1979
- Formed Damn Yankees in 1989. Sold 5 million albums
- Live at Hammersmith recording, on Sony, 1997
- Top 10 Grossing Tours of 2000 with KISS
- New York Times Best Selling Author, God, Guns, & Rock 'n' Roll, Regnery Publishing, August, 2000; Kill It & Grill It, Regnery Publishing, 2002
- Host of the #1-rated *Ted Nugent Morning Show*, WWBR, Detroit
- Creator and host of the *Ted Nugent Commando Radio Show* for 10 years, Detroit, Michigan
- Honored on the floor of the U.S. Senate, 1994
- Named Father of the Year at children's school
- Named Michigan Conservationist of the Year, 1999
- ALWAYS outspoken about drugs and alcohol throughout career
- Recipient of numerous commendations from state police, sheriff departments, FBI, DEA, U.S. Army and police agencies nationwide
- Editor/Publisher of *Ted Nugent Adventure Outdoors Magazine*
- President: Ted Nugent United Sportsmen of America
- Founder: Ted Nugent Kamp for Kids
- Founder: Ted Nugent Bowhunting School and SUNRIZE SAFARIS, booking, guiding and outfitting adventures worldwide
- Author, *Blood Trails: The Truth About Bowhunting,* 1990
- Creator and producer of award-winning Ted Nugent *Spirit of the Wild* PBS video series, raising in excess of three million dollars for PBS affiliates nationwide.
- Creator and producer of the Outdoor Channel's #1 Viewer's Choice, Ted Nugent *Spirit of the Wild*
- Outspoken pro-hunting media crusader, conducting 5-10 prime media interviews every week, impacting millions every day.
- Aggressive campaigner on lecture circuit promoting individualism through outdoor sports and conservation to the youth of America
- Creator of highly successful teleconferencing program to school systems nationwide
- Appointed to Board of Directors of the National Rifle Association, 1995-present
- Spokesman for National Field Archers Association, Mothers Against Drunk Driving, Big Brothers/Big Sisters, Drug Abuse Resistance Education (D.A.R.E.) law enforcement program
- Official Rock 'n' Roll, hunting, conservation representative of the Rush Limbaugh EIB Radio and Television Network
- Guest speaker at International Law Enforcement Convention by invitation from FBI Director William Webster, Edwin Meese and President Ronald Reagan
- Appointed to Michigan Year of the Family Council by Governor John Engler
- Named Man of the Year by Michigan Recreation and Parks Association
- Keynote Speaker for Native American Fish & Wildlife Society National Conference, Anchorage, Alaska, 1995
- Named Archery Commissioner by Governor John Engler for the Great Lakes State Games
- Appointee to Michigan's Hunting and Fishing Heritage Task Force
- Recipient of 1999 National Arbor Day Conservation Award

- Director, Quality Deer Management Association of Michigan, Three Rivers Chapter
- Appointee, Michigan State Parks Foundation
- Board of Directors, Lyme Alliance
- Michigan County Sheriff Deputy, 1978-present
- Nominee, Handgun Hunters Hall of Fame
- Nominee, Outstanding American Handgunner Award
- Inducted into the Native American Strongheart Society by the Lakota Sioux, Northern Cheyenne and Arapahoe Tribes
- Keynote Speaker for 1995 Governor's Symposium on North American Hunting Heritage, Green Bay, Wisconsin
- Certified Hunter Safety Instructor and International Bowhunter Education Foundation Instructor
- Honored in the Congressional Record by Congressman Jim Barcia, 1993
- Huron School District Student Youth Counselor
- Designer of Nugent Blade Broadhead, Ted Nugent Blood Brother Bow and signature line of hunting gear.
- Professional staff advisor for Browning, GameTracker, Mossy Oak, LaCrosse, Sims Vibration Labs
- Rock 'n' Rolls approximately six months per year, hunts six months per year
- Regular columnist and contributor to more than 30 publications
- **Life Member of:** The National Rifle Association (NRA), Michigan Bow Hunters, Citizen's Committee for the Right to Keep and Bear Arms, Second Amendment Foundation, Gun Owners of America, Gun Owners of California, Director Law Enforcement Alliance of America, New York City Benevolent Policeman's Association, National Wildlife Federation, Ducks Unlimited, Michigan United Conservation Clubs, Michigan Big Game Hunters Association, Handgun Hunters International, Michigan Sheriff's Association, National Trappers Association, U.S. Sportsmen's Alliance, Wisconsin Bowhunters Association, Mississippi Bowhunters, Drug Abuse Resistance Education (DARE) Spokesman, Outdoor Writers Association of America, Coalition of Michigan Hunters, National Field Archers Association (NFAA), Director Canadian Outdoor Heritage Alliance (COHA), Putting People First, South Dakota Archery Association, Maryland Bowhunters Society, Arizona Bowhunter Society, United Bowhunters of Connecticut, Massachusetts Bowhunting Association, United Bowhunters of Pennsylvania, Ohio Society of Traditional Archers (OSTA), South Carolina Bowhunters, Director: Michigan Bowhunting Conference and Vice President: American Shooting Sports Council

"Ted has his facts. He is very articulate and is also bold, honest, not shy or afraid to meet any challenge. He is carrying on the work which Fred Bear did so wisely and so well."

-Dick Mauch, Director of Archery Manufacturers Organization, lifelong personal friend of Fred Bear

MY SOARING QUALITY OF LIFE is possible only thru the teamwork of those gifted individuals who have dedicated themselves for so many years. Here I will attempt a comprehensive list of them all. I thank and salute: Doug Banker, Bob Quandt, Fred Bear, Linda Peterson, Charlton Heston, Kirk Gibson, Jim Lawson, Wayne LaPierre, Connie Strine, Paul Wilson, Bob Munger, Elmer Kieth, Ward Parker, Lee Fields, Dennis Arfa, John Kolodner, Pablo Gamboa, Erica Rogers, Gwen Nappi, Harry Crocker, Al Regnery, Marja Walker, Tommy Aldridge, Marco Mendoza, Kayne Robinson, Johnny Gunnel, Derek St. Holmes, Jack and Molly Blades, Steve Fortney, the Nallis, Jim Curnutt, Michael Cartellone, Tommy Shaw, John Rocker, Joe Vitale, Johnny Angelos. Rob Rusga, Michael Lutz, Benny Rappa, Gunnar Ross, Gary Hicks, Bob Lehnert, Gale Uptadale, Dick Treat, Andy Solomon, Dave Palmer, Dave Amato, Gabe Magno Tony Reale, Lew Futterman, Tom Werman, Charlie Huhn, Craig Colburn, John Conk, Jimmy Douglas, Jimmy Johnson, Mark Newman, Dan Beck, Doug Morris, David Krebs, Carmine Appice, Vic Mastrianni, Todd Howarth, Greg Arama, John Brake and family, John Finly, Tom Noel, Pete Prim, Pete DeYoung, Steve Farmer, K.J. Knight, Cliff Davies, Steve Brown, Rob DeLaGrange, Bill White, Rick Lober, Keith Johnstone, Mark

Ditzel, Bob Blevins, Dean Mitchell, Bill "Rip" Mayes, Calvin and Melissa Ross, Steve Sinden, Eric Web, Tony Dukes, Ronnie Bradford, Bob Hilts, Greg Price, Toby Francis, Jim Yakabuski, NiteBob, Bobby "OD" Oberdorsen, Willy Twork, Mark Vanderwall, Scooter Davis, Laura Kaufman, Mitch Snyder, Earl Miles, Bob Foulkrod, Scott Young, Larry and Celeste Pollack, Jack Brittingham and family, Dan and Kathy Countiss, Clint Starling, Chester Moore, Ken Moody and family, Mike Sohm, Steve and Greg Sims, Frank Mitchell, Mike Hoban, Larry Pratt, Paul Wilson, Bryan Schupbach, Chuck Buzzy, Louie, Randy and Cheryl Krick, Rod Peterson, Tom Minsel, Chip Stewart and family, Keith Baker, Brad Landwerlen, Phillip Carter, Kevin Kelly, David Allen, Jason Zins, Mike Kitner, Kevin Smart, Jim McCullough, Robin Stibb.

We apologize if we have forgotten anyone or misspelled names. All of our TNWB members and everyone associated with us are very important and we thank you for supporting the great American traditions of bowhunting and conservation.

Anyway Poem

People quite often are unreasonable, illogical, and self-centered. Love them anyway!

If you do good, people may accuse you of selfish, ulterior motives. Do good anyway!

If you are successful, you will win some false friends and true enemies. Succeed anyway!

The good you do today will be forgotten tomorrow. Do good anyway!

Honesty and frankness make you vulnerable. Be honest and frank anyway!

The biggest people with the biggest ideas can be shot down by the smallest people with the smallest minds. Think big anyway!

People favor underdogs, but follow only top dogs. Fight for some underdogs anyway!

What you spend years building may be destroyed overnight. Build anyway!

People really need help, but may attack you if you help them. Help them anyway!

Give the world the best you have and you might get kicked in the teeth. Give the world the best you've got anyway!

Good Luck and God Bless You!

You cannot bring about prosperity by discouraging thrift. You cannot strengthen the weak by weakening the strong. You cannot help the wage earner by pulling down the wage payer. You cannot further the brotherhood of man by encouraging class hatred. You cannot help the poor by discouraging the rich. You cannot establish sound security on borrowed money. You cannot keep out of trouble by spending more than you earn. You cannot build character and courage by taking away man's initiative and independence. You cannot help men permanently by doing for them what they could and should do for themselves. —Abraham Lincoln

WOODS N² WATER PRESS

Other Outdoorsman's Edge Books Available from

Woods N' Water Press

❏ **Wildlife & Woodlot Management**
  by Monte Burch

❏ **Sure-Fire Whitetail Tactics**
  by John Weiss

❏ **Hunting Big Woods Bucks: Secrets of Tracking and Stalking Whitetails**
  by Master Guide Hal Blood

❏ **Advanced Turkey Hunting**
  by Richard Combs

❏ **The Ultimate Guide to Planting Food Plots for Deer and Other Wildlife**
  by John Weiss

❏ **Hunting Rutting Bucks**
  by John Trout, Jr.

❏ **Complete Guide to Rabbit Hunting: Secrets of a Master Cottontail Hunter**
  by David Fisher

❏ **Butchering Deer: The Complete Manual of Field Dressing,
  Skinning, Aging, and Butchering Deer at Home**
  by John Weiss

❏ **The Art of Whitetail Deception: Calling, Rattling and Decoying**
  by Kathy Etling

❏ **Predator Hunting: Proven Strategies that Work from East to West**
  by Ron Spomer

❏ **A to Z Guide to White-tailed Deer and Deer Hunting**
  by Dr. Randall Gilbert

❏ **Hunting Bears: Black, Brown, Grizzly, and Polar Bears**
  by Kathy Etling

❏ **Do-It-Yourself Gun Repair: Gunsmithing at Home**
  by Ed Matunas

❏ **Moon Phase Whitetail Hunting**
  by Jeffrey Murray

❏ **Antler, Bone, Horn and Hide: Projects You Can Make at Home**
  by Monte Burch

❏ **Finding Wounded Deer**
  by John Trout, Jr.

TO ORDER,

Call us at 1-800-652-7527, write us at Woods N' Water Press, P.O. Box 550, Florida, NY 10921 or
visit us on the web at www.fiduccia.com or www.outdoorsmansedge.com.